Dr. Orenia Yaffe-Yanai

CAREER YOUR PASSION

On Love, Family Genograms,
Passion and Calling

Dr. Orenia Yaffe-Yanai

CAREER YOUR PASSION

On Love, Family Genograms,
Passion and Calling

··

Written in dialog with Dov Yanai

 **MODAN PUBLISHING HOUSE**

CAREER YOUR PASSION
Orenia Yaffe-Yanai

English Translation: Deborah Reich
English Copy Editor: Vanessa Rakin

© Copyright by Modan Publishing House Ltd.
Meshek 33, Moshav Ben-Shemen, 73115

ISBN: 978-965-7141-12-0

Printed in Israel

To my Father, Rachmiel (Mima) Yaffe,
Who gave me a love and yearning for words.

Contents

Love and Thanks

To my mother, Rachel Yaffe; and to the Krock-Sher family, who gave me the colors.

To my husband, business partner, and soul mate, Dov Yanai, who saw the possibilities, nurtured the roots with love, and worked tirelessly to give the effort wings.

To our children Goni, Nathalie, and Elad, who taught me about love and common sense.

To the friends who have been with me and have been there for me throughout the writing of this book: Ilana Kedron, Ayala Malach-Pines, Tzefi Gilad, Hannah Nir, Rivka Nardi, Ilana Revo, and Yehuda Atlas. To Yuval Stern for his painting. To the Strauss family who walk their talk in their family business and life. To Shula Modan, who believed; to Vanessa Rakin my copyeditor for the English version and who was determined to guide me towards this quest; and to Tamar Milo, my partner in AMI and in growing up.

To Shir Shavit for her clever view point.

And to all my patients and counselees, who joined with me and gave me their trust as they forged the paths for their journeys: making choices, reaching a little beyond themselves… a little beyond me…

Introduction to 2007 Edition

The path is wiser than the one who travels it.

Bedouin proverb

It seems like everything began with my father's death. First came the agony and the days of anguish; and then, even more painful, my awakening to a piercing revelation that was impossible to avoid. My father died in his prime because he no longer found meaning in his work. A wonderful, talented man, he never learned how to channel his abilities. His work, which was contrary to his calling, simply did him in.

Over the years, my father's "vocational death" became central to my own professional life. What began as a memorial to his death, now became my lighthouse. Over decades of work, I translated his pain into a broader human dimension and transformed it into my career. I met hundreds of unfulfilled people who were "vocationally stuck," and I gained a fresh perspective on their quest for the path to self-expression while sharing their struggles and basking in their victories. I learned that work or career can be either a disease, or a cure, depending on the choice an individual makes.

For most people, the simplest of questions always looms large.

"What profession suits me anyhow, and what is my true calling?"

I learned that the absence of self-realization can destroy a person, and not merely the individual alone. This kind of distress is often deeply engraved in the family psycho-genes, sometimes for generations. Through counseling people with vocational dilemmas and researching job seekers and those in search of career change, a striking revelation hit me. One of the greatest grudges that children harbor towards their parents, often exceeding anger over financial issues, infidelity, abuse, or even abandonment, is the resentment a child feels towards a parent who has missed the boat, who has not felt entitled to a meaningful life.

Career Your Passion was born from my yearning to inscribe the journeys I have travelled over decades. Solitary journeys, and journeys with others – journeys with people who became stuck in their work, in their career, and in fulfilling their life mission. The people whose journeys are shared here are people who chose to set out on a career quest, and it was the act of choice that inspired them to reach their respective destinations. This book was born from my long-standing belief that "The path is wiser than the one who travels it." I believe that deep down inside them, people know whether they are on the right track or if they have gone astray.

To fulfill your vision you may need a quest, like biblical Abraham when he left Ur, or what the Maori call a 'walkabout'. Leave the familiar and set out on a journey to discover yourself and your hidden inner worlds. By traveling far from your motherland, from all that is familiar and especially from your family home, you will be able to connect to your dreams and desires. Departures and farewells are critical along the path to fulfilling your vision, and the journey to a new land shall inspire you to reconnect creatively to your roots as well as to your family psycho-genes.

In order to facilitate career journeys I have used a three-generational family vocational tree as a working tool. When drawing a map of the family Genogram or even parts of it, a wider understanding of the vocational DNA reservoir is opened for the traveler.

Careers are not only born, they are often made by decoding automatic vocational patterns of behavior that enable free choice. However, when a person's career becomes their calling, this is when it is at its best, and so is its "owner" and leader...

Work, career, vocation, profession, job, or calling – all of these are different and they reflect diverse emotional work states of mind. I have used each of them according to the state of mind and emotions of my clients.

My approach is both analytical and intuitive. It strives at decoding personal career patterns; those who facilitate career fulfillment and those who lead to recurrent career impasse.

Impasse, or getting stuck, is sometimes mandatory for our growth and development. The human desire to work in a vocation that is personally fulfilling is an existential need. The struggle to carve out a meaningful life is difficult and painful; it demands tough choices traveling through rough terrain, yet it is filled with vitality and creativity. Missing out on this quest can lead to enormous suffering and sometimes can even be fatal.

I wish for each of you a personal journey that will be true, enduring, and fulfilling. Take a friend on your journey, for "The prisoner cannot surrender his own bonds." Learn from others and teach yourselves. Make your dreams come true. They know who you are.

Seek your path.

Trust its wisdom.

Follow your inner voice.

Go out there and find your Promised Land.

Orenia Yaffe-Yanai

Chapter One
Receiving the Green Light

I needed someone to give me permission to succeed.

Ever since I can remember, I nurtured hopes for a future of vocational bliss for my father. As a child, I remember closing my eyes and wishing, "Please let Dad wake up in the morning and do something that will make him happy, something that is right for him, something that gives him joy." I wanted him to feel that he had a reason to live. I wanted him to wake up without that beaten look of someone who experiences himself as a failure, unable to create, and incapable of self-expression. Above all, I could never understand why the great love he had for his family and especially for me, was never enough to grant him happiness and contentment.

After he died, I tried, as a clinical and vocational psychologist, to fathom the secret of his life and death. I discovered that two essential components had been lacking in his work environment. First, he had lacked a meaningful figure who would notice, even by way of criticism, the job he was doing. Second, it devastated him that his work had so little connection to his inner needs, and so little connection to his soul.

My father was a teacher who wanted to be an educator, a

mentor, who documents his experiences with students in order to pass them on to others. As a school teacher, he came home day after day increasingly frustrated. He thrived on unmediated interaction with people in a world unsuited to provide it. He felt passed over, a man without a future, a person doomed to the wrong profession.

More than anything else, my father yearned to express himself in writing, yet was unable to allow himself to put pen to paper. I, too, wished to write, but through years of counseling others, I learned that one can almost never get a green light from an unfulfilled parent. Being asked for this kind of blessing by one's child can bring both pain and happiness beyond what an unfulfilled parent can bear. The happiness that one's child is living the dream is mixed with the pain of envy. The conflict is too painful and thus parental permission is never granted. For consent to be given, one has to struggle on alone, which is never an easy task.

Curiously, it was I who gave him permission to write through a kind of unspoken, prearranged game we shared. When I had a composition to prepare for school I would come to him and say, "Daddy, I can't write this composition; maybe you can do it for me?" He would always gladly agree, seeming to take it for granted that I wasn't capable of it myself, and I, of course, was always willing to sacrifice my own self-expression to let him write for me.

Often, people feel that what they do for a living, or their career choice, is truly painful for them. Along with the pain comes a sense of having missed out, or of being stuck in a rut. Sometimes this distress can bring a person to despair and withdrawal from life, or in extreme cases, can even lead to death.

Over decades of counseling various people seeking vocational quests, I have discovered that those who touched me most were those who resembled my father. They were my comrades on the journey to fulfillment, and they touched an inner wound that never completely healed.

Daniel was one of those people. He had actually chosen the profession that was right for him, but neither he nor his employer knew it. Daniel was unaware that something important was missing in his life: that inner permission to find vocational fulfillment. And he had no parental figures to give him their blessing or their permission.

When he came to me he was thirty-five and had just been notified that he should start looking for another job. He was not overly surprised by being fired, yet something deep within brought him to me and made him begin asking himself questions even before beginning his job hunt or discussing with his superiors why he had been fired.

Daniel impressed me tremendously with his sensitivity to others. I was astonished by his superior intelligence and the tremendous courage he had mastered to confront the challenges he had set himself.

Although there was something pleasant about him, Daniel was not an especially impressive looking man. Squat and balding, he perspired a lot, dressed carelessly and moved clumsily, yet his eyes were attentive and accepting. An analytical man, Daniel asked precise questions and sought their answers diligently. Daniel felt his career was a failure, mainly because of lack of employer and peer recognition. My empathy was immediate as I recognized the distress that comes from sensing missed opportunities, and of being sidelined. After all, my entire life, I had watched my father suffer the same feelings.

Initially, Daniel was unable to pinpoint the problem. He could not explain why he was being let go by the multimedia company that had employed him from its first day in business. Yet somehow, he realized that something in the way he functioned within the company was flawed. When I asked him about his family, he responded that he lived with his girlfriend and that she was very important to him. They had no children.

Our first session was very tough. Daniel sat there, uneasy, dripping with sweat, smiling a polite, artificial smile. "I don't understand what's happening to me," he said. "I think I just have to find the right profession."

"How do you know that your profession doesn't suit you?" I asked.

"If people don't appreciate what I do, then maybe what I do just isn't right," he replied rapidly.

The words and the feelings struck a familiar chord…

So often, people who are stuck in their career sense only the need for changing the nature and content of their work; that other dimensions might require change simply never occurs to them.

Daniel told me how his career developed together with the growth of the software firm where he worked, and how he had come to specialize in communication arts and multimedia. It was not clear to him why the people he reported to were dissatisfied with him or what exactly they might be unhappy about.

"Are you good at what you do?" I asked him directly.

"Yes. I think I am. But nobody actually says so."

"Sometimes people don't hear because they don't know how to register approval. They avoid relationships with their colleagues and then miss out on all the compliments. Other people don't allow themselves to think well of themselves despite truly giving all they have to their work."

Daniel listened and took a moment to reply.

"I'm a fairly disorganized person, but I do listen to other people…"

"I've noticed that," I assented, "but do you also pay attention when people pay you compliments?"

"Not really," he replied, weighing his words. "I think that mainly I have been thinking about how good I am at it and not about if I like what I'm doing."

Daniel and I understood fairly quickly that his place in the organization was not very clear and that his relationships at work required special attention. He had systematically succeeded in neutralizing any attempt on the part of his employer or his customers to think well of him or relate to him constructively. He had even managed to persuade them that his work needed improvement. As a result, Daniel had achieved an ongoing attitude of lack of appreciation of his work.

All of that, however, seemed secondary to him in comparison to his new awareness of failing to take credit for his work in the world of communication arts and multimedia that he so loved.

"If I were to ask at your studio," I pressed him, "how happy you are with what you do, what would they tell me?"

Daniel was surprised and his brow creased as he answered with his usual candor. "I've never really thought about it, but now that you're asking, they would probably tell you that I'm not happy. As I say that, though, something in me objects, because deep down I'm really happy with what I do."

"And are others allowed to know that? Are you permitted to acknowledge it?" I refused to relent.

I vividly recollected my struggle to be happy with myself and with what I do, despite the tormented look my father wore, returning day after day frustrated from his job. It is not easy to be happy, so close to another person's grief.

These painful encounters taught me that a person's real or imagined career dissatisfaction is directly related to the level of the significant parent's feeling of dissatisfaction regarding his/her own career. Hence the son of an unfulfilled father may feel frustrated even if his work suits him and expresses his inner world. It was imperative for Daniel and me to understand his tremendous need to feel unfulfilled and dissatisfied; and why he felt the need to convey this message to his colleagues at work. Quite possibly this even made him create situations where his work would be negatively evaluated.

I told Daniel the story of my father and me, and I suggested he examine his parents' degree of satisfaction with their work.

Gradually we reacted the bottom of things. Daniel looked at me like a pilot coping with vertigo for the first time – the instruments in front of him reflected a reality different from the one conveyed to him by his senses... which was correct?

Daniel decided to trust me and began recounting the story of his parents' work histories for the first time in his life.

"I was born," he said ironically, "to unfulfilled parents. My father was a graphic artist whose talents went unrecognized. He was frustrated and lived with the feeling that he could have done anything. More than anything, he wanted to be an artist."

"Was your father sad?" I asked, remembering my own father's pain.

"Yes, very," he replied. "His work and talent were never acknowledged and eventually he gave in to melancholy and alcohol. When I was four, he left home."

"So in fact, he left you, too."

"Yes, but I loved him deeply and he loved me back," replied Daniel with certainty.

"And this hurt to see your father unable to find himself?"

"It was terrible," Daniel recalled, "and it was also incomprehensible. Why did he leave? What happened at home? Why wasn't he respected? What was wrong with him? Even now, it's not clear to me."

I saw my father right in front of me. How he secluded himself even within his marriage to my mother. How he abandoned both himself and her emotionally. How he was not there, despite living physically in their shared home. From my father, I also learned that a family can be either a training ground or a killing field for personal development and fulfillment. Sometimes, owing to unbearable distress, overwhelming despair, and a lack of career fulfillment, a person can destroy his/her family relationships.

"Tell me, do you think there are people who leave home because they haven't found meaning in their lives at work?" asked Daniel pensively.

"Yes," I replied. "I know that often when couples break up and people leave their homes and families, it's from a sense of despair, of having let things slip away in terms of their lack of work fulfillment."

"Why wasn't my father appreciated?" Daniel asked again.

"You came to me with the same issues," I said, trying to throw light on the link between the generations, "and that question could be asked about you, too."

"Yes," said Daniel. "When I was growing up I thought that my father had always wanted to be an artist and that he had renounced art by choosing graphic design. When I was little, I was afraid something would happen to him...could it be that my father left my mother because of his work frustration?" Daniel seemed frightened by his own words, as if he had now for the first time understood how likely that was.

I suggested that Daniel considered to what extent his parents could perceive his father as an occupational success. A useful tool for doing that can be done by checking the vocational family tree or vocational Genogram over three generations. I suggested that Daniel checked whether the men in his family were considered winners, what they did for a living, and how they related to other "male" occupations. Families tend to pass behavioral patterns and attitudes from one generation to the next. When these are not consciously identified, family members tend to relive them.

I shared my knowledge from life and literature with Daniel. We both sensed that he was stuck in the grip of a generational legacy, and not that he had chosen the wrong path. He was ready to get in touch with his new feelings involving "permission" to excel and the acceptance of that permission.

When Daniel and I parted at that stage in his journey, he had homework to do. He planned to talk with his mother and father about the work they had done in their lives and what they felt they had missed out on.

He came to our next session in a very emotional state. "You

know," he said, "I discovered that I am a loser, son of a loser, and grandson of a loser. Not only my father, his housepainter Father, too, had seen themselves as vocational failures, and that was the way their families also viewed them. And according to my mother, her father was also dubbed a loser. Do you think it's hereditary?"

"It can be, if you accept the family message as your destiny. But it's always possible to seize the permission to change," I replied. "What does your girlfriend think of your work?"

"She thinks I'm a genius," he said, with barely a pause for thought.

"A promising beginning," I noted, pleased. "You chose someone who believes in you."

I thought I heard a sigh of relief.

"You know," Daniel continued, "when I talked with my father he was really embarrassed. His whole connection with painting and graphics was unclear to him. Finally he told me: 'My father didn't value his work, because his father wanted him to become the artist he himself had never been... I told him that perhaps he didn't wish to be a painter, that he could have been happy becoming a successful graphic artist if his father had been supportive. I saw that he was as surprised as I was by that new possibility. He didn't deny it the next day either. I think he has started his own homework now..."

"And what about your mother?" I asked.

"At first Mom didn't delve too deeply into the question or her answer. She dismissed me with, 'Your father never made a living, just like your grandfather...' 'Like me?' I asked her, scared. That question pushed her buttons, 'Aren't things going well for you?' she asked, with renewed interest in my work. 'They want to fire me,' I told her. She looked at me sadly. And then, I asked her for the first time what expectations she had of me. She didn't really know what to say. At dinner, I felt she looked at me with a different perspective."

Daniel was moved. Our journey had brought him, as an adult, into a new encounter with his parents.

He sprawled a little more comfortably in his chair. I mused over how the ability to see one's parents and their work through both adult and children's eyes is one of the more useful tools on the journey towards growing up. The two views are never the same. Sometimes it is hard to decide which is the more telling. I lean toward the idea that the adult's view is more crucial for forgiveness, while the child's is more central in determining unconscious choices.

Daniel the child was sure that his mother, who gave up completing her engineering studies to become a housewife and gracious hostess, had sacrificed her career for him and the family. Daniel the adult could recognize that his talented mother could have finished her engineering studies had she so desired, but that she preferred being a homemaker and had found great satisfaction in that role. Daniel recalled that after his army service began studying tourism and even run a restaurant for a while. Possibly these were attempts to identify with his mother. At the same time Daniel was captivated by the world of computers. He created a software application for illustrating business cards and then created software for educational programs. Later, he joined the multimedia company where he currently worked.

"It has really worked out well for me, but…" he broke off.

"The son of the graphic artist who had not chosen communication arts became a communication arts expert …" said I, putting it bluntly. We both smiled.

At our next session, Daniel told me about some changes that were happening at work. A certain project he had undertaken to finish before leaving his job had been a huge success, and the head of his firm had offered him another chance. He even suggested that Daniel should think about taking on a more responsible position with greater scope, though more clearly defined. Daniel was considering the idea favorably, as it left him room for initiative and personal responsibility – which he needed, although he had not yet clearly discerned as much.

"And," he added excitedly, "my girlfriend is pregnant. We're expecting a son."

Daniel was bursting with pride. I thought to myself that becoming a parent was also probably connected with the transition he had made from his child's-eye view of his parents and the experiences he had shared with them, to seeing them from an adult perspective as people, and not simply as parents.

Daniel could now see the bigger picture. How he had been inwardly tied to his father's profession. How his father and grandfather had felt unfulfilled. How he had been unable to accept his choice of graphic design as his own choice. How he perceived himself as a loser, in a manner that paralleled the way his father and mother saw him. And how a veto which had passed down through generations had prevented him from feeling that he could be satisfied, fulfilled, or successful.

Daniel now understood that it was not in his work that he was at an impasse but in the way he related to his work. He also understood that ignorance and misunderstanding had pushed him into wanting to change his profession, and that he had neglected addressing the essential questions involving his profession and the way he related to it.

"People who live with high expectations of themselves," I shared with Daniel, "sometimes make do with the feeling that they haven't chosen. Meanwhile they enjoy greater freedom. One who has not chosen is not ranked in relation to some comparative yardstick or other benchmark. He or she gets the benefit of the doubt and can go on dreaming of perfection."

Daniel made a conscious decision to commit to success and free choice. After his son was born, he grew increasingly successful at selling multimedia services, and the list of his satisfied clients kept growing. Simultaneously, however, he still had many doubts: Am I good enough? Will I be able to maintain the momentum? The son's fear of success was juxtaposed against the pain of his "unfulfilled" and "unsuccessful" father, who so wanted his son to succeed, yet also envied him and had difficulty bestowing him with praise. Daniel's father's aspirations were, in fact, those of his own father. Given that he had never dared to take a good look at what he was all about, how could he have offered freedom of choice to his son?

Aside from this difficulty, the element of fear also exists uncomfortably alongside success. If I achieve what my father was unable to achieve, if I succeed – will I still be my father's son? If I succeed, how will I be judged in relationship to him? How will his failure look next to my success?

This brought me to thoughts of Greg, who had done well in his profession and was the successful son of an "unsuccessful" father. When yet another wave of success overtook him, Greg told me with pain: "The fact that I'm successful in my work is a daily reminder to my father of what he missed out on in life. It's terribly painful. But I'm not giving in because along with the pain is his pride in my accomplishments and my wonderful feelings of fulfillment. These are things I'm not willing to throw away!"

Towards the end of my journey together with Daniel, and only a month after his grandchild was born, Daniel's father died. Daniel had been able to spend time at his father's bedside, being close and caring for him with kindness. The father and son, for perhaps the first time in their lives, were able to talk and spend time together in friendship and reconciliation. His father was happy with his success.

I had often wondered how much the death of a beloved father – despite having lived with a feeling of having missed out – can make it easier for a child to change direction and take a new and different path.

Daniel's bereavement made me think that perhaps a person is fortunate to be able to bid his parents farewell and separate from them while they are still alive. Daniel was able to do that. In a gradual, conscious process, Daniel gleaned wisdom from his father about what was good in him, and came to terms with what was lacking, without paying too heavy a price for this reconciliation. I thought about how lucky people are who do not have to "kill off" their parents in order to live their own lives, to be free, to have a wide range of choices without losing their parents' love.

A year later, Daniel came to see me. He was tastefully dressed, twenty-five pounds thinner and sported an excellent haircut. He said, "I came back to tell you that now I finally know that I really love what I do." His face was all lit up with his recent revelation.

"And what are you working at now?" I asked with interest.

"These days I'm doing what I really love, and I'm enjoying every moment of it. I build applications for people who don't understand communication arts and multimedia, so I get to combine my passion for my work with my desire to help people and meet their needs. The dialogue I have with people as I'm working on their applications is very important to me. Maybe that's because of the dialogue you and I had – to ask, to answer, to respond, to provide, and to contribute in a creative, colorful way. This allows for self-expression, both for me and for my clients. Does that make any sense?"

I smiled. Both of us felt a great leap forward had been made.

"It's not just that you made it, you're also helping other people to express their abilities and their feelings by helping them give birth to their ideas and recycling them as graphic design."

"I guess. I really am happy to wake up in the mornings."

I sat there thinking. I have always seen myself as a kind of midwife; someone who enables others, in the midst of confusion and ignorance, to be reborn. Only when I came to terms with what my father had missed out on was I able to be reborn myself.

"And are you still bothered if other people don't appreciate what you do?" I asked.

"Less than I used to be," he said, "but the truth is that now the people around me also appreciate me more."

"And you yourself know that you're good at what you do," I noted.

"Definitely!"

At our last meeting, Daniel told me about his desire to go into business for himself and about realizing his dream of setting up his own multimedia company. "My company," he said proudly, "even has a name already. Image Ltd." As an only child who grew up almost without a father; and as an entrepreneur (he selected a typical "fatherless" career path), Daniel felt that having his own company would provide him with the right kind of incubator. This would be a new opportunity for trusting his vision. Permission had not only been seized by Daniel, but stretched and expanded.

Working with Daniel was for me a journey of seeking the path from darkness to light, from silence to speech. I felt, as he did, that what had emerged from the pain of impasse and from identifying the forbidden, were permission, fulfillment, timing, acknowledgement, and self-expression. All of this in turn had given birth to joy and satisfaction, for both Daniel and me.

As a partner in enabling permission for another person to succeed, my own permission had expanded a little, too.

Chapter Two
Illness as a Cry for Help

My headaches forced me to revaluate my career path

My mother used to tell me about my grandmother, who would take to her bed and hibernate before and after what my mother called her "creativity attacks." These would happen, for example, after she came down with spring-cleaning fever. Twice a year, when the weather changed, in spring and in fall, she would systematically begin cleaning the house while changing around winter and summer wardrobes. She would reorganize the entire house – new colors, different furniture, fresh flowers as if she were setting the stage for a new performance. Everyone in town, my mother said, used to come by to see the new scenery. And when the performance was over, the hibernation began.

In due course, my grandmother's daughter, my mother, began to display similar behavior. Before and after giving birth to a painting, she slept like Rip Van Winkle in her bed. It was as if the creative event demanded her disconnection from day-to-day affairs. Sometimes, this hibernation was accompanied by headaches, general weakness, vomiting, or depression.

As the years passed, I found that these episodes also occurred whenever my mother was faced with the difficulties of extending her unique talents beyond the scope of a one-time event or when she needed to present her creativity to the outside world. These events terrified me.

Many years ago, I fell ill and underwent surgery. I experienced a feeling that was new to me. I felt weighed down. All of a sudden, I was forced to take a time-out from life. I reacted with a combination of relief and panic. After vain attempts at denial, I realized that I had actually become a work addict, and that this in itself was a kind of career impasse. Gradually, I came to realize that this addiction gave me no scope for choice and no room for creativity, both of which I needed desperately. I felt that I wanted to examine myself from within, to engage in a kind of introspection that results from being at liberty to choose, rather than from necessity or force of habit.

The reality of my illness evoked in me a desire to practice moving from a productive mode to a creative one, from intensive activity to allowing space for leisure and inactivity. I wanted to make space to engage in self-debate and undergo new experiences so as to give roots to new opportunities. I decided to move with my family to the country. This was a leave-taking that was to facilitate profound changes in my life. I wanted to shift from a place of meeting with dozens of people every month, to a place where I would have time to think in solitude. I wanted to change from focused activity to entire days of doing nothing at all. I wanted to face up to questions and adversity. I wanted to go to sleep at night even though I hadn't accomplished any "meaningful" deeds throughout the day. I wanted to enable an idea to ripen so that creativity and accomplishment would evolve. And gradually, from within the illness, from within that place of hibernation inherited from both my mother and my grandmother, from within the empty space, from false starts and wondering – there emerged a flowering of creativity, a period of writing, and an experience of fulfillment.

Thus when Alan came to me, I was ready to set out with him on a journey. I was ready to take on the meaning of "hibernation."

I understood that it could be an incubator that enables the core personality to take root, grow, and reach out to the light.

In general, people tend to deny themselves the benefit of a time-out from life. People fear wasting time and worry that they might get sidelined if they aren't active for a while. Thus, they think twice before opting out for any significant period of time. Moreover, many people are afraid of the idea of being with themselves, without an agenda, without structure, without a goal. And society around us exerts pressure, too. "What? You're not working?".

In many cases, when there's no way out of a vocational crisis, the physical body crashes. This is actually how the body struggles toward reason and sense, by going public with its inability to function properly at work.

Alan came to me when he was thirty-nine years old. He was a scion of a well-connected European family who immigrated to the United States in the early 1960s. Shortly after, Alan married the daughter of an aristocratic French family. Since both families were affluent, there was no need for Alan to work for a living, and he didn't. This talented, inspiring man limited himself to civic and philanthropic activities. His schedule was crammed full, but he never earned a penny. His bank balance was enviable, but very few people knew that his talent, charm, and good looks contributed nothing to increasing it from month to month.

Alan lacked for nothing, but also had nothing. True, he was respected in the community and the gossip columns were full of his activities, but he felt empty and unfulfilled. He worked without passion, received no direct recognition for his work, and had no outlet for his many talents. He felt powerless and worn out, with little ability to explain precisely what was wrong.

This refined and handsome man, with his sensitive discerning eyes, came to me on the threshold of forty, after immigrating to Israel, to reevaluate his professional future. He sat down in an armchair facing me. After laying aside his Christian Dior sunglasses and the keys to his Land Rover parked outside, he said to me sadly: "I've come to the end of the line."

He seemed profoundly depressed and helpless. He was also exhausted by the effort of playing the ultimate high achiever in a highly demanding social environment, a role for which he'd been educated over many years. Very few people were aware that he had attempted suicide. The attempt was actually a cry for help that hadn't been adequately heard. Thus, after long months of depression and loneliness, Alan sank into a terrible silence, yet finally succeeded, just barely, in mustering the strength to seek out professional help.

Fairly quickly, we both realized that the crisis was vocational in nature. In one of our early meetings, after we'd begun raising questions and examining paths taken and those to come, I was bold enough to ask, "If you had to make a change in your life today, what event would you choose?"

"An earthquake," replied Alan. Shoulders slumped, he appeared the very personification of ruin and collapse. "I mean to tear down the dam," he said, and something decisive flickered briefly in his lost gaze.

At that moment, I saw clearly. This was global, not an event to be addressed as a single incident. We were not talking about a trickle here, but a deluge.

"If we're dealing with a flood here," I asked him, "how would you like to get ready for it?"

Alan began to play along with me. "I would like to build an ark and climb aboard," he answered, relaxing slightly.

"And what would you take on board with you?" I asked.

"I'd take my wife and children. I can't allow myself to lose them," he replied, and smiled. I in turn smiled inwardly. I knew that when the family anchor remains stable and steadfast, whatever's been cut adrift can be tied to it.

"What else would you take with you onto the ark?" I asked.

I wanted to exploit the fact that the flood had yet to arrive, and the ark still waited, empty. Alan had stumbled on a chance to get himself in shape, to change things for himself and his environment. True, he still didn't know how his ark would float, or in which direction, but he knew that an opportunity had arisen that couldn't be missed. Alan had no intention of allowing it to slip away. His life was about to change, of that he was acutely aware.

"Aside from your wife and children, what else would you take with you onto the ark? What would you choose to take from home?"

"Which home?" he asked.

"Your mother and father's home," I replied.

Alan told me that his father had been an officer in the French Foreign Legion, and his mother a member of the glitterati in France. Together we understood that on his long journey into the unknown, he would carry with him both his father's courage and his mother's determination.

From this point onward, Alan began attempting to formulate his new path. "I'll also take onto the ark with me the feeling that there's no going back," he said.

"And what else?" I continued pushing, reminding him that in his inner house were many resources that could aid him on his way.

To Alan, as with many of us, it wasn't clear just how far his talents could take him. He suffered from dyslexia, yet he was blessed with amazing gifts. Though exceptionally quick-witted, he had done poorly at school. The problem with dyslectic children like Alan is that they are constantly frustrated by the daily challenges of conventional school demands. so much so, that they can hardly understand that their challenges may turn out to be their blessings. Alan was one of those people whose rare intuition seemed to contradict prevailing common sense in school terms. This was a tragic situation that grew directly out of his learning disabilities. Thus, although he had grown up to be a wonderful, smart, even wise man, he was defeated on the academic level, mainly in terms of his self-image. His financial status didn't force him to deal with work that had real consequences for himself.

"You barely have the skills required to get a university degree," I told him, "and yet you have terrific capabilities for succeeding in a place where your wisdom and your personality are more important than a degree."

The atmosphere in the room became a little less tense. Alan's "education block" still seemed highly threatening. Nevertheless, it was now clear to both of us that his learning problems were not damming up the flow of his life. I decided to push him further and asked him again what else he would bring to the ark.

He closed his eyes briefly. "I'd take with me," he said, "my need and my ability to be with people, to influence them, to move them to action, and to do good for them. But something still bothers me, something still stops me from packing all these things together in one bag." Again his shoulders slumped and his brow was furrowed.

"You want to do good for people," I said, relentlessly, "but you can't. What's stopping you? What's stopping all that from happening?"

"Something is forbidding all that from happening," he explained.

"Something?" I queried, trying to help him out of the prickly undergrowth, "Or someone?"

Alan burst into tears. The flood of weeping had begun. Some of the thorny layers trapping him in were opening up a little.

That was the first time Alan had cried since the age of five. I gradually learned that behind the aristocratic façade of the house where he grew up, dark demons were hiding. Alan was an abused child. He had learned that his very existence was forbidden to him. The blows were not always physical. Mainly, the battering was in the form of outbursts of vitriolic criticism on the part of his father, a military man who was full of sullen anger. Alan's father was a lone Jewish soldier among gentiles, doing his utmost to pursue promotion. The Jewish officer internalized the rigid superstructure others forced on him, and recreated it, to the misfortune of his family, at home. His father was not a man without love. He was basically warm and loving, but the circumstances of his life had taught him that sternness and discipline were the path to survival. His thinking was educational. He wanted to prepare his little boy for the big bad world outside.

Alongside this rigid, military father was Alan's mother, a calm presence in the home. She was a beautiful woman who had passionately adopted the culture of hospitality with which she had been raised in her grandfather's hotel. In her scale of values, hosting and welcoming people reigned supreme. Over the years, hospitality became something indispensable, and obedience to its laws a prime objective.

The little boy Alan grew up in this environment. He was a sensitive child who learned to behave as expected of him, without rebellion and without exploring or expressing his own desires. Alan experienced childhood in a home where no adult ever stopped to ask him even once, "Alan, maybe there's something special you'd like to do today?" Outwardly, the family's life was all smiles, fun parties, fabulous picnics. But inwardly, inside the house, all was sterile and rigid. Love had been vanquished in favor of a slavish surrender to social norms.

Thus, I was not surprised when in subsequent sessions we found ourselves stalled on the subject of his parents' unfulfilled marriage. Experience has taught me that when parents are divorced, either physically or psychologically, or when from a psychological standpoint they have never learned to pull together in a unified direction, their child will have trouble later on in choosing a profession. Such a child is often afraid to answer the question, "Who do you love more? Mommy or Daddy?" A child whose parents have a successfully functioning marriage is rarely afraid to reply, because deep down these children sense that no response they could make, in either direction, could threaten the stability of their parents' marriage.

The challenge in Alan's case was daunting. The first trickle of the flood to come had already appeared, and we had yet to finish stocking up Alan's ark. At the end of our next session, we were able to close the gap just in time. The flood was already upon us. Alan had taken with him everything he needed for the journey, yet neither of us could guess what convoluted seas he would have to travel before a rainbow would emerge through the clouds.

Alan didn't appear for our next scheduled session. His wife notified me the next day that Alan had been hospitalized due to high fever and pains of unknown origin. "The doctors have no diagnosis as yet," she told me on the phone, and I became anxious. I feared that Alan's body had proceeded onward from the point at which the words had stopped. I also feared that this was possibly a kind of signal from his body that his endurance had been overreached and he was looking for an armistice for the conflicting forces at war inside him.

Later on, we understood. The hospital was the ark. The hospital was a legitimate address where Alan could contend with the flood without having to make any unnecessary explanations, neither to his inner world, nor to his outer world. To provide an adequate explanation, he had succeeded in developing real pains and an actual fever – concrete symptoms sufficient to get him sent straight to the hospital for a time-out from life.

Alan had played his part perfectly. Over the years, I've learned that proper attention must be given to whatever time a person takes for the processes going on in his life. That was the situation with Alan. His sophisticated personality had supplied him with a perfect alibi for a sojourn in an institution for healing physical ailments.

The doctors searched at length in an attempt to come up with a diagnosis that addressed the pain Alan was experiencing. The medical staff had no way of guessing that the pains in question had actually been "selected" for a specific purpose. Alan had found it necessary to drop out of life for a period of time in order to be able, later on, to begin living a different life. The hospital was called on to provide suitable cover, and performed its role splendidly.

The hospital also prescribed the required therapeutic healing in the form of a young doctor. During Alan's long hospitalization, a young physician took Alan under his wing, and a special relationship developed between the two. Each time this young doctor examined Alan or gave him medication, he would sit at Alan's bedside and talk with him. In that way he hoped to learn the history of this patient's mysterious disease, and in the meantime he was also learning about everything else that had gone on in Alan's life in the past, when the patient had been considered healthy.

These long discussions during Alan's stay on the ward were useful to both men, proving fertile ground for each of them to develop along their own path, and a warm friendship grew between the two men. When they talked about the right to be a separate person and the right to be attached to others, the two were unknowingly acting out a classic model. Increasingly, today's psychologists believe that a successful course of treatment works only when the caregiver grows along with the client – and that real change evokes reciprocity for both partners in the dialogue and the growth process.

I had no doubt that this is what had happened between the young doctor and Alan in the hospital – one with a stethoscope around his neck and the other in hospital pajamas. One was a young man with a quasi-paternal and professional authority;

the other, an adult who had a small child's desperate need for official approval and for the crucial permission that would enable him to set out on his new road.

Nine months passed until the waters receded. In the interim, Alan received the safeguard and official authorization he needed. He didn't have to cope with the world and its demands. He wasn't required to look smart and successful, rich and glittering. Finally he was able to be himself. After nine months, Alan took his wife and children, and left the ark, equipped with renewed courage and survival skills.

Alan's illness accounts for a widespread phenomenon. Often, a physical illness or trauma can enable or even demand that a person examines his life from a new vantage point. Usually this angle is different or in complete contrast to the way his life has been viewed up to that point. His priorities may very well change, as may his attitude towards those around him. During an illness and while fighting for the right to live, patients often examine their lives repeatedly, generating endless questions. Am I satisfied with my personal and professional life? Am I making the right choices and the correct decisions? Am I truly fulfilled according to my innermost desires?

Not infrequently, such a period is characterized by total ruin. The patient arrives at the decisive moment with the foundations of his house collapsing or destruction already around him and with no way out except to raze them. Later on, when it becomes possible, a completely new beginning must be made. Surveying the debris of a lifetime, some people lack the strength to start over and instead decide to waive the privilege.

When Alan emerged from the cataclysm onto safe ground at last, he understood that his earlier life was now in ruins. He realized that the spiritual assets he had taken with him on the ark were still with him, disconnected though they might be to the vast material resources that had once seemed to constitute the foundations of his life. During the long months of his hospitalization, Alan had succeeded in losing most of what he owned in a material sense. We both knew that the neglect of his material assets and his consequential financial losses was something that he had brought upon himself. Alan evidently had some kind of unconquerable urge towards a personal reconstruction from within, rather than one based on material assets.

Alan could have taken care of his financial affairs from within the hospital, but he had chosen not to. Sometimes people have to lose everything – at least, everything acquired by good fortune rather than by right – in order to reconstruct their lives to include the missing elements. Alan needed to lose more than his abundant possessions. He needed to break free, once and for all, from his father's brutal criticism and from the long list of thou-shalt-nots that bound him to a lifestyle which he would never had chosen of his own free will.

Now, choice became easier. Since he had virtually shed all his possessions, Alan couldn't very well continue all the philanthropic projects that formerly had filled his days and provided his life with substance. In that sense the financial and business losses he suffered were liberating and healing. For the first time ever, Alan was now obliged to begin supporting himself. Yet at the same time, he was finally free to shape his life and devote himself to his family as he saw fit.

The rents in the fabric of Alan's existence began closing. First, a circle was closed with his father. It was no coincidence that the supportive doctor had been recruited to play a healing role. He was a comrade and a soul mate still searching for his way. Yet simultaneously, he represented an authority figure that sanctions healing of the original father to enable his son to alter the course of life that his ark is sailing. Now, Alan had found a different father figure, complete and complementary, who although an authority was also more sensitive and understanding of Alan's needs and desires. The dialogue between them was not merely comforting; it also facilitated construction of a strong foundation for Alan to build new dimensions of identification of his inner self. Now he could aspire to the identity of a person who creates, and – for the first time – one who is able to be fulfilled and happy with his life.

There I was in this drama, keeping an eye on him from afar. I felt like Miriam, sister to Moses, who walked along watching the baby's little floating ark until it reached a safe shore, yet did not steer it herself. In my weekly sessions with Alan, I mostly listened, but was also very supportive. I constantly reminded him, at his request, to consider what was really important to him; to be authentic and to explore his calling. I became a partner in the quest to fulfill his vision and the midwife for Alan's right to pursue his destiny and build a meaningful life.

For the first time ever, Alan felt that now, after the flood, he could till his soil and harvest the fruits of his labor. He felt ready to go off in search of his heart's desire and as the weeks went by, he began to realize that his calling involved working with people connected in some way to hosting or entertaining. So he placed the discovery of his calling on a slow back burner until his dream finally crystallized into shape.

One fine spring day, Alan arrived for his session dressed in jeans and a T-shirt. His face was open and his eyes were shining. "I had a dream," he told me. "I dreamed that, like you, I created a place for people where they could realize their dreams. I dreamed that I was the proprietor of a hotel; a place full of color, art, flowers and soft carpets. People from all over the world came to stay with me… Tell me, could that be a career?"

I smiled happily. "As an occupation it already exists, at least in your vision. Now, all you have to do is get vocational about it and make your dream come true."

Alan smiled back at me. "You know, ever since I recovered, I am feeling much stronger and I'm not afraid of my father any more. I don't feel guilty anymore; it's as if I've paid my dues."

Alan understood that his hospitalization had been simultaneously a period of recovery and a time-out. Gradually, he became more and more certain that his true calling involved hosting guests and hotel management, and that all of this was connected to his family roots: his grandfather, his mother, and his parents' hospitable establishment.

Behind these conciliatory statements, a man who was whole and certain of himself began to emerge. Alan felt confident enough to choose, to move on, to grow and flourish in the hotel industry. He felt connected to his sources, yet in his own way. And he now felt more secure in his masculinity than ever before.

It was clear that this period of illness and recovery had provided the major emotional building blocks that Alan needed to put his life back together. He decided to pursue professional development through various courses in hotel management and in general business management. He chose a community college that demanded less in theoretical study and stressed the acquisition of practical skills.

Aside from taking these courses, Alan was improving his ability to understand people, and learning to use the connections and good faith accumulated in his former philanthropic work. He was further leveraging his father's courage and his mother's determination, both qualities that he had internalized.

All this helped him to slowly establish, beginning with almost nothing, a hotel, that quickly became widely popular. This happened before he'd even finished his hotel management studies. "If it hadn't been for the crisis and my hospitalization," he told me at our session just before the opening ceremony of his hotel, "I would have missed all of this."

So the flood had been rehabilitative. Only through crisis could Alan have discovered that beneath the surface, sustenance awaited. Fallow land that for years had produced nothing due to a lack of cultivation, proved in the end to be outstandingly fertile. What was waiting inside Alan enabled him, in the end, to reorganize his life and his livelihood. And those qualities were his all along; they merely rearranged and reorganized themselves. When the flood was over, the sun shone brightly down on a process of creativity and rebirth.

I learned from Alan that perspective is everything. What is perceived as a catastrophe, a financial disaster, a ruined career, a physical collapse, may ultimately turn out for many people to be beginning of a new road, a more appropriate way – more like the right path.

In many ways Alan reminded me of Danny, a handsome soldier, who came to Hadassah Hospital in Jerusalem where I was working at the height of the Yom Kippur War during the autumn of 1973. In the context of war, Danny's wound was not considered serious. His ankle had been shattered by a bullet. As a result, his right leg had been somewhat shortened, leaving him with a slight limp. With a minor modification in his right shoe, however, his limp was barely noticeable.

Although this was a disaster for his family, for Danny it was a release. "On my part," he told me a few days after I met him on the ward and was having trouble understanding the contradiction between his plaster-enclosed leg and his smiling face, "this wound is a once-in-a-lifetime opportunity, made to order, especially for me."

Initially, I didn't understand. Comprehension soon dawned with the arrival of an over-elegantly-dressed woman, who stormed hysterically onto the scene. The contrast between her precise appearance and the scene of wounded men and bloodstained sheets all around us was almost surreal. She charged into the orthopedic ward and, having located her wounded son, began shouting: "My son Danny is perfect and that's how he's going to leave this place. P-E-R-F-E-C-T! If not, he'll die!"

We on the ward were bleary-eyed, in pain and surrounded by

it, and had been doing our best for endless nights to keep our heads clear and retain our professionalism, despite the inhuman face of war. We sat Danny's mother down on a chair in a corner and gave her a glass of cold water. We also made sure that, despite how understaffed we were, she had a chance to talk with a social worker.

Ruth, Danny's mother, was not the sort of person to whom one gives instructions. She was the pampered daughter of a leading Israeli family. The tremendous effort she was making not to shut down emotionally was painfully obvious. Her chilly facial expression masked her fear for Danny's fate. She maintained a look of superiority and treated the medical staff with contempt. "That's how it is with people like us," she told me when I asked. "Everything with us is always fine." She carefully smoothed her perfectly pressed blue skirt.

I wondered ironically about the contrast she presented to the wounded with their missing limbs. They couldn't feel because they'd lost parts of themselves. She couldn't feel because emotionally, she had lost parts of herself.

I spent many hours with Danny that day. I noticed that he was embarrassed by his mother – by the drama she provoked, by her inability to understand what was going on around her, and by her inability to understand both Danny and herself.

Day became night. We were both exhausted and broke the codes of professional behavior. I, the psychologist, sat with a cigarette in my hand; he, an officer and a gentleman, couldn't stop crying. "You know," he said to me a little before midnight, "I've never cried. That is, as a child maybe I cried, but after that, as a young man? Never!"

"Weeping disturbs the perfection," I suggested, recalling his exaggeratedly refined mother.

But Danny went on crying. Tired as I was, I could see that this weeping must not be interrupted.

Later that night, past crying, Danny was unflagging in his

effort to seize the opportunity that had fallen his way. He talked and talked. Even with the approach of dawn, eyelids drooping, Danny kept at it enthusiastically: "Now, finally, I feel that because I'm wounded, I'll be able to escape this perfection trap. I feel like I may be able to be a regular, ordinary guy. You know," he whispered with a look in his eyes I still remember more than thirty years later, "I have never let myself fall in love with a woman. I have never failed an exam. I have never made mistakes. I couldn't do anything wrong, because I'd never brought myself to the point where I could make mistakes."

Danny was the raw material from which the troubadours of that war wove their melancholy ballads. He was handsome, wise, and captivating. He was the vulnerable warrior, the wounded conqueror. The nurses on the ward chased after him from the first moment they saw him. But even then, there was a strange, incomprehensible contradiction between the graceful way he moved and his cold, almost arrogant glance. This was the veneer he had maintained for so many years. "It was so scary," he told me after a week, as if finally decoding the mystery of the contradiction, "when people would suddenly perceive uncertainty in my voice or a lack of determination. So I always acted the tough guy and ended up being that way; nothing moved me."

And now, here was his opportunity. His limp would constantly accompany his life, and his "perfect" mother's behavior in a ward full of wounded soldiers, helped him reach a decision. A daunting array of challenges awaited Danny around the corner. He decided to come out of the perfection closet into the big, wide, flawed world. Now he would have to find new tools to reflect the reality out there and the new plans he was making for himself. Danny was slowly identifying the components he would choose and those he would reject from his life. Danny was one of the brave ones.

Once he had decided, the curtain lifted that had separated

him from life and from people. "Life for me was always a front, like scenery," he told me a few months later when he returned to the ward for a routine follow-up. "The big curtain kept me from looking at life. I was able to see everything but always through this screen. Now, things are slowly changing."

I warned Danny against removing the curtain all at once. I suggested that he made it more flexible, lighter, and thereby, easier to roll up. I suggested that he protected himself, but without letting go of what he was experiencing.

It was a long process of learning and understanding. Danny's life really did change. When he was able to connect with life in all its variety, he was able to open the real estate business he had always dreamed of but never permitted himself to.

We parted, but periodically Danny would echo through my thoughts. Thirty years later, when I sat down with Alan the hotelier, Danny was there again. Alan's path had been a much tougher one than Danny's, and his choices were tougher, too. He was older, and the sacrifices he was required to make were heavy. Both these men needed the connection via their ailing bodies to a new identity rather than progressing through emotional pain and growth .

With illness and physical wounds, there are, of course, two sides to the coin. Men like Danny and Alan used them as instruments of change in their lives, to achieve impressive breakthroughs. Others do differently. Some barricade themselves behind an illness and make it a sanctuary, a camouflaged braking system that brings their vocational growth to a halt. There are people of great talent among us, people of extraordinary strengths, who lack the tools to express the range of their abilities. Their situation is reminiscent of a man wearing explosives taped to his body. He knows that the slightest start can transform the explosives into a destructive bomb. He decides to limit his trips, not go so far afield and stay closer to home, all so as not to jeopardize his existence with the prospect of that explosion. Alan found his way by first losing nearly all he had. Danny, the younger man, was able to use his wound and his disability as an opportunity to forge a new path for himself.

In contrast to Alan and Danny, Beth managed to restrict the scope of her abilities without being consciously aware of doing so.

Beth was an outstanding executive manager. She came to me in the wake of severe, recurring panic attacks and an obsessive need to examine and reexamine things. These symptoms stole a great many of her working hours and gave her terrible headaches. Medical tests turned up no pathology. Psychological evaluation indicated an outstanding manager whose ability to improvise solutions and overcome crises was impressive. Moreover, she developed creative and original ways to inspire her team to follow her, no matter what. It was clear to us that the headaches and the repetitive examination rituals were a means for her to tie her hands so as to hold something back. I asked myself what was she damming up in this fashion. Perhaps the flood of her abilities, or possibly feelings of which she was unaware?

In our second session, there was nothing to do but to keep on asking: Why was she so deeply mired in pain? What in fact was blocking the flow? I believed that, deep down, she knew the true answer and that this knowledge would help her to move forward via a process of inner clarification.

"The pain is like a lighthouse," I told her. "To use it properly means being able to see the cliff from a distance. If you didn't feel the need to examine everything all the time, and if these headaches weren't bothering you," I asked, "what would have been happening in your career?"

Her reply didn't surprise me. "My career would have been really taking off," she said, without hesitation.

"And what would have happened with such a meteoric rise in your career?" I pushed.

"I would have exploded, I would have crashed," she said.

"Why?"

"I have no idea, but it's absolutely clear to me that this is what would have happened," she said.

Beth felt trapped. She felt like a power station, small but full of energy, where powerful forces had changed direction and were exploding internally instead of performing their job externally. Paradoxical as it may sound, these dynamic and powerful personal resources were precisely the problem. They threatened her vulnerable sense of self, which wasn't mature enough in emotional terms. She lacked sophisticated tools to deal with the depth of the feelings she was experiencing. This is how, in extreme cases, an imbalance in energies can become a physical ailment.

Beth set out to learn how to succeed by compartmentalizing her various channels and building the appropriate systems for utilizing her time and energy. She took her headaches seriously, as if they were alarm bells, warning her of impending perils.

As a general rule, a bad mood or a mild depression is not sufficient justification for missing work or functioning poorly. A stomachache sounds better, or a high fever. Fever is a good excuse to permit ourselves to be ourselves. A physical illness is a genuine opportunity to be released from our duties, and it carries a pleasant bonus. We get everybody's attention, and our workplace has lowered expectations of us in the near future.

Beth's choice was to get down to learning about her needs and limitations. She came to realize her fear of big-time success and her desire to stay small and needy. The power of her personality and her talents represented a threat to her needs. Having recognized her limitations, she felt it would be permissible to make choices and to grow at a suitable rate, in line with her needs. Once Beth achieved the right balance, her fear threshold improved together with her ability to manage her vocational life.

Things that we have yet to discover are apparently already known to our unconscious – the emotional substratum that has been communicating all these years with our physical systems. Hence, when confronted with overload, some people suddenly find themselves struck with a physical ailment. They honestly believe the illness to be a negative occurrence, and the fact that they could possibly have made this "choice," strikes them as horrendous. Others, however, in a flash of insight, understand the dimensions of the opportunity that has presented itself. They can make use of the illness to go on an adventure, or to tackle tasks they would never have considered at the peak of health. All Beth needed was this sudden realization.

Illness is frightening and sometimes signifies the end of the road. The signals sent by lesser ailments, however, are perceptible much earlier. Today, with our universal awareness of ourselves so drastically heightened, many of us understand that it's possible to simply say: "I want it to be this way." More and more people sense a need to be able to say: "I don't want to go on working at this career," without having to offer a suitable excuse or explanation. The world has become more accepting and tolerant. Today we see more clearly that once we cease the fear of acknowledging limitations, even a Hydra can turn into a sweet princess with whom one can build a better and more fulfilling life.

The image of the princess is associative. It is taken from fairy tales that draw on life-wisdom learned in our childhood. We know the story of the beautiful princess who, because of her parents' insensitivity, was cursed by the witch and forbidden to ever to touch a spinning wheel again. One interpretation holds that the princess suffered from over-loving parents. They didn't pay attention to her real needs, and thus prevented her from having meaningful activity in her life. So a curse was laid on her that prevented her from real activity or else she would die. How can one live without being productive? It's impossible. The fables knew this, too. The princess, however, following some unclear impulse and against her parents' wish, searched endlessly for a spindle to spin some thread so as to do something meaningful. Since she had been forbidden to act, she had neither the permission, nor the tools for performing such an action. When she tried anyway – she pricked herself with the needle. Since she had never been trained to cope with pain, she was turned into stone, and sank into a deep trance that lasted a hundred years. Her parents' restrictions had been so harsh that they stifled not only her ability to act, but that of everything around her. Only unconditional love could free the princess from her deep sleep.

From personal experience, I know that in order to perform, one must acquire tools for development that go beyond one's natural skills and talents. Sometimes, to grow and flourish, one must wake up and undergo inner processes such as those the princess underwent. Often internalized parental prohibition is liable to torpedo our ability to do and to actualize. Only our mature, authentic love for ourselves or the love of another that is attentive and alert to our real needs, can awaken us and push us onward to renewed action. By contrast, when there is no love but only criticism, despair, and missed opportunities, we find it hard to muster the tools we need to develop creatively and meaningfully. Successful executives and organizational consultants know this well. An embittered, dissatisfied employee, mired in a state of inaction, can have a destructive influence not only on himself but also on those in his immediate work environment, and sometimes even on the organization as a whole.

The princess is the quintessential illustration, due to a lack of tools for coping with new conflicts, of the flow of life coming to a standstill. She is frozen, body and soul, for one hundred long years. Nonetheless, our bodies and souls are far more sophisticated and flexible than we imagine. Often we are not required to shut down our entire system. Sometimes, indeed, we are wise enough to isolate only one physical component that is crucial to the vocational functioning we subconsciously wish to leave behind, and our bodies cleverly isolate that single component.

Many of the lecturers and schoolteachers who have come to me over the years for help in changing careers in the wake of chronic laryngitis were not, in fact, happy in their profession. Most of them, however, reported difficulty in abandoning a profession that represented tenure and a measure of financial stability. Despite their difficulty in leaving teaching, they reported that they were no longer able to identify with it. They needed permission to make the change, and the body provided it. Coming down with laryngitis enabled many of them to develop a new career and to bid farewell to an activity they no longer found fulfilling. Laryngitis paved a socially acceptable way to leave what they had once viewed as a noble profession and a worthy calling.

This is how it was for Karen, who ended up in teaching as the result of parental pressure. Her parents were sure that teaching would enable her to be a good mother and a fine wife. Her students, however, knew as well as she did, that she wasn't a real teacher in her soul and that she hadn't become a teacher by choice or in search of her own fulfillment. "My outrage was stuck in my throat," she told me at our first session. "I knew that I was stuck in the profession, against my will and contrary to my personality, but I was a good girl and therefore I kept quiet." After Karen was able to identify her impasse, which cleverly manifested itself as laryngitis, she never returned to school. Today she runs a successful real estate agency in Chicago.

Alan, Danny, Beth, and Karen chose to view the message of illness sent by their bodies as an opportunity to rethink their lives. Their body systems demanded a reorganization of their life performance, drawing support from the soul. In each case, the patients identified the body's signals as indicators of a loss of balance or a flaw of some kind that needed repair.

Isaac, on the other hand, responded in a different way to the persistent signals being given off by his body. He came to me during a period of rehabilitation he was undergoing following a workplace accident. His fingers had been chopped off by the grinding machine he worked with, and he had lost all feeling in his arm.

Isaac, who had dyslexia, was the oldest child in a large family that immigrated to Israel from Iraq. Since he barely knew how to read and write his vocational options were limited. He had never been satisfied with the manual labor he did for a living. His social life compensated for the lack of satisfaction he felt in his work. Isaac, who had never read a word in his life, was active in civil affairs in his community and had received considerable recognition for his efforts – the kind of acknowledgement he never received at work.

What was surprising was his relative passivity in the face of his injury. Sometimes it even seemed to me that Isaac was pleased by what had befallen him. When I tried to discuss new ways for him to earn a living, he refused to cooperate. In time, I began to understand that Isaac had absolutely no interest in finding himself a rehabilitation solution, because he had already worked out his own. Still, I felt that it was important to clarify how a skilled worker like him could have had such an accident.

"It just happened," he answered.

Something in his eyes prompted me to persist: "So tell me about it anyway."

He looked at me with wise eyes. "You know something? I never liked my job as a production worker. I never concentrated enough, most of the time I didn't pay attention to what was going on with the machine. I knew that some day it would happen."

"And when you thought about the consequences, did you know what you would do?" I asked.

"I didn't know what I'd do but I knew that I wouldn't have to go to work anymore," he said.

"And you didn't want to be there?"

"The truth? Being a production worker wasn't right for me."

"And what would be?"

"If I'd studied and if I knew how to read and write?" he asked.

"If you could choose," I said.

"I think I would be a teacher," he answered confidently.

Despite having been asked a direct question, Isaac was no longer afraid of the answer. It turned out that the answer had always been there, waiting to be discovered. At the same time, his response surprised even me. Isaac chose something that seemed to be at the opposite pole of his range of ability. He, who had never studied, dreamed of how he would impart learning to others. Yet once I began to comprehend the story of his life, things became a bit clearer. Isaac had been orphaned young, and after coming to Israel, already as an eight-year-old he had gone out into the world to help support the family.

"I didn't know anything," he told me at our next session. "I didn't even speak Hebrew. I began working as a bellboy at a small hotel but after a few years my back began hurting and I found work in a factory that was close to home. I worked there for many years, and always looked forward to evening, to the prayers in the synagogue, to the Jewish Studies Lessons, to studying and the talking to the old men. I wanted to go home and watch television. I learned a lot from television."

"Do you enjoy studying?" I asked.

"Very much," he replied.

"And if you got a stipend?"

"That would be great," he said.

Isaac is a fine example of a man who was self-aware, and who, in the context of his limitations and the limited degree of freedom life had offered him, was able to make a choice.

In all of our sessions, Isaac denied that the accident had been anything but completely accidental. As a disabled person, he was eligible for insurance compensation; and he knew how to satisfy his enduring hunger to learn by exploiting his new found freedom. He reconnected to generations of his family roots by teaching bar mitzvah boys how to sing ancient cantillation notes from the Old Testament.

"That comes from my musical memory," he told me with a smile. And at the same time, he joined an aural class for studying the Holy Scriptures.

Isaac understood that he was not qualified to develop a career on a high level. He had embarked on a spiritual path by leveraging his naturally inherent skills. His thirst for learning was very powerful and to satisfy it, he had been ready to pay – even at the price of becoming disabled.

The deal, from his standpoint, had been worth it. The lost fingers and the lost job represented his ticket to freedom, to expression, and to fulfillment.

Chapter Three
Cutting Loose Bonds between the Generations

Decoding my family genes helped me choose my true calling

My mother never stopped talking about him. Over the years, the vision of her grandfather increasingly became a family legend never to be queried. Mendl Krock belonged to a world that was passing into oblivion.

According to the stories, he was a wealthy timber merchant in Poland who transported fallen tree trunks down the Vistula River, giving his family every comfort, at a time when the Jews of the town were never certain where their daily bread was coming from.

Mendl Krock, a person who could be depended on in all situations, appeared to be the consummate businessman. It was obvious to everyone that generations of the family would follow in his footsteps, and in the flourishing Europe of the 1920s, it seemed the dynasty of His Excellency Krock was assured of perpetuity. However, somewhere along the way, something went wrong.

As a little girl, I never stopped asking my mother why she didn't have any money if her grandfather had been so wealthy. My mother had no problem with what appeared to me as a clear paradox. She pinned the blame on one person.

"My father," she told me, "grandfather's son-in-law, was a terrible businessman. In fact, he was a loser and lazy. Over the years he managed to lose most of grandfather's money through a string of unsuccessful ventures."

I heard what my mother said, yet the problem remained.

The myth of my fabulously successful great-grandfather was finally wiped out for me by my husband Dov. "If there had been a talented businessman in your family," the grandson-in-law explained to me patiently, "it's reasonable to assume that there would be more businessmen somewhere around in your family. Why don't you look into it and check for a business gene somewhere in your family. Possibly this gene found itself a home with some relative of yours. Go and search for a businessman somewhere on your vocational family tree. Because in your entire family, I have never met a single one," he added with a wink, "and maybe there never was a business gene in the family to start with. Maybe not even in the case of your 'fabulously successful great-grandfather.'"

These were my first steps in building a vocational family tree and in learning how to utilize it as a tool for my clients.

Dov was right. A search of my family roots raised startling findings. There were teachers, educators, clowns, artists, humanists – but not one single businessman. It appeared as though great-grandfather had made sure to distribute a variety of psycho-genetic qualities among his many descendents, but the quality of making money was nowhere in evidence. What my grandmother and my mother had refused to acknowledge for half a century, I began to discern as I clarified things for myself. I realized that great-grandfather had actually been an "indentured merchant." He received a great deal of money from his in-laws, and instead of going to study what he really wanted such as architecture or art, he had been forced to become a man of business.

At first I tried to cling to the idea that maybe the difficult war years had killed off the elusive business gene, but I soon learned that it wasn't so.

Over years of decoding hundreds of people's vocational family trees, I became convinced that career choices are linked to the significant figures in a person's life story. These links are intergenerational, suggesting that individual vocational inclinations are passed on from generation to generation. Pursuing this notion, I began examining the hypothesis that the choice of a career in general, and the way a person does things in particular, are very closely tied to psycho-genetics and "vocational inheritance."

So perhaps my dear grandfather never succeeded in business because he wasn't suited to that world. That's why he apparently passed on this lack of talent to his children. Yet, it seems reasonable to assume that he had passed on to them plenty of his core talents in the arts, in handiwork, and in home renovations.

Over the years, my conviction grew stronger that a person's vocational choice is derived from his identity and that his calling is influenced by the significant others in his family. The sense of being indentured to a particular profession can also be passed on as a legacy, becoming a path to non-choice.

One day, I discovered another gene in my mother's family. This psycho-gene had been passed down to the males through at least three generations on my mother's side. And then, to my surprise, I found a similar gene in my father's family...

My mother saw my father the same way her mother had seen her husband, and blamed him for a lack of success in his career. And my father, like his father before him, came to terms with his wife's negative evaluation of him – she clearly expected both of them to be "career losers."

Richard Dawkins, in his book *The Human Gene* (1989),

speaks of "memes" as the unit containing the psycho-cultural inheritance. Edward Beck and Christopher Cohen, in their book *Spiral Dynamics* (1996), broaden this notion, saying that just as biochemical genes involve biochemical DNA, "memes" involve a psycho-cultural DNA of their own. Thus the concept of the "meme" refers to a kind of psycho-gene or unit of psycho-cultural information that is passed along in the collective unconscious among individuals, families, organizations, and nations.

In my experience, it is also possible to speak of a vocational meme, or of a psycho-vocational gene. Thus, a child who grows up in a family of career success stories will internalize the message of success, and a child who grows up in a family of losers will internalize that of failure. If the father of the family is a businessman in his soul, it's quite reasonable to presume that at least one of his children will carry on his vocational torch, and may even pass it along further to successive generations. But what happens when a man who is an artist in his soul becomes a failed businessman? At least one of his children has the potential to adopt the model and pass it on down the generations.

Can this "defective gene" be reengineered? Absolutely yes, but not easily. The chain of family vocational inheritance can be broken when its genetic code is cracked; when family members become aware of it, and move carefully to re-channel it. In order to identify hidden components affecting one's vocational direction, a family Genogram can be an important tool and can facilitate real vocational choices. Breaking a family's genetic career code and enabling authentic vocational choices requires perseverance, optimism, and especially courage – the courage to change what has been deemed hereditary or learned automatically.

It was the American psychologist Virginia Satir who first enabled me to understand how family behavior can be inherited. With her help, I learned how new characteristics – positive ones, for a change – can be implanted into the hereditary chain, once we are willing to acknowledge the preexisting conceptions. Prior to that point, the very mention of a person's career being linked in any way to the family genes sent me into a rage of angry denial.

I experienced a revelation during a family therapy workshop run by Virginia Satir in Tel Aviv many years ago. A world renowned therapist, Satir requested a volunteer to come up on stage. The volunteer, a woman, was a fifty-year-old psychologist named Nina. "I have a terrible problem with my three daughters-in-law," she related. "I feel like I'm losing my mind. I'm always trying to get close to them and help them, yet they reject me as a person and exploit me unfairly. I've become angry and embittered about our relationship and I feel helpless in so many ways. I simply don't have a clue what to do about it."

The microphone passed to Satir. She asked Nina to analyze her family over three generations, mainly in terms of mothers-in-law and daughters-in-law. Nina's story, which had begun with complaints and helplessness, suddenly developed a fascinating twist. It turned out that, due to historical circumstances of war, death, and bereavement, Nina's family had lacked any mother-in-law relationships for three generations! When the daughters-in-law arrived, the mothers-in-law were already gone. Due to these tragic circumstances, no daughter-in-law/mother-in-law traditions had ever been formed, and thus no behavioral patterns were passed along down the line.

Nina simply did not know how to behave: she had no models to emulate in managing a relationship between a mother-in-law and a daughter-in-law. She read books on mothers-in-law and rounded out this questionable theoretical foundation by watching films and talking with friends. The mother-in-law figure was a fantasy figure for her. Although she desperately tried to be the ideal mother-in-law, she had no concept of the ordinary day-to-day relationship between daughters-in-law and mothers-in-law.

In the workshop, Nina learned for the first time that the way she related to her daughters-in-law wasn't natural. Although she always went out of her way for them, she never actually listened to them or paid attention to their needs. Nor did she listen to herself. She placed herself and her daughters-in-law into boxes that allowed no room for feelings of anger, no room for arguments. From her own standpoint, her relationship with them allowed for no clarification, no negotiation.

At the time I had no idea what a gift for the future Virginia and Nina had given me. Only after Nina finished speaking and left the podium did I suddenly see the light. In my family, too, there had been no mothers-in-law for three generations! It flashed through my brain that the issue would become problematical if I were to marry, and I made a mental note to remember that when the time came.

At the time, I had no idea that I would end up marrying an orphan myself...

Later I came to understand that someone who lacks an emotional psycho-gene in a given family-emotional area, such as love or marriage, is likely to have a similar experience on a career level, or with other issues. A person whose parental figures didn't reflect meaningful vocational models is liable to be unaware of this lack in himself. I also learned that identifying what is missing, like recognizing what is present and pinpointing its source, is crucial for diagnosing the problem and evolving toward a satisfactory solution in order to reach career fulfillment. When a family's vocational genealogy is straightforward, and their way of relating to various professions is clearly understood, this facilitates an understanding of how to cope with vocational identity.

Years after that workshop, when I was already married, I met Nina at a professional conference. The meeting was enlightening. When I reminded her of the workshop with Virginia, she smiled and said: "After that workshop, I decided to go home and break the hereditary chain. I had a huge fight with my daughters-in-law during which I made clear to them that things were about to change and that I expected a little give-and-take from them. "And," she added, "you know what? After that things became easier for them, too."

Now it was my turn to smile. I told her that her story had evoked in me a desire to understand my own hereditary family baggage. I told her how much my work, particularly my understanding of career impasse, had been enriched by virtue of this heightened awareness of how family genes can impact our work and our careers. Choice of a vocation and one's personal vision are very closely linked with the myths and the emotional experiences of previous generations. Thus a young woman who chooses a teaching career is likely to find that her mother, though illiterate, taught young brides how to run a household, and that her grandmother was a well-known story-teller...

The important thing is that awareness enables us freedom of choice so that while our destinies are predetermined, free will can always be exercised.

Michael White (1991), a creative Australian therapist and researcher who studied families, wrote that families are like states or tribes. Each family is unique in its laws and values, its behavioral norms, language, leadership, and secrets. Thus beyond the strictly genetic inheritance of a family, there is a psycho-genetic pool or an occupational "meme pool," to paraphrase Dawkins. Researching your family is an anthropological journey of discovery. A child born into a given family is suffused with its atmosphere and norms, and contributes its own uniqueness to the family infrastructure. Understanding our family-tribal baggage enables us to identify our uniqueness and exercise our freedom of choice, while helping us to recognize the limitations and restrictions that are imposed on our choices.

Murray Bowen (1980) wrote about a trans-generational psycho-genetic bequeathing process, mostly unconscious, that enables personal qualities, emotional messages, and modes of functioning to pass like a silk thread from one generation to another. When we are unaware of these, we continue the family line without the possibility of choice and, sometimes, without even knowing that our choices are not made consciously of our own free will.

In their book *Genograms in Family Assessment* (1985), Monica McGoldrik and Randy Gerson use family trees to study the structure and psychodynamic traits of families. They evaluate how a family functions, the sibling roles within the family, and the emotional and interpersonal coping styles between family members.

In this context, they analyzed the vocations of some well-known families. They looked, for example, at the family tree of Alexander Graham Bell, inventor of the telephone, revealing a surprising finding. Over three generations, the Bell family displayed interesting phenomena of stuttering and deafness among its women. The grandfather, the fathers, and the sons all dealt in phonetics, stuttering, and the art of pronunciation. Integration of the family talents occurred only in the third generation. Alexander, son of a deaf mother and married to a deaf woman, studied and taught hearing-impaired people as had his brother, his father, and his grandfather – and he ended up inventing the telephone.

Thus, down through the generations of the Bell family, the men became experts in hearing and speech, as if trying to compensate the impaired members of the family by finding solutions to their communication problems.

In the Bell family, the confrontation with weakness and disability was transformed into an inspired source of vocational creativity and invention over several generations of males.

Every family is a system with an emotional and value structure of its own, involving its own unique model of interrelatedness. Hence, via a superficial analysis of the family's vocational tree, one can see how other family members can be influenced by one member's courage to change.

It's amazing how unaware we are of the many behavioral models that so greatly impact upon our career choices and the activities we end up pursuing. Clearly, ignorance concerning the sources of our influences makes it so much more powerful. Lack of awareness of influences rooted in the past can thwart our ability to recognize choices made and opportunities for change, and this can leave us relatively defenseless in the face of what I have termed Chronic Vocational Impasse.

When people acquire awareness, and hence a clearer picture of their vocational history, their range of choice expands. Thus, it becomes easier to accept the limitations of what is feasible or not. If, for example, we are dealing with a man's vocational choices, we would be well advised to thoroughly check not only which occupations were chosen by the men of the family, but also how those vocational choices were made and how they were viewed. Were the men's occupations valued within the family? For a full understanding, it's useful to check whether there are other "inherited" variables as well. We can ask questions like: What activities or hobbies did they have that were not income-producing? How successful were they? Were the eldest boys' professions viewed favorably, or those of the younger boys? It is also worthwhile to find out what vocations were chosen by the women of the family.

Sometimes it turns out that a hobby can bring a person respect and increased satisfaction while inducing feelings of achievement and success. Significance can be attached to what a person loved doing and not necessarily how a living was made. Thus, for example, I would recommend that a woman whose grandmother was a housewife try to find out what talents her grandmother was known for among members of the family. For example: chef (she was a "great cook"); public relations ("she was great at hosting affairs"); advising (she was the family "psychotherapist"), and so on.

By looking at the recognition your family members awarded a particular vocation, you can learn which professions were valued in your family over the generations. You may even learn something about the worth you assign a particular profession.

A family vocational tree or Genogram is a simple, but very powerful, mapping device. It enables the searcher to find the hidden talents – "lost" vocations, "forbidden" occupations, and professions that became family standard-bearers.

Terah, father of the biblical Abraham, was a maker of idols. His son Abraham followed family tradition in the sense that he "created" the Jewish God, an abstract god, but not before he smashed all of his father's idol-gods … He didn't smash the god-building "gene," he merely found his god according to his own beliefs. He didn't completely break free of the genetic constraints that threatened to bind him, yet he elevated them to an abstract level.

The vocational journey of two sisters, Hannah and Gail, involved breaking the trans-generational chain that had relegated the men in the family to miss out on their appropriate vocation, one generation after another. This case, however, is a model of the quest for vocational fulfillment waged by the women in a family, in which the men struggled and failed, whilst the women struggled and succeeded.

When Hannah came to me, she was in the last stages of pregnancy. A good-looking woman, Hannah camouflaged herself completely under a facade of neglect and tasteless dress, giving the impression of a simple sort of person who had allowed life to pass her by. If not for the fluency of her speech, one could have mistaken Hannah for someone from a highly disadvantaged neighborhood. She spoke about how she felt suffocated and left behind from a vocational perspective.

Immediatly, in our first session, I explained the unique

difficulties in advising pregnant women, but she claimed that it was the pregnancy that had prompted her to come. Sometimes, women feel confused between their vocational activities and their motherhood, and instead of seeking fulfillment through work they take a legitimate time-out via pregnancy. There are cases when they even use such a break as a training ground for moving up a notch. Sometimes women exploit their pregnancy interlude to repair their relationship with their partners, or to settle accounts and open more constructive modes of communication with significant others in their lives. Other women use this time to examine their vocational situation. There are even some men who do so vicariously via pregnancy and parenthood but, in the nature of things, less directly than in the case of women.

The longer we talked, the more we realized that from a certain standpoint Hannah's current pregnancy was preparing her to give birth to herself. She had been the second child in her family and now was about to give birth to her second child. We both understood that there was significance in the fact that she had come for counseling precisely at this particular stage of her life.

"Very often, we identify with the child whose place in the birth order is the same as ours, and tend to have unique, strong feelings for that child," I told Hannah, from long experience. "Often the two children get mixed up – the one who is about to be born, with the one who was already born, but still doesn't know where their life is going."

Hannah listened closely, but stood her ground. She felt that the urgency here was because of the infant. "You see," she said, "if I don't solve my vocational problems by the time I give birth, I'll be causing a situation where my daughter may inherit my lack of choice."

Only very rarely have I had the opportunity to set out on a journey with a woman who spoke my own language even before we met…

At the voyage's outset, we first attempted to gain information and a better awareness of her origins. Hannah and I began constructing her family's vocational tree in order to throw light on which of the family's activities had been successful, and which not.

She knew right away that her own work aspirations were identical to the dream both her grandmother and her mother had cherished – all three had wanted very much to work in the arts. Her grandmother and her mother hadn't found the way to live that dream. Hannah, however, had decided to discover her path.

Hannah knew clearly where she was stuck. Though she had run her husband's business for many years, she had always been irresistibly drawn to anything involving weaving, painting, and sculpture.

"I know that I want to paint," she insisted at our second meeting, "Deep down, I know that I am an artist. I want to express myself with color and form. And yet, something in me is stuck. Now I understand that part of that is a result of the weight of generations, or maybe it's even a curse across the generations."

Hannah understood that she had still not broken the chain, and she had not even identified all its components.

We continued with our analysis of her vocational Genogram.

"Though my mother worked as a teacher," she told me, "she always dreamed of painting."

"And what about you?" I asked.

"I… I also have dreams… but I will fulfill them… and maybe that way, my daughter will be able to fulfill her own dreams when the time comes…"

At that time we did not yet know that her personal fulfillment would make it easier for both her mother and her sister to go ahead and pursue their respective vocational dreams.

"My father worked in national security," Hannah said, turning immediately to a discussion of her father, as if to maintain a delicate balance between him and her mother. "As far as I know, he loved his work and would come home all smiles. After my sister and I were born, my mother got tired of moving around from place to place, from city to city, from one army base to another. She suggested that we move to a kibbutz, permanently. I found out," said Hannah, her face suddenly appearing to age, "that a kibbutz can be an excellent incubator for vocationally stuck people." At that time, most kibbutz members worked at a job that was needed by the collective, rather than in a job that fulfilled a person's calling.

After moving to the kibbutz, her mother became a caregiver for children and a cook, while her father worked in the kibbutz plastics factory.

"My father," related Hannah, "who until the move to the kibbutz was a dynamic military man, gradually became embittered and frustrated. He moved about dejectedly from one job to another, but never found his niche. Meanwhile, due to the anger and dissatisfaction, he gradually distanced himself from my mother, and over time, the alienation between them grew."

"And that's the story of your father?" I asked. I wondered about the father's version and whether he had left a successful career or not? He couldn't have done it only for his wife and children.

"Of course not," agreed Hannah bitterly. "Just before his death, some of the secrets came out."

We continued with our journey. We wanted to go deeper, to peel back another layer in the family story. Hannah knew how to do this. She, like her father, had the psycho-genes of a researcher in the secret service.

Hannah thought some sort of crisis had occurred in her father's vaunted military career.

"When we moved to the kibbutz," she said, sharing her thoughts with me, "it was as if we were avoiding coping with the crisis and the frustration. My father had a difficult orphaned childhood. When he was two, his mother died right after his brother was born. Three years later, when he was about five, he lost his father, who himself had lost his own parents in a car accident. Thus, for my father, death was tied to births and parenting. My father yearned to be a better father but didn't know how to come to terms with being a parent or how to approach it. In some way, the kibbutz gave him a kind of release from the need to cope with life."

At that stage I understood that Hannah, too, was afraid of losing parts of herself by virtue of her impending parenthood.

"Actually," she summed up, "my parents didn't face up to their real problems, and so our major systems deteriorated – their marriage, the family, and their careers."

Hannah understood that career choice is part of an overall functional emotional whole.

"In the end," I added, "your father relived the story of his life as an orphan with you. Perhaps he was consciously trying to get closer to you, but in practice he distanced himself from all of you."

"Yes," she agreed, "and in the end he became chronically ill and gave up everything… almost killing himself…"

Hannah's story had by now generated an anguished heaviness in the atmosphere of the room. I mulled over how cautious one must be, and how much effort is required, when confronting such immense pain. So much has to be changed in order to prevent a fall that seems preordained, even when there is an awareness of potential breakthroughs.

At my next session with Hannah, I noticed a change. She had the special beauty of a young woman about to give birth, almost a look of fulfillment and satisfaction. Hannah, unlike her father, could look at the difficulties, get past them, and move on. She was also the child of a different generation for whom career fulfillment was more acceptable and even necessary.

"You're not willing to give up your dream?" I said, rephrasing her wish.

"No. That's the main thing," she said. "I understand that it involves a lot of pain. I feel a need to go back in time and understand what happened to my father and mother who had desires and dreams but weren't able to find fulfillment. I have to understand what happened to me, their little girl, who dreams as they did, and who has such a hard time making her dreams come true."

Hannah was silent for a moment, and then, hesitantly, continued: "I think my father and mother had no idea where their impasse came from, and they began to hate each other because of it. My sister Gail and I were both little girls and found ourselves constantly on high alert." The creases in her face deepened, especially the one along the ridge of her nose, which became very pronounced.

Where was she getting the courage and determination to change the code handed down over generations? I asked myself, and then asked her.

"My older sister Gail had it worse than me," Hannah continued, "though my situation was pretty bad, too, but at least I was my father's favorite. Gail was really an abused child. My mother didn't hit her, but she found fault with everything she did.

"My father paid attention to me only because of my studies," she went on. "I knew that if I came to him with my math homework, I'd get a little love and attention. Beyond that, nothing. As if I weren't his little girl. Anything that went through my head and that I tried to share with him, any interesting encounter I'd had with a friend and came to tell him – it was as though he closed his eyes to it.

"When I grew older," she continued, as if to herself, "I asked myself, how had I managed to find a father within a father who had himself been orphaned and hardly experienced parental love? The struggle was doomed ahead of time," she whispered, and tears appeared for the first time. "You know, I haven't cried for many years," she whispered. I took her hand.

She gripped mine in return, and held on hard.

Several minutes passed. Behind the screen of tears, a smile appeared. We both felt that Hannah was wrapped in a new aura of tranquility. Thereafter, the way forward was somewhat simpler. Hannah understood that her desire to be a mother was linked with her desire for wholeness and fulfillment of her need to express herself through the arts. She wanted to connect the two manifestations of her authentic self. When she understood this, she made a commitment to the quest for fulfillment.

It took us several long months of work to arrive at the point at which Hannah had built herself a successful multi-media company and was managing it happily, while creating and moving forward. The painting came even later.

A short time after my journey of discovery with Hannah, her older sister Gail came to see me.

"My sister Hannah sent me," Gail whispered, as if she had come to tell me a story about someone else.

Gail had left her boyfriend John behind in Zimbabwe. John was an alcoholic and a drug addict. He had never earned a living, indeed had never done much of anything; trying to repair him was, as Gail put it, "her life's work."

"What attracted you to John?" I asked her. From her story I understood that John was the masculine aspect of Gail, the rejected, abused daughter.

"Perhaps loving John was like loving Gail," I suggested.

"Could be," she murmured, and paused for a long time, finally adding: "Only after I was able to take care of John and accept him as he was, with all his flaws, was I able to accept myself... as if I was the accepting mother to Gail the rejected child."

Gail, like Hannah, had a rich and sharply expressive vocabulary and manner of speaking.

"From a young age no one wanted me," she told me. "No one could bear having me around – neither my mother, nor my family, nor the kibbutz. I was an awful child. No one could stand me."

"There are no awful children!" I interrupted, "there is only an environment that brands a child as 'awful.'"

Gail gazed at me and burst into bitter tears, and she wept intermittently throughout the entire session.

As Gail talked, the family portrait that Hannah had already begun sketching for me became clearer. "My father was never at home. And when he would finally show up, he never stayed there. His presence wasn't discernible. He would sit with us in the living room, but his thoughts were always elsewhere."

"Then you were an orphan, too," I mused aloud.

"Yes," she answered, "I was an orphan – on both sides. My sister at least had a father. When Hannah asked him to help her solve her math problems, he would sit with her for hours. He helped her and she, in return, delivered him excellent grades. Whereas I – he never even looked at me. All I remember about him is his hollow eyes and angry glances. My father didn't take care of his little girl. I was no more than air, to him. Sometimes, I even felt that I repelled him."

"And what about your mother?" I asked.

Gail's eyes were fearful, her shoulders hunched, her lips tight, and she spoke in a muted tone as if trying hard to hide the storm raging inside her. "My mother was worse," she whispered. "My mother named me after her mother, with whom she had a poor relationship; and she simply hated me. Every time she saw me, she became aggravated. Whatever I did or didn't do, was a disaster."

At our next session, Gail described for me how she used to neglect herself. "I didn't comb my hair, I didn't brush my teeth, I didn't cut my fingernails," she said.

Gail judged herself very harshly and sentenced herself to a social exile that followed from her self-neglect. She had no guardian, no mother and no father. The angel of salvation appeared to her, in fact, at the boarding school to which she had been sent.

Gail told me that one day, while she was sitting in class, gazing into space as usual, a heavy and unfamiliar hand landed on her shoulder, and a low feminine voice said to her: "I am going to be your teacher. I can see you have intelligent eyes. With me, you will learn and you will get good grades."

"This amazing sentence had tremendous power," related Gail. "It caused me to take showers, cut my nails, study on a regular basis, and get top grades. That teacher was the first person who stopped to actually look at me. She was the first person who really saw me. The problem was that after I finished boarding school, I went back home."

But this time, Gail understood what she had to do. She decided to run away. "I didn't understand it then," she told me. "Now, when I relive all that, I remember my father, always angry at me, and my mother, fading away at his side. Only in Zimbabwe, thousands of miles from my parents, did I finally feel that I could be myself."

What her parents couldn't give her, she decided to give to herself.

Like Hannah, Gail was deeply attracted to the arts yet was afraid to touch the subject. In Zimbabwe, she worked at whatever jobs came along and later went from being a waitress to managing a restaurant. Immediately after her return to Israel, she received an offer to return to her traditional vocation: running a restaurant. This time, however, Gail decided to refuse. Though she had no other source of income at the time, she decided to rely on herself. She came to me with the goal of learning about her origins and figuring out her dreams and how to realize them.

Slowly but surely, she began wanting to integrate her capability in the business management field with her ability to express herself creatively, an ability she decided to develop from within herself. Positive evaluation from aptitude tests led her to realize that she had many talents and this reinforced her new and healthier self-perception.

Gradually Gail was able to combine her two loves: creative arts and management. She took some courses in cooking, and became a chef in a small, well-thought-of restaurant. Later on she studied in France and was hired as a chef in a renowned French restaurant.

The little girl who had been hungry all her life repaired her soul through the nourishment of others, through creative giving. And she didn't let go of her dream to open her own restaurant.

Gail understood, and showed me, part of the special bond that chefs feel with their vocation. "My renewal was from my roots," she explained in her own special language. "For me, food is tied to giving and to nurturing."

I thought about three-year-olds who build sand castles on the shore, and make "meatballs" from the sand to feed their guests.

I remembered how, along with their first colorful scribbles, nursery school children bake mud pies. Food and drawing have their source in a common essence. Perhaps that is why the artist and graphic artist construct what they say from the materials of their childhood. It wasn't coincidental that Gail began sculpting only after she had become a master chef.

Hannah and Gail began their recovery process through the feminine side of themselves. And they helped one another.

Hannah's recovery process also made good use of her pregnancy and the birth of her daughter, her second child. Her sister Gail restored herself through cooking, and through her partnership in her sister's journey.

Nonetheless, at that stage the recovery was not yet complete. As tragic as it may sound, the two sisters were unable to close the circle of their renewed lives without their father's illness, which presented another opportunity for healing. When her father fell ill, Gail again left the country. She was unable to care for him on his sickbed. She knew that she was still too weak and angry. I helped her to respect this inability and to continue her search for a new path to self-expression.

Hannah, in contrast, was determined to let the past go and take care of her father. He had paid her sufficient attention for her to reciprocate.

"He literally faded away in front of our eyes," she recalled, "but it was then, in his weakness, that he began to finally see me as a person. So I was able to take care of him and communicate with him."

I understood Hannah, because I had made a mess of things at the exact point where she had succeeded. When my father fell ill, I sat next to his bed for three months, but his anger at himself, and my fear, were too strong, and we missed our chance. Still, some aspect of giving, some facet of the closeness and our shared period of inverted parenting, provided a measure of comfort to both of us. After three months of mutual caring, my ability to love grew into a devotion that was new to me.

Hannah forgave her father and was freed to turn to her vocation, to the world of graphic art and multimedia. She felt that she did so out of choice, and that she was not coerced. She felt none of the guilt that can come when permission to seek fulfillment is withheld. She was able to do this without getting stuck, by coming into direct contact with her ability to express herself profoundly.

Hannah knew that there had been no malicious intent on her father's side. But she also realized that the impasse had not arisen because of some flaw in her. Her impasse was tied to her father's sense that he lacked permission for personal expression and for real dialogue, with himself and with her. Hannah now knew that his ability to choose and to feel alive was constricted, just as his vocational creativity had been constricted.

I suggested that Hannah should ask her father what he had wanted to do when he was young.

"As you suggested, I asked my father what he really had wanted to do," she told me, "and he answered, 'Not only did I not know what I wanted to do, I didn't even ask myself that question. In my generation, we didn't ask such questions.' After that, he died."

Hannah understood that there had been a new look of wholeness and reconciliation in his last glance. "Suddenly, there with me, he stopped being an orphan," she said. "Only then was he able to relate to himself some other way, more positively. Through him, I developed and grew, too. Certainly it was an opportune interlude for both of us."

In that way, Hannah gained a father for a few short months, and he found the "parent" he'd never had. During their last weeks together, they were both restoring their souls, together.

Thus Hannah, through this new experience, was able to alter the structure of the weighty psycho-genetic chain of orphan-hood and parental neglect, which for years had threatened her future, both emotionally and vocationally. She was able to grant herself what her father had never allowed himself – to be accepted. Only from this perspective could Hannah allow herself real fulfillment.

Thus things came full circle and a new chapter was opened, Hannah's birth as a complete human being. On our journey, we had understood the profound importance of Hannah being able to undertake this process before giving birth to her daughter. Completing her feeling of being "someone's daughter" gave her the space to be "someone's mother."

"Now, after a long pregnancy of thirty-four years, I can finally give birth to my tremendous hunger for creative self-expression!" said Hannah, with joy.

Gail's path was a longer one. Seeing her younger sister Hannah seize the permission she required offered Gail a beacon of hope in her own quest for fulfillment.

Hannah and Gail were the children of unfulfilled parents whose ignorance and vocational impasse had been handed down, in hereditary fashion, to their daughters.

"I always knew what I would do when I grew up," said Hannah. "Even in first grade, I used to scribble drawings in the margins of my notebooks. I needed only justification and permission. In the end, I received the go-ahead through my ability to be my father's daughter, and thanks to the journey we took together, hand in hand, phase by phase, and thanks to your determination to make it possible for me to express myself."

"And there was also your mother, who contributed something, wasn't there?" I added, somewhere between asking and stating.

The anger had by then waned somewhat.

"Mother also gave us the creative urge," replied Hannah. "She gave us the ability to survive and the right to fight for our lives…"

Not in vain did Hannah, and later on Gail, tell themselves what millions of people all over the world say to themselves quietly: "If I can't do what I really want to do with my life, I will cease to exist." The problem is that millions of others continue to give up on their dreams.

The distance between Gail and her father was greater than in Hannah's case and the recovery, therefore, was longer and more difficult. But Gail, too, even if only unconsciously, knew what could help spring her out of impasse. By caring for John, the drug-addicted orphan who lacked everything, by caring for this down-and-out man, Gail had been able to find a bit of salvation.

Once, when I asked her if she had loved John, she looked at me in surprise. "Do you think I know how to love?" she asked. I was embarrassed. I understood how desperately hard it had been for Gail to cope with her continual quest for love.

After two years or so, Gail told me, "I need more. I'm no longer satisfied with preparing food, which disappears immediately afterwards. I want to make 'food' that will last. I want to create something that will be respected and remain forever and ever."

Gradually, Gail moved toward the world of creative arts until she discovered sculpting. This, she felt was her true calling.

"Statues are forever," said Gail at our final session. In her hands, she held one of her sculptures – the figure of a woman, every line radiating unmistakable independence and self-sufficiency.

Hannah needed the infant she was raising. Gail, on the other hand, chose not to have children. Instead she sculpted them.

Hannah, who had ultimately experienced her father's acceptance directly, told me at the close of our last meeting, "I am going to raise a daughter who was born to a mother who gave herself permission to be born. To this child, so much more will be acceptable. She will be able to be, to express, to do. And most important – she will be her mother's child, a mother who allows herself to choose and who is in touch with her needs and boundaries."

Hannah and Gail dared to break the genetic chains that bound the generations of their family. They were helped by decoding their career barriers and by life processes. They chose to reach for self-fulfillment, and they chose to consciously undergo the process of renewal almost simultaneously with each other. This is unusual but is more common among children whose parents failed both at parenting and in self-fulfillment.

Most of us go through unconscious parallel processes when one of our family members begins a process of search and change. A change in one system is a change in all. Families, like organizations, are built like systems, so when a part of the arrangement changes, the whole system changes – for better or for worse.

Chapter Four
Know Thyself

Awareness of my identity was the gateway to a meaningful career

I have always felt that people know quite well where they are stuck. Some people at an impasse even know where they would like to go, and they sense which route they must choose to move towards self-actualization. What they lack is an understanding of precisely what is bothering them, how to put it behind them, and how to acquire tools for coping with the issues they encounter along the road to fulfillment.

When I was five years old, my only brother, Zorick, was born. For a third of his brief life he was gravely ill, and when I was six-and-a-half, he died. His death filled my parents with guilt, despair, and helplessness at their failure to save him. All this changed my place in the family, and afterwards in the world. I became an invisible observer. The child I was and the person I grew up to be – was no longer seen. In their mourning, my parents bequeathed me only half a life: the active half. The feeling half, for many years, stood honor guard over the family's bereavement.

A child's emotional niche and history in the family can be a springboard to achievement, but also an obstacle. As a child matures, he or she needs to have someone provide a kind of supervised "training program" to help overcome the pain and the obstacles scattered like stones in the field of life – in order for the child's destiny to germinate, develop, and flower.

My encounter with Nathan was such a voyage of growth. It was a journey from have-not to have; a voyage from the inner world of Nathan, born to a reality in which his existence was acknowledged and permitted only when he was absent and erased from sight, towards the experience of an existence filled with work, satisfaction, and fulfillment.

I first met Nathan soon after he had undergone vocational testing. He asked me to take a look at the results.

They were astonishing. The report placed on my desk that day unequivocally indicated: "The subject has exceptional ability in all realms of endeavor: technical, mathematical, verbal, creative, etc. If he so desires, he could excel as a top journalist, electronics engineer, or accountant."

"This man has a rare breadth of talent," stated the counselor who brought me the report. "He must be a top executive, right?"

I had a hard time replying. The gap between the test results and the reality of Nathan's situation was so vast that I needed time to assimilate the information. In fact, it was almost impossible to connect the data with Nathan, who appeared lethargic and spoke in a dry, distant monotone. Perhaps it was his very alienation that drew me to him.

Later on, with Nathan poised to embark on his road to self-actualization, I realized how commonly the death of a sibling turns out to be a deciding factor in a child's life. Often parents are blind to a child's existence and ignore the child's needs, feeling, or talents.

"I've always wanted to work in accounting," said Nathan bluntly, and a bit awkwardly, "but I'm nowhere near that. And I don't understand why or where I'm stuck."

I wondered to myself why he didn't bother to ask if that was the right profession for him; the information was lying there from the psychological assessment he had just undergone. Clearly Nathan knew that at that point it was not yet relevant.

I realized right from the outset that Nathan was trapped in the maze of his life. He was up against that great riddle. Why, despite his impressive range of talents and the fact that he recognized his life direction quite clearly, had Nathan worked for all those years as a junior technician in a small refrigeration company?

There was no doubt that Nathan was going to be a professional challenge for me. Yet beyond that, he seemed like a small island of sadness. I wanted to rescue him from his private prison, but I had no idea how to go about it.

Our first session resembled shots fired in desperation through a fog. I fired off volley after volley at what appeared to be an impenetrable thicket, hoping that somehow I would connect and create an opening. At the beginning I asked Nathan routine questions: family status, age, type of employment, education, and the other getting-acquainted questions that frame the beginning of a long, drawn-out quest. I asked, and he answered. Pale and listless, Nathan's eyes remained vacant and his shoulders slumped.

"My wife sent me," he eventually told me.

I kept still, focused on hearing that voice breaking through.

"I don't know exactly why I came to you," he continued. "Maybe I came to get counseling or direction. Truthfully, I don't have the slightest idea what I'm going to be when I grow up… and I've been grown up already for so many years," he said, with a forlorn, resigned look in his eyes.

"What do you do?" I asked.

"I'm a technician," he answered immediately.

"A good one?"

"Yes, but so what?" he added belligerently, as if the words were being torn from his mouth. "I've never liked to study!"

Those appeared to be Nathan's first words to me uttered on his own initiative.

"So how do you learn?" I asked, hoping to hear another voice from among the ruins of his wishes and desires.

I tried to relate to him with a series of typical psychotherapist's questions. What kind of a reader is he? What sort of breaks does he take? What does he do with his eyes? How fast does he read? Does he make spelling mistakes, and if so, of what nature? What kind of temperament does he have?

We both got bored, however, and were unable to generate any momentum. Nathan slumped further and further down. The maze seemed more complicated than ever.

And then, suddenly, Nathan said: "Something inside me puts me off."

I looked at him. Suddenly I recognized, in the slumped shoulders and the vacant eyes, the type of person who had been forbidden to succeed.

I looked at Nathan again and knew that I had discovered the solitary confinement in which he was imprisoned. Now I would have to find the key to free him. I wanted to learn something about the background to this imprisonment. From my experience, it is often the case that this kind of a prison sentence is connected to family patterns of free choice.

"Tell me, Nathan," I went on conventionally, "what did your parents do? Were they satisfied with their work? How good was your relationship with them?"

Nathan smiled in embarrassment and scratched his head. "My father was a blue-collar worker all his life," he said. "He always used to tell us that work was work, leisure was leisure, and that they shouldn't be confused with one another. 'You don't go to work to enjoy yourself,' he used to say. The truth is that I had a problem with my father. Until I was grown up, I had no relationship with him at all. He was a man with no aspirations – stubborn, indifferent – and highly skilled with his hands."

"Okay, so what did you two do together?" I prodded him.

Despite everything, I believed in the ability of fathers and sons to communicate along various channels. Nathan's reply surprised me: "We played soccer together. Every Saturday. We used to play on a little field behind our old house."

I breathed easier. I sensed that I had succeeded, if only for a moment, in making contact with the source of Nathan's vitality.

"And what about your father's work?" I pressed on.

"My father wasn't much of a success at work."

"And your mother?"

"My mother was a cleaning lady. She was a warm, friendly person."

"Who do you take after?" I asked.

"To some extent, I'm like my mother – I'm a worrier, and I want to help, like her."

I smiled. There was a note of success in the way Nathan spoke. He talked of his mother warmly and with pride, and the metaphorical dungeon was suddenly illuminated with a flash of light.

The riddle was not yet completely solved, but parts of it were becoming clearer. My experience inclined me to press on. I knew that we were approaching the goal. I pursued a line of questioning about his parents' parents and we discovered that the psycho-genetics, although complicated, were not an obstacle. Something else was clanking around the cell – something murky, heavy and threatening, some bond that had hold of Nathan. He did not have enough strength to break those heavy iron chains by himself.

I tried to break in by referring to his married life and asked him about his wife.

"My wife?" he repeated, his eyes lighting up for a moment. "My wife has always urged me to study – workshops, seminars, new projects – everything. But somehow, it hasn't taken me anywhere."

Nathan's expression once again became indifferent.

"What does your wife do?" I asked, moving on with my interrogation.

"Carol's a dental technician, very successful, and she's a very optimistic person."

"What about your siblings?" I asked. I wanted to become familiar with a broader cross-section of his vocational family tree. Moreover, I knew that there were only so many avenues of inquiry left to me. My brain was working feverishly as I tried to puzzle it out.

Nathan didn't understand my distress. "There are three of us..." he began, "though actually, I had an older brother who died when he was a year old. At the time, I wasn't on the scene yet... I came into the picture only after his death."

The fact that it was so important to him to be precise about the timing of his own conception was, for me, a green light.

I asked him to tell me a little more about it. "My brother Mickey died because the doctors made a mistake. He was a year old. He had appendicitis and there were complications. I never asked about the details," he said. "Because of him I guess I'm special," he added in a near whisper. "I think I came into the world, well, sort of to take his place."

Nathan didn't know how right he was. Not infrequently, parents who lose a child tend to have a "replacement" baby to fill the space left by the loss. Often, this replacement child does not have, indeed must not have, a real space of his own in the world. Serving as the stand-in is his designated role. The hopes his parents had nurtured for his sibling are now passed onto the tender shoulders of the replacement child. Sometimes the demands are so strenuous that the replacement child relinquishes the impossible mission in advance. When we factor in this sort of psychogenetic inheritance of a failed struggle for existence, clearly such a person needs tremendous powers to attain any forward movement at all.

Such children are born into immediate distress. They sense the demand that they become two, or even three, individuals. Sadness and depression mark the loss of the dead sibling, while the living child's very existence compensates for the dead child's absence. As another patient of mine, who had also lost a sibling in childhood, once said, "I am a walking memorial." Still another bereaved brother once told me, "I am a living grave."

Nathan, in fact, had had an additional heavy burden to bear. "A year after me my brother Max was born," he related. "Max always wanted what I had, and I always gave it to him. I always deferred to him."

"Why did you? Did you ever think about that?" I asked, mainly to hear him give voice to the unfairness of it.

"Because of my mother. My mother was so sad, and all I wanted was for her to be happy, I wanted her not to worry so much."

"Your mother loved you."

"I was a special child. Only now talking with you, I'm beginning to figure out that I filled the place of two sons – the living one and the dead one."

"In my experience," I told him, "you aren't the only one to respond in this way. You must remember that it's impossible to live for two – it's hard to be satisfied with what you do, however great it is, if the expectations are doubled. A child who is expected to fill the role of his dead brother is doomed to failure: no matter what he does, he will never be able to fulfill people's hopes."

I explained to Nathan that people in this situation tend towards inaction, reaching conclusions like "I don't know what I want to be when I grow up" or "I have to do something special that no one else has ever done" or "I have to do something especially wonderful and anything less will be a disappointment."

Nathan seemed embarrassed. "That's exactly how I feel," he said. "I want to do something special. Maybe for my mother more than for my dead brother. She always did everything for me, but I couldn't pay her back. I couldn't. I even tried to bring my dead brother to life. Once I asked her to call me Mickey and she cried. I asked her to be happy about what I said, and she was sad and said nothing. Finally, I guess I chose to kill off the living child – myself."

"That's where the 'giving up' comes in," I said in agreement. "Renouncing need, forgoing the search, and especially renouncing actualization – which is doomed in advance to be inadequate, and maybe impossible."

"You know what? I've never thought about it in that way," he said, sitting up straighter. "It's not easy to see things from the inside. I… I've hardly talked at all in my life. With my father, never. I always kept quiet. With my mother, most of our relationship didn't involve words. All she had to do was look at me, and I'd do whatever she wanted, out of love."

I sensed that it was still too early to deal with the inevitable anger and frustration, too soon to go into the burden of the legacy that had been laid on Nathan.

"After me, two more brothers were born," he continued. "None of us is really educated. I'm sure that all three of us could at least have finished university."

"Nathan, comforter of the bereaved. You still don't know what you can achieve. In spite of the fact that, at our first session, you hinted that you do know the field you'd choose, for self-actualization…."

"Evidently," he said, and stopped.

"Even before you came to me," I emphasized, "you pretty much knew what you wanted to do. It seems that your problem is in trying to define what you want for yourself, not for your mother or your dead brother."

I saw clearly that Nathan, like many other people who come to me for counseling, knew quite well his own worth and what he wanted. For such people psychological testing and vocational evaluation merely serve as confirmation.

Children also know what they want. Nathan's desires were buried deep inside him. He knew his direction and had the necessary spark for adequate action. I was worried that the existence of that spark might be in danger.

A month passed. Nathan thought things over and continued to digest them. "When I was an adolescent, I used to write," he recalled. "I wrote about all sorts of things. My thoughts, experiences, ideas that came to me. I put it all in a drawer. Now, I don't write, and I don't have any other kind of outlet either. Nothing."

"Nothing?"

"Well, not really. I knew that a confrontation with my mother would be hard for her, not for me. I can't do that to her," said Nathan, almost to himself.

Nathan was born to a fragile mother and, thus, that is how he perceived her as a woman, too. He could not take the risk of losing her. He could not allow himself to accuse her or be angry with her for having forced him to bear the burden of his dead brother.

When a small child dies, the parent carries a tremendous amount of guilt and anger. These feelings connect with a certain rage at oneself for daring to try to be a good parent to a living child. After the failure to parent the child who died, how can one be happy about the child who's alive? How can one be happy at all?

The child who serves as a replacement imbibes these feelings with his mother's milk. His mother, in fact, conveys a dangerously mixed message. Anything is possible, and nothing is possible. Be both dead and alive. In Nathan's terms, it went like this: "If I wrote, they would expect me to be, at the very least, a Wordsworth or a Shakespeare, and at the same time they would expect me to be incapable of writing anything at all. I wrote poems that impressed people, but I stopped pretty quickly," he noted candidly. "I just gave it up. That's exactly the old pain that's been chasing me ever since. I'm dying to write, and it never happens. Giving it up is killing me."

"What else have you given up?" I asked.

Nathan surprised me further. "You won't believe this, but I was the school's champion runner. After I took first prize I stopped running."

We were back to the fear of success and the guilt feelings that success engenders.

"I stopped painting after I won a prize for one of my drawings when I was fifteen," I told him. "I was petrified by success. It took me almost another forty years to come back to it... and to start all over again."

Three forces can prevent us from performing: the will to achieve, the fear of failure, and the fear of success. The first two are understandable, the third less so. It is connected with having (or not having) permission to actualize deep yearnings. The price of our success can be exacting. Our relationships with the people we love and depend on can sometimes be damaged by their reaction to our success. If happiness at Nathan's success, for example, evokes his mother's sadness and guilt in relation to the lost son and the lost brother, then it is preferable to be without such happiness...

I very much wanted to connect with that spark of urgency in Nathan, to the fact that he was once a winner. I suggested that he continued his journey and moved forward.

Gradually Nathan and I learned more about him. We learned that he was gifted, stubborn, sad, and blocked, a person who perseveres out of habit, but never really commits. We also uncovered colossal anger, and a deep longing to simply be an ordinary child, one who is not expected to be a champion athlete, a Shakespeare, and simultaneously a vocational failure, but a child whose mother sees him as he is. We focused mainly on two special components of his personality. His determination and his depth of character, which he had never allowed himself to recognize. It appeared as if Nathan had chosen to become acquainted with only part of himself. Just as his mother related to him by seeing him as a reflection of his dead brother, so did Nathan stash away parts of his personality and his feelings, never learning to acknowledge or value them. Still, deep down, he knew they were there.

It was actually his father, who though unable to talk with him, gave him permission – through their shared soccer games – to exist. This was obviously important, limited though it was. Yet Nathan's father did not bequeath him a direction in life any more than his mother had.

Nathan's emotional life was a reflection of his extended identity. He felt that only his absence made his existence felt. When he was present and dared to show signs of life, he never got any real feedback. Alive, Nathan was ignored. There was simply too much guilt.

I thought of my dead brother. It was he who connected me with Nathan. After my brother's death, my mother took to her bed, covering herself up in depression and despair. I was forgotten. After about a year, when she had no more strength left, the doctor told her, "You have a living daughter who needs you. If you don't take care of her again, she will die, too."

When I was older, my mother told me that she had been so frightened by what he said that she chose to live again. Nonetheless, I too, had to invest years of work on myself and my family in order to build a good life with joy and creativity and not be satisfied merely with the fact of my sheer existence. Somehow, with their last remaining strength and with great courage, my parents were able to reach out and push me ahead to a safer shore.

During my journey with Nathan, I asked myself more than once whether mine was the hand that was pushing Nathan toward that shore. But it wasn't. I only helped him find it. It was his wife Carol who was the warrior. She set the direction and was there for him to lean on. I sensed that behind the phrase "my wife sent me" was great power, not weakness. These were the words that expressed Nathan's strength. For years Carol had been his engine. She was the woman who permitted him to exist and who bequeathed him life.

After Carol was openly recruited for the journey, Nathan became stronger, "My wife believes in me and she's no fool," he told me, and later on he said: "You are always asking me what I would like to be. I actually have known for a long time."

"Both of us know that you know," I replied confidently. What we did not yet know was what had to be released in order to fulfill his desires. I asked Nathan to try to describe what he wanted.

"I want to begin living life," he said with conviction. "I want to study accounting. Accounting is connected with bringing order to commerce and finance. What you get and what you give and what remains…"

The force of his clarity shocked both of us. So banal, so simple.

"Now comes the question: How are you, Nathan, going to do that," I said. It was clear to me that he also knew what path he needed to choose to reach his goal. Another thing was clear to me, and apparently to him as well. In the technical field in which he was then employed, the same field that had been his father's and in which his father had failed, Nathan could not cope with success.

"In accounting, I will succeed," he responded.

In the evaluation Nathan had undergone, his accounting talent had been conspicuous, as had his need to bring order to things and put them in suitable frameworks and possibly advise people how to put their own accounts in order. Evidently, accounting was the field in which he could provide financial counseling and enjoy doing so.

Nathan raised a thumb skyward: "Not a mere tax adviser but an accountant. Writing as a hobby will be an expression of my soul."

I leaned back and sighed in relief. The rescue squad's tough mission was about to conclude. The freed party was present and accounted for. Now he would have to shake off all that dust, change his clothes, and go out and rehabilitate his vocational life. Accounting would be an excellent solution. We both clearly saw that Nathan would perform better as a self-employed professional than as an employee. I suggested that he not invest too much energy in integrating himself into a big corporation. "Going it alone will shorten the way for you," I recommended.

These things are true for many people for whom their families never served as functionally constructive systems for promoting their progress, often requiring them to blaze their own trails to success. These people do well as self-employed professionals, where they and they alone are responsible for their fate.

Chapter Five
Anger is Career Sabotage

Frustration and rage disrupted my career

Deeply buried anger, unresolved rebellion, or prolonged frustration can stop us in our vocational tracks. It's as simple as that. I remember situations where I couldn't bear something or I was so furious at someone... and I hit impasse. Despite wanting desperately to perform, to prove myself, to succeed – ultimately, I was paralyzed. My brain was blocked and my memory sealed shut.

I remember, for instance, an especially frightening incident when I was taking a literature exam. For two hours, I stubbornly went on sitting there in despair, with my eyes on the empty answer sheet, unable to remember a single answer. My brain emptied out. When my impotent rage really got underway, I began filling in line after line, page after page, with liberating phrases: "Guy is stupid," "Guy is disgusting," "Guy is a sadist"... (Plus other expletives not fit to print here, and certainly this is not the time or place to explain who Guy was.) After about fifteen minutes, a stream of memory that had been temporarily blocked by rage and anger, suddenly, and miraculously came flowing back to me.

Albert and Muriel, whose stories I will tell in this chapter, were born to parents who had accumulated tremendous anger over the years in the context of their work. Both had parents who cultivated larger-than-life expectations regarding their children. Over the course of my journey with Albert and Muriel, I learned that the seeds of their parents' anger had sprouted in the fertile fields of their children's lives, stunting their abilities and even their willingness to work at all.

Albert appeared to have been born to succeed. He was a very good-looking man and won the hearts of men and women alike. He had completed a Bachelor's degree in Economics and Business Administration and a Master's degree in Philosophy. He had an unusual ability to spot a business opportunity and rapidly exploit its financial possibilities. Albert was the kind of child every mother would be proud of. He had been born into an affluent environment and lacked for nothing. It was clear to all that one day he would make it, and make it big.

Yet, Albert disappointed everyone. A short time after his twenty-eighth birthday, he resigned from his position, began collecting unemployment benefits, and started looking for a new job in a desultory fashion. He seemed to be in no hurry and appeared to have no special objective or goal. It was as if he had been sentenced to an enforced idleness. He read the want ads but his efforts never really amounted to anything.

The days passed. Weeks became months and months turned into years. For eight years, in fact, Albert sat at home, until finally his wife called me. "Do something!" she pleaded, her voice at the other end of the line full of despair. "I have no idea what to do anymore."

It often happens that a partner or parent calls on behalf of their significant other to request help. When Albert arrived at our first session, I was duly surprised by how presentable he looked for a man who had been unemployed for so long. He had an athletic build, wore well-tailored sports clothes, and his short hair was neatly cut and combed. Other than a kind of dullness in his eyes and a nervous tic that appeared occasionally at the corner of his mouth, there was nothing to suggest that he had been out of work for nearly a decade.

Albert, unlike most people who come for counseling, skipped the denial stage. "I'm here because I'm stuck," he said forcefully. "It's been eight years now that I haven't earned anything. My life is like a wagon, mired in the mud. It's time to drag the wagon out of the mud."

"Is this painful for you?" I asked.

"Until now, it hasn't really been. But now, it's starting to be."

"What changed?" I pressed him.

Albert thought about it. After long minutes of silence, he said: "Maybe it was the birth of my son."

I learned a long time ago that the birth of a child and the transition to parenthood can change a person's perspective concerning many aspects of their commitment to a career and career satisfaction.

"So only the wagon is stuck in the mud?" I went on, by way of clarification.

"Not exactly the wagon," Albert said. "I think it's more a question of the horses. Evidently they aren't trying hard enough to pull the wagon out. The wagon is mechanically sound, and the horses are well trained and in good shape. I don't have a clear idea why it won't budge. Do you think you can help me?"

"I can try," I said, taken aback at his directness. I considered how many complicated vocational puzzles I had succeeded in figuring out in the past, and thought about how each time I had been forced to begin from scratch. The same question always popped up. If almost everything seems to be in such good shape, then how is it that nothing is okay? What is stuck? What is the connection between the cart and the horse? What about the driver?

Albert's state of impasse raises once again the matter of the quintessentially human challenge inherent in the notion of a calling and its actualization. Why does Albert have no idea of what he wants to do? Does he really not know what he wants to do? Why has he never addressed this question before?

The findings from the psychological evaluation that Albert had undergone pointed to impressive talents, a striking ability to think and calculate in financial terms, and the sensitivities of a veteran media man. In addition, Albert had a wife who wouldn't give up. I wondered how his parents fit into the picture. I asked Albert how one keeps a family afloat during eight years of unemployment.

"My parents have been supporting us," Albert responded, shamefacedly, like a child caught misbehaving – but there was also a momentary flash of something akin to gloating in his expression. "Without them, I would have been lost," he went on. "My father is in finance. At least there's someone left in the family who works successfully in his field and is satisfied with his job."

I smiled to myself. I felt hyper-alert, like an interrogator waiting for a stubborn witness to slip up somewhere. Albert had given me the tip of the first thread to unravel, because those few innocent statements conveyed important information. Albert's father was also a talented man who was deeply respected by those around him. I asked myself if this might be an extended adolescent paralysis that grew out of having parents who were overachievers. Perhaps I'd stumbled by accident on a case of the grass and the ficus tree?

The grass-and-ficus theory was something I'd learned from my old friend George, a gardener by trade. He taught me that grass always seeks a bit of shade to get out of the burning sun. The shade gives the grass respite from the sun during its first years of growth. The problem is that sometimes there's too much shade, and the ficus tree, while protecting the grass, doesn't let through a single ray of sunshine. In that event the grass won't grow on its own in its natural way.

Was Albert's father, the successful financial wizard at the top like a ficus tree casting his shadow on his children so that they were unable to do anything at all under his patronage?

The grass-and-ficus theory reminded me of Muriel. Muriel was a gifted sculptor and a single mother. After her daughter was born, she had an attack of eczema that covered the palms of her hands. She was virtually unable to touch her daughter and had to stop working for many years. Like Albert who had been sent by his wife, similarly Muriel came to me accompanied by her parents, who were already in their sixties and found supporting their daughter very hard.

Both Albert and Muriel, as a result of parenthood, had reached the point where they wanted to deal with changing their vocational situation. Albert felt that the time had come for him to get going when his first son was about to be born. Muriel, on the other hand, was ready to make the trek to a better understanding of her situation when her daughter, then ten years old, began distancing herself from her mother and doing poorly at school.

It was Muriel who taught me to look at the environment in which grown children are raised and to check in what sort of shade they attempt to blossom. The picture was clearer with respect to Muriel's childhood than Albert's. In Muriel's case, the problem was her field; her work itself. This type of vocational impasse – not working and being supported by parents ran in her family on the women's side.

As noted in prior chapters, I have found a connetion between the gender of the parent and that of the child and the vocational drama they enact, which is often more dramatic when both are the same gender.

Muriel's mother had been obliged to begin working as a child. At the age of nine, she began taking care of children and cleaning houses. Gradually, she became the primary breadwinner in her family – a family of Iraqi immigrants who had had a hard time adjusting to life in Tel Aviv. Hard work, however, had not affected Muriel's mother's thirst for learning. Not long after she finished high school, she became a receptionist at a bookkeeping firm while attending night school and earned a degree in accounting, with honors.

Muriel's mother was not extraordinarily talented, but her tremendous dedication to work, her impressive achievements, and her absolute loyalty to her firm earned her considerable respect at the textile company where she served as controller. Despite this, Muriel's mother was never satisfied. She went on feeling that she hadn't really chosen her field. And she felt that in spite of all that she had invested, no one really appreciated her.

The turning point came when Muriel's mother was forty. Angry and frustrated by what she believed was inadequate recognition of her talents, drained by years of inner exhaustion, her relations with company executives became conspicuously tense, and loud arguments ensued. At a certain stage, deeply disappointed with the disgruntled controller, the firm's CEO called her in for a brief talk and fired her. Muriel's mother was in shock. Although aware of such a possibility, she had never really taken seriously what it would mean. Her rage was so deep that for the next ten years she was unable to find another job. Muriel at the time was nine years old! Her entire adolescence unfolded in the shadow of her mother's gloom and rage, which cast the little household under a large shadow of despair, fury, bitterness, anger, and hopelessness. "I deserve better than this," her mother used to say, at first to her husband, and later to her children. "I don't understand why my talents aren't recognized and why I don't get the positions I deserve."

For ten years, the household was mired in emotional and financial distress. Finally, when Muriel was nineteen, she began asking the million-dollar question – "What will I do when I grow up?" Only then did her mother comprehend that she had to get a grip and acquire a different perspective of the world of work. She began giving financial advice to individual clients and, gradually, built up a base of satisfied customers. Muriel's mother realized that the voluntary period of at-home convalescence was over, and that she was ready to move on from the status of employee to that of an independent, self-employed professional.

Though the house regained an air of financial stability, it lacked an atmosphere of personal fulfillment.

"There was always this feeling that things could have been a little better," Muriel related. "There was a feeling that Mom could move up a little more and make more money. In our house, there were always feelings of having missed out and of something lacking in our lives."

There was another piece to Muriel's puzzle – the story of her father. Muriel's father had a faceless, drab clerical job in a human resources firm. In his leisure time, at home with his family, he was an outstanding cook and baker. He enjoyed creative cooking, and his family appreciated his talent and let him know it.

"That was the only ray of light in my life. In fact, in all our lives," said Muriel, when I tried to understand how events had unfolded and what it meant in terms of impasse. "Maybe," she added hesitantly, "my father's happiness and satisfaction from cooking and baking were the basis for my aspirations, for my feeling that I had permission for creativity…"

Muriel and I sensed that indeed her satisfying work as a sculptor had its source in her father's side of the family. Still, it seemed that as an adult woman, Muriel had relived her mother's experience of vocational catastrophe. Later on, we came to see that the combination of emotional identification with her mother and her choice of sculpture that continued her father's work in "sculpting" food, were in harmony until the moment she became a mother. When she gave birth to her daughter, the balance shifted.

As she began another step in the process of separating from the sort of activity her family had engaged in, the conflict deepened. Muriel wanted to be more fulfilled than her mother had been, but she also wanted to choose something like her father's cooking – something he had so loved.

She succeeded both in choosing something she wanted and in finding great satisfaction. "Yet, still I reached impasse," Muriel said. "Even if it was called 'an allergic reaction to sculpting materials,' the eczema was there. Suddenly, I was stuck. I couldn't sculpt or touch anything connected to my work. All this happened just when my daughter was born – I'd waited so long for her, and I desperately wanted to touch her. And so, just like my mother, I sat at home for ten years, in my innocence, and didn't touch any of the materials I worked with… and didn't do anything else, either."

Still, over these years something important did happen to Muriel. She gradually began to confront the rage and anger she had accumulated inside herself for all those years – feelings that she didn't even know existed. Muriel discovered that this internalized rage was directed mainly at her mother.

"Suddenly I understood that nothing that I had done was ever good enough for her," Muriel said angrily. "She especially couldn't come to terms with the fact that I'd chosen art as my career. 'You call sculpting a profession?' she would ask me, half mockingly, half provokingly. I made a good living creating functional, decorative pottery and I also taught art. Nonetheless, Mom was always in a state of turmoil about my work. 'If you're not a real artist like Picasso or Michelangelo – it's a waste of time!' she always claimed."

At the end of a long journey Muriel had confronted her rage at her mother and finally came to terms with her mother's limitations. After that she was able to make the distinction between her identity and that of her mother ("I'm not my mother; I'm only her daughter…"). Muriel improved her ability to identify with her mother's great desire for more substantial self-actualization and fulfillment and along the way, she learned to forgive her. All of this was necessary for Muriel to break through her paralysis and permit herself to be a supportive and healthy mother for her own preadolescent daughter.

On further analysis, it became clear that Muriel's grandmother had become ill when she gave birth to Muriel's mother and that she, too, for ten years, had stopped doing the housework she did so well. It turned out that her granddaughter, Muriel, had assimilated the family psycho-gene and reenacted the same script. But Muriel, unlike her mother and grandmother, found a way to look into herself and dared to decode the genetic links that bound her to her past. She was able to ascertain that she was different. She saw that she was not compelled to proceed automatically as just another link in the intergenerational chain. Muriel came to believe that the power to choose was in her own hands. After she had moved beyond these obstacles, she was able to resume creative work, earn a living, and be a proud mother to her daughter. With Muriel closing the cycle, the path was wide open for her own daughter to excel at school. Muriel had chosen to cease being the victim of the rage and frustration that her mother and grandmother had been unable to relinquish.

With Albert, at least initially, things appeared otherwise. Only later did we find out that Albert, like Muriel, was dealing with the frustration and rage of a dissatisfied and unfulfilled parent, and with the great things expected of him, irrespective of his own real needs.

When first asked about his successful father's level of vocational satisfaction, Albert was sure that his dad was a happy man, fulfilled in his work. "My father is a success story. He's happy with his achievements," insisted Albert.

Further along in our journey, Albert began to see his father from a slightly different perspective. "Dad was a financial executive at a major corporation," Albert related. "He was the sort whose accounting wizardry saved the firm at critical junctures, and he was respected accordingly. The problems started when a new CEO came in and began making far-reaching organizational changes at the company. When my father decided to resign, he received a substantial severance package, and went charging off into the private market. Together with Mom, he set up a firm investing in new business ventures. Everything seemed set to go. But still, at home there was this feeling that he wasn't satisfied, that he wasn't so much traveling around the world as getting lost, set adrift. This man, whom we had always seen as a rock of stability, began vacillating suddenly between two poles – enthusiasm at one extreme, and abdication at the other."

"Just as you seem to have been doing lately," I commented cautiously. "As your father did back then, you haven't even tried to find out what you really want to do."

"Truthfully? Not at this point," he responded.

Albert was silent, as was I.

"Perhaps," I offered finally, "you could give some thought to what is keeping you from knowing what you want to do. Try to think about what your dream is."

The thought behind the question was simple. I wanted to try to connect with Albert the dreamer, Albert the creative, Albert the chooser. I wanted to understand who or what was restraining his dreams and blocking his creativity. The question was too advanced for this preliminary stage of our work together. It needed to be approached gradually.

"It's a little bit like when people who are on a diet go to a gourmet restaurant," I said, trying to explain. "They know what they aren't supposed to order, but staring them in the face are all those pastas, steaks, fantastic-smelling baked goods. They feel stuck in every direction. Instead of choosing something they really want and are permitted to eat, they lose all direction and become frustrated. The same thing happens to people who find themselves in a restaurant that's a little bit over their budget. Instead of thinking about what they'd like to eat, they're preoccupied with thoughts of all the things they can't have because they're too broke. Do you understand, Albert? In the restaurant, like in life, a lot of energy is invested in what is forbidden."

Albert said nothing, but his face reddened. I thought I'd gone ahead too fast. I decided to try from another direction.

"Tell me," I asked, feeling my way, "what did your mother do when your father was busy with business issues?"

"Oh, well, my mother," he said, breaking into an ironic smile. "Mom was an agile, sleight-of-hand artist. She was tops at dividing her time between her various roles – a senior educational advisor and a popular lecturer, unflagging helpmate to my father, and perfect mother at home. Are you getting the picture? I had two parents, both driven by success... but we three kids, we grew up any which way, without any drive to achieve."

"No drive? What do you mean?"

"Look at the three of us," he answered, "which of us has achieved anything?"

I found that he was right. The two boys and their older sister had never disappointed as students. Their school grades were high and their college entrance test scores guaranteed them admission to any institution of higher education. A problem arose when they had to begin actualizing all that potential on a vocational level as adults. So long as the game was to bring a good report card home – mission accomplished, no problem. But once they went out into the adult world and had to apply their talents to some form of employment – to choose and commit – all three failed, time after time. Eventually we realized that they had all been overpowered by identifying too closely with their exceptionally talented parents whose powerful internal prohibition on identifying authentic personal motivation had been passed on to all three children.

Once again I was facing the familiar pattern of unfulfilled parents who had demanded of their children great things that bore no relation to the children's essential selves. In Albert's case, both highly successful parents hadn't managed to listen to and fulfill their own needs, and both held high expectations of their children.

The data from Albert's psychological testing showed that he could excel in almost any field: "Consider the frustration you have to contend with," I told him at our next session, "with so many talents, and so little space to express them."

Albert looked at me. Suddenly, I saw a gleam in his eyes. Albert had begun to put two and two together.

"Look," he said, weighing each word, "what I need to know is not what to do. That, I already know. And I don't need someone to tell me what I'm good at, because I'm well aware of that.

"I needed someone who could tell me to stop and give me direction. I needed someone who could set limits to the uncompromising demand for achievement, to the exaggerated expectations that I would always be successful. I knew that I had to succeed, but I didn't know to what degree I was supposed to. It was very frustrating."

"And it was on account of this frustration that you developed this blunt edged indifference?" I asked.

"I guess so," he said, the pent-up pain visible in his eyes. "As time went by," he added quietly, "this ambiguity spread beyond the boundaries of work and took over my entire life."

"Can you go inward, into your own depths, and try to get past the ambiguity?"

"I can, but I don't want to. There's too much anger and pain there."

"What kind of pain?"

"The pain of wasted talents, frustration at lost working years and the wonderful things I could have done, and didn't do. True, there were years when I wanted things and I achieved them, but it was never enough. There was always another rung to climb, another level to reach for."

"Was that how you saw things? Or could it be that other people expected you to go up another level?"

Albert was impatient. Apparently he'd decided that it was time to change the rules of the game. "In case you still don't understand, I'm not talking about other people. I'm talking about my parents. I'm talking about my father and mother. My brother, my sister, and I grew up with the feeling that no matter what we did, we could always have done better. When we brought home good grades, even if they were the top grades in the class, my father would be at pains to explain to us that, 'In this family, we get straight As.' If we were in second place, my father would casually ask, 'And who came first?' We felt that we always had to conquer a new summit, but we never knew just what it was or how high up it was, because there would always be another level, one step higher."

"When you don't know where the sky begins," I commented, "its better not to take off at all."

"Evidently," he replied.

"So," I said, anxious to close the circle, "because you didn't work, your father had to go on working to support you and your family."

"I didn't think about that," Albert replied. "I only felt that the endless pressure was too much for me, and that something was definitely screwed up, but I didn't know what."

I could really feel Albert's pain. I empathized with where and how he was stuck, drowning in rage and helplessness at his parents for their coercive stance and impossible expectations. I asked myself what children can realistically be expected to know about the very powerful, if covert, competition between themselves and their parents. The problem is more severe if the parent was abandoned in childhood, as in the case of Muriel's mother. Muriel's mother herself, because she did not have supportive parents, had trouble coping with negative feelings like jealousy and possessiveness. Moreover, the feeling of growing competitiveness can be so frightening and threatening that it leaves no room for give-and-take and mutual support. This can happen between parents and children and also among siblings. Quitting the race often seems like a way out of the competition.

There are families who keep their achievement orientation at a reasonable level, so that competitiveness and striving for success is balanced by mutual assistance and support. Sometimes, indeed, a constructive and complementary contest can emerge between parents and their children. In such a family, competition exists within defined boundaries, and there are set rules by which to play. Only in that way can all the family members enjoy the rivalry, and turn it into a useful tool for their own development and the attainment of their goals.

Families attuned towards over-achievement, in contrast, tend to suppress problems and lack clear boundaries. The very scope of the achievements sought, and the threat of drastic falls from grace, if success is not accomplished, engenders frustration and disappointment. In this context, children become unable to create tools that will help them deal with "real life" and manage their lives in a fulfilling way; they may even become unable to accept or take permission for vocational fulfillment.

Children who come from a family background of over-achievement generally have a very difficult time accomplishing things without external help and support. The problem is especially magnified if the parents' accomplishments are considered unusual while, at the same time, there are covert contradictory feelings of low self-esteem, self-denigration, or a sense that they could really have done better and succeeded even more. In such a case, by a kind of osmosis, the children absorb those feelings from their parents and are outraged that their parents ignored their true personalities and desires... Years later, identification with these intense feelings can grow so powerful that complete vocational paralysis can ensue.

How can we ensure conditions of competition that enable proper, healthy growth? How can we encourage the development of a desire for achievement suited to the individual's needs and abilities? How can we develop an awareness of basic, fundamental needs? How can we learn to compete with, yet simultaneously support one another? And the really fundamental question: How can we facilitate this for someone whose parents are, or were, overly achievement-oriented, lacking in confidence, restless, and living with a pervasive sense of having lost out on what they were meant to be or do?

These were the questions I tried to address with Albert. "First of all, it's important to identify all the components of your inner needs. After that, it's advisable to try to lead a healthy life with a reasonable, sensible level of achievement," I said, trying to define what we were after.

Albert listened very attentively.

"Do you mean," he finally asked me, "that I can define reasonable measures of achievement that will be logical for me? You think that I can make a list of reasonable goals, ones I can try to achieve?"

"You must prepare a list of objectives that you would like to achieve," I told him, trying to emphasize the aspect of choice and the commitment it implies.

"Maybe I can also find some kind of framework, even if at first it's just an external one, that will serve as a surrogate parent – rational, supportive, and encouraging," Albert said.

I liked his description. "Right. Some work environments fill that role, at one level or another. A job should reward you for your achievements – ones that are defined in advance. Furthermore, a job should create new codes for you, different than the ones that ruled in the quagmire of your family life. And another thing, just as important, is that an efficient workplace will ensure you don't receive double messages."

Albert was ready to take this a little further. "You know," he said, "this is exactly what my parents never did. They were proud of the articles I wrote but they kept on saying that the main thing was to study law or finance. A good profession was essential in order to support myself later on in life."

"On the one hand, they were proud of your 'creations,' and on the other hand they stressed the worth of a different profession," I restated it for him. "They ignored your core need and negated the existence of your spontaneous urge to create, which comes from your inner self. In their confusion," I explained, "and given their own personal renunciation of fulfillment, they really confused you, didn't they?"

Albert gazed at me, perplexed.

"Wait a second, I don't really understand what you're talking about. They wanted things to be good for me, didn't they?"

"What I'm talking about is that they presented a contradiction between your core creativity and practicality, so to speak. Possibly all that pragmatic talk imprisoned your freedom and your right to create. Maybe the key to your internal bonds is lying in a little glass case called 'Permission to Get in Touch with Needs and Desires.' This permission is something your father himself did not experience, and possibly neither your mother. There are many families like yours where people suffer from paralytic pragmatism."

"Look," he said defensively, still trying to fend off the understanding that was fast encroaching, "I do have a Bachelor's degree in Economics, but my Master's is in Philosophy."

"Philosophy," I said, "is also all about pragmatism. You can lecture about philosophy in schools, at university, in workshops, write books about it; be an advisor on a television program, and so on."

Heavy silence hung in the air. Albert seemed to shrink. For just a second, he was that little boy again, the class genius, about to take another test. This time he wasn't standing in front of the blackboard in the classroom, but in front of his parents, and possibly me...As understanding dawned, his rage began to boil over.

"Don't you see? It's not just the contradiction between my real wishes and pragmatism. There was also a decree that said: 'It doesn't matter what you achieve, the main thing is to be a good human being,'" he said, very agitated.

"And that's a little too much..." I countered, daring to go the next step.

The picture was becoming clearer and clearer. Albert was out of touch with his true abilities, lacked the tools of self-discovery, and had no idea how to connect the two. All his life he had received double messages, so that finding a profession became an impossible mission.

Beneath his hidden anger, Albert suffered from not knowing what gift of happiness he could offer his parents. He had no way of knowing what they would really appreciate. The mixed messages made it impossible to guess.

When contemplating one's work, the pleasure of creative satisfaction is usually followed by the desire for appreciation and recognition. When there's no one to value our accomplishments, a critical part of our creative impulse wilts. There's nothing and no one to exert ourselves for, to think, to produce... In that event, people tend to feel that passivity is preferable – not to initiate, not to create – the main issue being not to risk offering a gift that no one wants.

Work and family; family and work. Actually, the nuclear family is our first workplace. There we learn to deliver results, and to compete with friendly, loving, and/or persistent competitors. There we learn to work within a framework that makes demands, but also gives love. There we learn to accept criticism along with admiration and support. The family nest is the soil in which we do our first growing. When that nest is damaged or does not provide the necessary raw materials and tools for growth, we may be expected to encounter problems. We find ourselves unprepared to meet the real world outside, including the working world.

Albert, regardless of his super-achievements, had never learned to conduct an authentic, in-depth inner dialogue. As his world gradually became more complicated, Albert slowly became petrified, running from one inappropriate job to another. Finally –

angry, bewildered, and in despair – he simply stopped in his tracks and refused to do anything at all.

The high point of the drama came with the birth of his first son. Then finally, everything fell apart. Perhaps Albert could have gone on lying to himself when he was alone, but not now, as a father, in front of his son. He had reached his limit. When his son was born, Albert decided he would no longer concede his right to be a free and creative person within his environment. "At that very moment," he said, summing up his 36 years of life, "I felt that I wanted to be a father who supports his family. I didn't want to be financially dependent on my parents any longer."

"That's not surprising," I said. "It seems that super-achieving parents like yours, for whom nothing is ever enough, often function from deprivation and a lack of basic self-confidence. Such people have difficulty letting their child live in a child's space. Often fear lurks behind their excessive demands. That's how they live their lives, and almost certainly their parents lived that way, too. If they don't make up their minds to choose to live otherwise – then their children will live their lives that way, too. And incidentally," I said, "while we're on the subject of children, what kind of a child were you?"

"I was afraid you would never ask," Albert grinned. "I was a child who played a lot of games with his imagination."

"And what about ordinary childhood games?"

"Not really. I was considered delicate, a kind of a wimp. My games weren't very realistic and didn't involve other children."

"Did you get dirty once in a while at the playground?"

Albert gazed at me, piqued. "Let's not exaggerate," he said humorously. "I was one of those clean children, a child who wasn't really involved in the world around him."

"You probably know how much children need to play. Children who don't experience the joy of play – the freedom to laugh, to get dirty, will have a hard time later on fitting into the real playground of living by trial and error. This is also true of people who refuse to let themselves 'get dirty' and cannot allow themselves to fall down and pick themselves up again. A person like that will have trouble progressing normally in life and at work, where the dirt doesn't always come off easily, and the falls can be really painful. And if you didn't play," I went on, interested in seeing how far his abilities and his excellence went, "perhaps you had the opportunity to 'play' in a different sense? To play an instrument, maybe?"

"In a family like mine, a question like that is almost redundant," Albert said, smiling. "Of course I studied an instrument. I played the piano for ten years."

"And did you continue playing?" I pursued.

"Until ninth grade, and then I gave up."

"Why? Didn't you enjoy it?" I insisted.

"Actually, yes, I did, but playing the piano was synonymous with musical genius in our house. I wanted to play for fun, not to be the next Artur Rubenstein. For me it was fine to play an hour every day, even two hours, but then I wanted to go to the park near the house. I wanted to be one of the kids. I wanted to play like everyone else. It's strange, but I only understand that now. My parents were always drilling it into me: 'You're an exceptional child, you have great potential. It would be a shame to waste that just playing like other kids. You must take advantage of your spare time to practice.' So I would practice, and suffer. I was always looking out the window at the park, and at the kids who called me from downstairs. Bit by bit, my love for playing just dried up. I was angry that they made me play more than I needed to. I guess, gradually, I became indifferent and finally, just stopped playing."

"You stopped playing, and after that, you also stopped feeling," I said quietly, summing up that mini-drama typical of so many children of demanding parents.

"Right," Albert said. His face was frozen, and only his focused gaze held back the force of his feelings. "If you don't want to feel, you go into a kind of dull place, you sleep a lot. Just as I did, until recently. But, and this is why I came to you, lately even sleep has suddenly been deprived from me. I've had it up to here. I feel like I have a real problem, and I must solve it."

Albert decided to take a risk and open up the subject with each of his parents. An amazing surprise awaited him. He never knew that, but he wasn't the only one with a secret. The entire family had a secret. His highly successful and accomplished parents had never felt that they had fulfilled their true desires. Mainly it was his father who bore this inner sense of failure, and felt a lack of meaning in his life. The feeling was strong, but labeling it was forbidden.

For his parents not to be portrayed in their own eyes as losers, the inner failure to find their true calling and the powerful need for original expression of the self were transformed into a well-kept secret. The glittering external trappings – the new car, the luxurious villa – smothered any doubts. Albert's parents were ensnared in an emotional and vocational trap. Though they worked and were successful, they had no passion for their work. Because they didn't know any other way to live, they felt obliged to go on maintaining the facade of success. It was as if their inner longings counted for nothing. Money and the need to show that all was well – reigned supreme.

"I am not willing to be like that," Albert said. "I want to follow my heart. I want to find my true creative direction."

Albert was silent. Then, feeling his way slowly, he added: "I'm uncomfortable about my father. There he was working hard all the time and giving up his true desires, if he still had any. Maybe he wants to find fulfillment now too, but doesn't dare? Why is it okay for me? …It's a luxury after all…"

"And maybe you are both stuck in the same place? If so, maybe you can liberate one another? What do you think," I suggested daringly, "about inviting your father to our next session?"

A look of complete astonishment crossed Albert's face. The

truth is I was no less surprised myself. I'd spoken from a natural impulse rather than from logical consideration. Nonetheless, even in hindsight, the idea was a good one.

Father and son arrived for the next session. The question of earning a living arose almost immediately.

"Do you think," asked the father of his son, accusingly, "that work is some kind of child's game, that people always enjoy their work? Your great-grandfather died when he was caught stealing food for his family. Work is food, and food is not a game. You go to work – and that's that."

Albert didn't give in. I could see the child in him cringing, afraid, but he also knew that this was his moment – it was now or never. The choice was his. He could stay angry and indifferent in his glass cage and gaze longingly at the rest of the world. Or he could sever the multi-generational lock, and request or even take the longed-for permission, that was his by right to a livelihood filled with creativity and meaning – within a supportive and caring framework that made reasonable demands on him.

Albert chose to go all the way. "I'm prepared to earn a living," he said, standing up straight and facing his father, "but I'm not ready to give up who I am. I'm not prepared to give up on writing. I'm not willing to give up on the happiness I derive from an article on philosophy or a really good lecture. You want to work and suffer? Fine. That's your choice. But don't interfere with my life choices."

Albert was no less surprised than his father by the force of what he had said and the evident determination behind it. When did that happen I wondered?

All three of us were silent. This was the beginning of the end of that dull cloud that had muffled the accumulated anger and frustration all those years. Breaking through that cloud, for the two of them, meant laying their nerve endings bare and coming into direct contact with their mutual pain.

Albert's father was openly astonished, and Albert even more so, at his ability to address the issue of fulfilling his own wishes and at the same time requesting his father's blessing. Possibly Albert was also trying to enable his father to make the change that he himself had been struggling with for ten years.

In the silence, with lips trembling, Albert's father said brokenly, almost in a whisper, "Do you think I really wanted a venture capital company? Do you think I wanted the travel abroad and the struggles over marketing and sales with global competitors? No. Like you, I wanted to study and teach philosophy. But then I got married, and everyone told me that philosophy is fun but it won't support a wife and children..."

"And that's why you studied finance?" asked Albert in a fatherly tone, with a smile that seemed at once cynical and bitter, yet somehow encouraging.

"Precisely for that reason," his father confirmed. "If you think I love number crunching, you're wrong. I'm good at it, and that's why a friend offered me a job as a controller. The offer was a tempting one, and I did well and went ahead almost against my will. But I didn't really like what I was doing. Later, I started the venture capital business with your mother. Between the two of us, to this day I don't really enjoy it. Maybe your mother doesn't really find it satisfying either. That's why it's not growing any more. Still, it gives me power and money, and it brings me a lot of respect wherever I go."

I was surprised at the candor and courage Albert's father showed. I decided to strike while the iron was hot. "Perhaps you'd join your son on his journey? Perhaps you may even discover a source of true satisfaction that you could develop into some kind of activity that would enrich your life?"

Albert's father was confused and kept scratching his head. "You want to know the truth? I have never allowed myself to dream. But," he said, turning almost accusingly to Albert, "that didn't stop me from working and supporting my family; maybe it even helped..."

Albert burst out, "I don't understand why I have to wait until

I'm sixty-five to talk about lost dreams! I want to learn now how to figure out what I want, and I want to choose a work environment that will suit me, right now, and I want to decide how far I'll go, and how high!"

After a brief silence, Albert added, "I apologize that I reached this point only after being 'on strike' for so long and doing nothing, and that you had to support me all that time."

"Yes. Why in fact are you punishing me and your mother? Why is it our problem to support you?" jabbed his father.

I decided to intervene. "Maybe because it's so painful? Maybe because Albert didn't know how to ask permission of you and didn't know how to take it by himself? It seems to me that this was Albert's way of fighting with you and pressing you for a response, for some change, a way to deal with the hidden conflict."

Albert interrupted immediately: "Maybe this was my way of settling accounts with both of you, but mainly you, Dad, for the burning frustration and anger that I was feeling inside all those years, when everything I did was never good enough for both of you, and the sky was the limit, but even that was unclear!"

"Was that the debt we paid to you and your family?" asked his father quietly.

"Perhaps that was also reparative parenting. You created the opportunity to support him so that he would begin a healing process," I suggested cautiously.

"Are you trying to say," began Albert's father, still disbelieving, "that Albert's not wanting to work and support himself was some kind of responsible statement? That maybe that was even his opportunity?"

"Yes!" I said. "Albert refuses to continue as he was and isn't able to go your way either. He isn't familiar with the path of inner choice and wants to learn it. He will have to learn new things, sever his dependencies, and build a new world of his own. You can help him by granting him the permission to do what comes from his own inner needs; what comes from love. If you give him your blessing for inner achievements and not only for external excellence, maybe he will be able to start earning a living for the sake of earning a living, and live his life in a manner that you can respect. Maybe in the end, what he does will be through genuine choice, either in a work environment or in any other sphere… It's a chance for you, too, to be a partner on his journey."

His father understood. At last he turned to Albert and smiled: "You've taught me a hard lesson."

"A hard lesson was dealt to me," Albert replied.

I smiled at both of them. I knew that this meeting had been another step forward. Albert, thanks to himself, had received two wonderful gifts – permission to be angry at his father and permission to distinguish between anger, love, and concern. Later on, Albert began writing and he signed up for a class in futurology. Meanwhile, he also began earning a living by managing investment portfolios. Perhaps this was his way of telling the world, and especially his father, that his achievements were designed to earn a decent living. He asked for support and encouragement and gradually received them. Eventually he even learned to negotiate respect.

Albert knew that a long, careful, planned process of learning awaited him as he worked to distinguish between his abilities and his limitations. He would learn to estimate how much gas he had in the tank, the range of his abilities, and how high he could fly. Albert was aware that a long and burdensome road lay ahead. But he also had no doubt that he had begun constructing a way for himself that enabled his calling and his self-actualization to be top priority. And above all, Albert felt that, for him, hope had been reborn.

Chapter Six
The War killed my Dreams

Trauma destroyed my passion for life

There are cases of impasse so severe that we could describe them as "Functional-Vocational Invalidism" or even "Functional-Vocational Death." Sometimes, finding oneself in this situation can give rise to such intense feelings of guilt and shame as to completely confuse the issue, effectively disguising the fact that a paralysis of productive work has occurred – a vocational or career impasse.

At one time, I experienced this kind of vocational incapacitation in terms of my ability to function emotionally. It happened sometime between the Six-Day War in June 1967 and the Yom Kippur War in October 1973. My emotional functioning had short-circuited, yet I went on working. Somehow, during those intervening years, I performed professionally and yet, without being aware of it, I had shut down a great many feelings and sensations. It was only on the second day of the Yom Kippur War, after encountering a soldier with an amputated leg and fainting at his bedside, that I understood how for six years I had been mortally afraid of experiencing fear. All that time, I had ignored my fear and hidden it away.

When the Six-Day War broke out in 1967, I was a young

psychologist. I volunteered for emergency duty at Soroka Hospital in the Negev. Neither my personal nor my professional training had prepared me in any way to deal with wounded soldiers. Given my particular field, my training had exposed me to all kinds of mental distress, rather than amputated limbs. I felt competent to deal with injured souls, not injured bodies. I found the encounter with death particularly hard. I had no idea how to deal with the helplessness of the physically wounded, and had immense difficulty dealing with my own feelings of inadequacy.

One night, a wounded soldier arrived at the emergency room. I don't remember his name. All I remember is his red hair. He was shell-shocked and wounded along the right side of his face. His remaining hazel eye gazed at me in bewilderment. He read the horror on my face and playfully teased: "Let's see if you can guess what color my other eye was!" We both burst into crazy laughter which rapidly turned to tears. The weeping released some of the pent-up feelings raging inside me. During the long days of that war, I never allowed myself to take inventory of things in a personal way. I felt that it wasn't the time or the place to examine what I was feeling and what was happening to me. I just kept on going; no horrifying dreams, no nightmares.

When the 1967 war was over, I went back to my studies. I felt that something was stuck emotionally, yet I didn't connect it to the war because after all, I hadn't been a soldier.

But the trauma was there, biding its time. The years passed and the 1973 Yom Kippur War broke out. This time, I was assigned to work as a counselor in the orthopedic ward at Hadassah Hospital in Jerusalem. Wearing my white jacket, amid a highly skilled team of doctors and nurses, I entered the first room on the ward. I stopped next to the first bed, where a young man was lying on his side facing the wall. A large white sheet covered him up to the neck. "He refuses to speak," the nurse told me. His chart read: "Amputated above the knee." At that moment the room began to spin. Unexpectedly, I had a series of vivid flashbacks to scenes from the 1967 war of the emergency room at Soroka Hospital. I saw those dozens of stretchers full of soldiers evacuated from the Sinai Desert – wounded, torn open, their internal organs exposed, no sheets to cover them. I fainted and slumped to the floor.

It was astounding that during the seven years that separated those two wars, although I had counseled dozens of soldiers suffering from shell-shock and other wounds of the soul, I had never permitted myself to fully feel the pain and the fear. Like the white sheet covering the stump of that soldier's leg in the first bed, I too had gone on with life covering up my pain with a sheet of words and a veneer of understanding.

I tried... until betrayed by my own soul. I was mortified by having fainted. I was also shocked to realize how profoundly I had repressed my denial. I sat down next to the wounded soldier's bed and told him that I, too, had been covering myself up. Thanks to him, my denial began to peel away...

Later, I was able to tell him that although he was now lying in a clean bed on clean white sheets, I still saw him with his wound – torn, bleeding, fighting to remain conscious, not to go under. I told him about my inner war. I told him about my fear of looking at that terrible wound. I told him about the embarrassment that asking for help evoked in me. And I spoke with him about how hard it was for him to grasp his situation, to overcome his embarrassment and accept the fact that he was at the beginning of a new life – a life with one leg gone.

This wounded soldier's struggle was bound up for me with my own. It was not an easy thing to acknowledge the wounds pain had caused and to deal with them instead of covering them up.

After I'd shared all of this with him, the young man turned around to face me. Moving very slowly, he removed his fist from his mouth and burst out crying.

When you've been through a difficult, painful event, you don't deal with this singular event only. Inside you, all your memories of prior painful experiences are rolling around. The more you've repressed those earlier feelings, the heavier they will weigh on you and the more burdensome they will become as you try to move on with your life.

David came to me twenty years after the Yom Kippur War had cut short his career. David was suffering from battlefield-related PTSD (post-traumatic stress disorder). He didn't know this; it came to light quite by accident. Someone in the army decided to do a follow-up study of the surviving members of one of the units that had lost most of its soldiers. David was from that unit. The researchers wanted to learn how heroes from that war were faring now: Have they been rehabilitated? Have they established families of their own? Have they been able to settle on a career? And have they found fulfillment, from a vocational standpoint, in their civilian lives? The follow-up data on David revealed that, in the two decades since the war, he hadn't found work that suited his talents. He was married, had a house and children, but had never really found a satisfying career. His friends from high school had finished bachelor's and master's degrees and established themselves in one field or another. David, however, had been left behind. He had survived on the battlefield thanks to his intuitive resourcefulness and yet had failed to find a place in the working world commensurate with his potential. He worked as a butcher, slaughtering fowl on the night shift.

The discovery that he was suffering from PTSD came as a complete surprise to him. "I suspect that you are still suffering from shell shock," he was told by a clinical psychologist at a large army base in the center of the country. "I would recommend that you also consult a vocational psychologist. They have experience with cases like yours and will be glad to help you." David was completely taken aback. So many years had passed since he was rescued from that inferno, and he believed that he had rehabilitated himself. He never made the connection between post-war effects and his career failure. And now the embarrassment of shell shock! He was David the hero on whose broad chest the Chief of Staff himself had pinned a medal.

"It seems to me," I said to David at our first meeting, "that your choosing to work at slaughtering chickens is overly ironic."

At this stage, David had still not absorbed the symbolic significance of his choice of occupation.

"After I realized that my nightmares were preventing me from falling asleep at night, I looked for night work," David explained in a matter-of-fact tone. "For a while I worked at all sorts of jobs, whatever came along, and then found work at the poultry slaughterhouse, where I could work the night shift."

"The bloody battlefield was replaced by the bloody slaughterhouse. You ran away from the nightmares that were haunting you, only to be reunited with them once more at the slaughterhouse," I said, unable to contain myself.

David had been stuck twice. He was at an impasse when he found himself working at the slaughterhouse, and then he became stuck when he found a niche for himself as a clerk at the plant. People came and went on the staff, clerks became managers and managers left the slaughterhouse for more attractive positions elsewhere. Only he stayed on as a junior clerk doing routine work, yet not succeeding in moving up the ladder to a better position.

His vocational choice seemed, on the face of it, to have a logical explanation. Since David was free to do as he liked during the day, he could devote time to his home and children, and the income he brought home was reasonable as well. Outwardly all appeared calm.

That was merely on the surface, however. David confessed at our first meeting that even he could see that his situation was a little strange, yet he had no explanation for his lack of vocational success. There seemed to be no other reason why a young man, with good grades, and clearly defined plans to graduate one day, should come to such a career standstill. How else could he explain finding himself stuck night after night in a dead-end job he hated – a job he had never dreamed he would end up doing, a job way beneath his abilities?

Could it be that in a place where people killed one another, something in David had also been killed? Had the war also "killed" his chances of choosing a profession of his liking?

David and I sensed that we would need some time to get to know one another better before we could understand the real significance of the "slaughter." We began with what happened after the war ended, after the nightmare, and after David returned to civilian life.

"After the war, I wanted to realize a dream that had been with me ever since I can remember," he said. "I wanted to study medicine. When the war ended, it was clear to me that I was going to Italy to study. When I failed the entrance exams the first time, I was surprised. But, as usual, I didn't give up. When I kept on failing again and again, year after year – it became a nightmare. I failed five times. For five years I tried. It was like death... that's when I went to the slaughtering..."

"And what do you think happened there?" I asked quietly.

"My profession was slaughtered... Until then, there was no challenge I hadn't accomplished. Even in the war, I beat death against all odds. Then reaching for my life's dream – I failed."

"How did that happen, how did your profession get slaughtered?" I pressed him.

David went on, characteristically brave: "When I see an ill or injured person, I see other things... wounded comrades... everything comes back to me. I, who never fainted back then, who came through all those scenes of childhood friends blasted to pulp, would faint when I saw someone injured who needed to be operated on..."

"Maybe giving up on medicine is part of an admission of disability?" I asked.

"That is the disability," he stressed.

"And going to work as a butcher?"

"That's being angry at the disability…. being angry at death… Butchering is a statement about being cut off from sympathy for suffering and physical pain… What's hard is to live with the feeling that everyone can see my fear written all over me."

"Maybe," I conjectured, "working at butchering is actually a kind of statement that the disability exists and that you are no longer willing to be afraid of people seeing it?"

"Perhaps," murmured David, "the war killed my emotional side – not the part with my family and children, but the desire for work and self-expression. It killed my future as a human being who dreams and creates – and serves society."

"But still you tried to go on, even after the war," I reminded him, citing his stubborn struggle to be accepted to medical school.

"Yes… as if everything was fine," said David, speaking rapidly, in a loud voice. "As opposed to the emotional turmoil and the horde of questions playing and replaying themselves inside me, on the outside everything was in order. I tried to ignore the inner commotion. I tried to bypass it in all kinds of ways, and generally I succeeded. But it broke through in terms of my career. That area, for some reason, was the most difficult."

David stopped speaking, his breathing became heavy. I, too, was silent, awed yet again by the close connection between a person's work and his core being.

"How long will it go on this way?" asked David when he had calmed down somewhat.

"The deeper the pain, the longer it takes…" I told him quietly.

I suggested that David recount the story of his war.

I should note that, while I have listened to many war stories, David's was the most shocking of them all. David had been saved from death an incredible number of times, and he was willing to retell his story over and over again.

"Death was right there beside me, all the time," he began.

"People kept dying all around me. You know, on one occasion, a tank crew refused to move out after the tank was ready to go because the guys manning it weren't willing to have me on board. Can you imagine that? Do you know what it is for a tank crew to refuse to move out? Every tank then was a precious treasure. A rumor circulated that being near me was the kiss of death. Everyone believed that wherever I was, that's where death would come…"

"And did you believe it, too?"

"Yes, I did. It was already way beyond coincidence."

A heavy silence pervaded the room.

"Silence is the worst," said David finally.

"Apparently it's so tough that it's simply impossible to digest," I said, quietly.

"Yes… it's like a dark secret," said David, echoing my thoughts.

Little wonder that David, right from the start, did not fit the classic pattern of the shell-shocked soldier… He was a good-looking man, caring, full of life. His conversation was elegant, almost literary. He was curious, quick on the uptake and very open about himself. And yet, for more than twenty years David had hidden the secret of his vocational death from himself, from his family, and from other people.

Sometimes there is a feeling that a secret pain is in fact a forbidden secret, a kind of sin. I was reminded of Ari, who also suffered from war-related PTSD and who represented for me in a special way how pain can be repressed and a person become stuck within a trauma. For Ari, the dread induced by shell shock was linked mainly to a feeling of sin and shame accompanied by his fear and impotence.

"When I feel helpless, it's as if someone is attacking me, penetrating me violently and taking over my soul. And it's not logical, because I should have been able to prevent a brutal assault of that kind," Ari had explained when I counseled him. "I should have been

strong and prevented the violence and the fear from invading me…"
For Ari, the trauma of the unexpected artillery barrage that shell-shocked him was like a double assault – rape from within and rape from without. He felt that not only did he not succeed in preventing this assault, but that he may have cooperated with it. He wanted so much to live, and not to die. Why was he letting this happen to him? He and those around him had become passive participants in the sin, and none of them prevented it… No one averted the shame.

"Events" like these are kept secret to avoid any suspicion of having participated in the crime and to prevent oneself and others from remembering how one failed the test. In many cases, this kind of secret is so powerful that the energy required for keeping it becomes so disproportionate that impasse in other realms is nearly unavoidable. Often the sphere most conspicuously affected is that of one's work.

The phenomenon of a trauma becoming a repressed secret that can hold back a person's career development is familiar to most people in terms of sexual abuse. Children who have undergone such experiences often "forget" the feelings that accompanied the incidents, thus recording the events in the memory unaccompanied by the traumatic feelings that were originally attached to them. In many cases, this is followed by a reduced capacity to perform and a loss of the right to self-actualization. This is what happened to Susan.

Susan was sexually abused by her grandfather, whom she deeply loved. Only after she was past the initial obstacle of remembering the pain – just like soldiers with PTSD – was Susan able to speak of the traumatic incident she had experienced. Susan, too, was unable to feel the actual incident itself. It was a secret. The shame, the terror, the disappointment, the desire, the outrage, all these and more were locked away in a secret place and forgotten. Thus, although she married, raised four wonderful children, and lived happily with her husband, she never knew what to do with herself. Susan came to me when she was fifty, at the request of her husband. She had never thought that there might be a connection between her secret and her inability to find meaningful work. Once she recognized and pinpointed where she was stuck, her depression and her sense of "I am nothing," began to surface. Only then could she start her journey in search of a vision of her own. Eventually, Susan found fulfillment working with families who had suffered through sexual abuse.

The secret that comprises trauma, pain, and forgetting has come up at various points in the course of my professional journey. A few years ago, I was the key-note speaker leading a seminar on the treatment of PTSD at the University of Munich. Some of the participants had been children during the Holocaust. That conference taught me that Germans, too, had "been stuck" in their inner traumas, and had covered up the pain of the past together with future plans and career quests.

At that seminar, we dealt with a very difficult case of professional impasse afflicting a German therapist called Renate. It turned out that Renate's father, whom she loved and admired, had disappeared for five years during the war when she was a child. She knew that there was a secret about that period, but she didn't want to remember or acknowledge it.

When the war was over, her father came home and life returned to normal without a word about the war. Ever since, until that same morning I met her, no word had ever been spoken – no memory ever mentioned – about where her father had been and what he had done during the war.

During the very difficult and painful process we underwent in the course of that day at the workshop, it turned out that Renate had always "known" but hadn't wanted to know. Gradually, she uncovered the details. She remembered her father's extensive knowledge of foreign languages, money they received from an unknown source, her mother who was always afraid to look straight forward, and her father who all her life had never once looked her in the eye. Along with the fear, the horror, the disgust, and the shame, she remembered the love as well. Without understanding why, Renate had locked these feelings away inside her. The secret of silence had been transferred to the therapy room where she received her clients. "To sense these feelings myself," Renate said, "would have been like telling myself that my father was with the Gestapo, with all the hidden implications. It was impossible. The secret had to be kept."

In Renate's case, as with David's, there was a forbidden memory. Any attempt to breach that forbidden zone threatened to destroy a crucial part of the person harboring the secret. Consigning such a secret and the emotions surrounding it to oblivion exacts a heavy toll, silencing an important part of the self in the process.

"The Germans didn't kill only the Jews among them," Renate wrote to me a year later. "They also murdered the soul of their own people. As the soul withered, their emotional memory began to die. Perhaps for that reason I became a therapist. I tried to transpose forgetting into remembering. I tried to come to grips with my father, all of him, so as to understand more and more of the link between pain, accountability, forgetting, and remembering. I wanted to be a complete mother… a person… but truthfully, until the secret came out, I was like a robot. I spoke the right words but didn't feel them."

From David, I learned more about the "forgetting" that can never obstruct the "remembering." When I spoke with David, my mind was full of all the other soldiers with whom I'd worked who could neither remember nor forget the terrors of war. Like David, they too felt vocationally paralyzed.

Bringing shell-shocked ex-soldiers back into the working world is a very difficult thing to accomplish. In 1973, Dr. Shalom Litman and I worked at Hadassah Hospital in Jerusalem with groups of former soldiers suffering from PTSD. Most of our efforts were directed at their reentry into the working world. We were attempting to help them relearn how to give of themselves and to create, and then to allow themselves to be respected and admired for it.

These men refused to resume business as usual, "as if nothing had happened." Along with feelings of powerlessness, they angrily refused to return to the daily routine of life. "After what I went through," Michael, told me, "I have nothing left to offer."

No wonder it took four years of therapy before Michael dared to begin writing down some of his experiences. He required another two years before he could return to his studies, and only ten years after the end of the war did he go back to work. It was not for nothing that the late Yitzhak Rabin said, in 1975, during a conference in Israel on war and peace: "We Israelis have a shell-shocked view of things. This perspective governs how we reach our decisions, perform our deeds of heroism, draw our strength, and how we see ourselves both on the day-to-day level and in battle."

When I looked into David's eyes at forty years of age, and when we went down memory lane to the sands of the Sinai desert, twenty years earlier, I sensed how long the road had taken. Together we searched for a spark of life energy to rekindle his basic need to pursue his calling. Sometimes that spark showed itself when we talked of his children – his eyes would radiate a love of life that didn't mesh with his being completely stuck vocationally.

Many sessions passed before David dared relate his nightmares from the first three days of battle. Finally it seemed that he was ready to open up and reveal his secrets.

During his first three days under fire, David didn't eat or sleep. He served in four tanks during those days of hell. Four tanks that were hit, exploded, and burned in turn. He saw his friends burnt alive. And as if to spite him, he alone was spared. When he wanted to join the crew of the fifth tank, the soldiers were afraid to let him in. "You bring bad luck," he was told.

"I felt alone and rejected. I was angry at everyone. At the same time, I felt guilty and ashamed," he related. "I was ashamed to be glad that I'd survived. I worried that fate was toying with me. One day, I was standing in a long line of men waiting for water. I stooped down for a second to tie my shoelaces and at that precise moment, a barrage hit us. The soldiers ahead of me and behind me were beheaded, one after another... I was left behind again... traumatized and alone. I felt so alone. And most of all, I was terribly afraid. After fear, came anger. I was furious at the leaders and the politicians who had consigned us to this terror, permitted all this to happen, and allowed us to face this nightmare exposed and helpless. They sat in their comfortable armchairs in their offices and made mistakes, and we on the battlefield paid with our blood. I was left without a commanding officer and I was so totally alone... When I was all by myself, me and the tank, facing dozens of enemy tanks, nothing at all mattered to me anymore. What kind of big hero was I, for God's sake? I was nothing more than a bewildered kid who had been turned into an automaton with a weapon... and can you believe that I got a medal of honor for that?"

Outrage shrieked from every part of David's body.

This fury of helplessness and loneliness was the central topic of the ensuing sessions. David was finally able to grapple with his anger at everyone. He was enraged at those who had died and left him behind. He was angry at having been awarded a medal for his unwitting heroism. He was furious at his superiors, who hadn't prepared him for what was coming. His previous commanding officer had fallen, and he didn't know the new one so he was incensed at both of them. He was angry at himself for surviving; and he was simultaneously happy to be alive, yet embarrassed to be happy.

From within his anger, a rebellious protest began rising that clarified somewhat his state of impasse concerning work. "Today I am unwilling to do anything for anyone," he said.

"And for yourself?" I said with emphasis, as if in clarification.

"Not that either," he answered, calming down somewhat.

The picture slowly came into focus. After David witnessed slaughtering before his very eyes, he decided, however unconsciously, to remain metaphorically in the killing fields from which he hadn't been able to flee inwardly. The meaning of his peculiar vocational choice began to emerge. I thought to myself that perhaps all professions are really a kind of ongoing act of creation in a successful or unsuccessful quest for work of emotional significance and of value.

The term "profession" in Latin means "to make a public declaration" (as in taking a vow, religious or otherwise). David "declared against," as it were – and that was precisely where he had been stuck for so long. His rage, fear, guilt, and repressed memory subverted his natural inclination to perform and may even had injured his emotional capacity to fulfill his dream and become a physician. David had continuously impeded and frustrated his own activity. It was as if his natural desire to create and to give had been killed within him.

My thoughts turned again to that 1975 War and Peace Conference. Its guiding principle had been that every nation must deal with its own trauma. Every nation must provide its citizens and soldiers with various ways of coping in order for each to alleviate their own private trauma. When a nation understands and accepts the fact that their history – whether as a nation or an individual – is not only a part of their collective memory but also of their present – only then can they be liberated from the trauma, consign it to the archives of history, and use that freedom to discover their individual potential.

This statement is true not only regarding victims of war-related shell shock but also regarding some people who experience "job-firing shock" when dismissed from a job. An employee who is dismissed, goes to his next job interview, not only with a desire to be hired, but also with a wide range of feelings regarding his dismissed – anger, rage, fear, a sense of injustice, insecurity, grief, hurt, despair… All these are echoing around his soul and intertwining, until the accumulated result is liable to destroy the normal process of being accepted at a new job, and even ruin his subsequent professional advancement.

David succeeded in metaphorically cleansing many areas of his life. His career was bound up in what remained, figuratively speaking soiled. As on the battlefield, David had marvelous good luck in most areas of his life. I have known many others damaged by the trauma of war who were unable to find their way to rehabilitation. David did better than that. After ten years, he even came to see that another battle lay ahead of him – the battle to make peace with society around him. Only after that would he be ready for the decisive battle – fulfillment in his work.

By confronting the rage surrounding his trauma, we were able to connect with the ostensibly simpler anger of David the boy and David the youth towards his parents. Even farther along in the process, other weighty feelings began to emerge, feelings that David had kept confined within himself all those years.

"I was like a child whose parent-commanders had assigned him after a single night of raging battle to the rank of an officer, almost a parent," protested David, "without any training for the sudden promotion to adult. I didn't go through the intermediate stages of later childhood, adolescence, and autonomous authority."

Now that David had permission, he felt a terrible anger at the situation of helplessness into which he'd been cast and the dreadful reality his commanders had forced on him. Anything that struck him as vaguely capricious, infuriated him.

This new understanding paved the way for further discoveries. David had memorialized the horror of the battlefield at the slaughterhouse, but he continued to tempt fate elsewhere as well. He drove his car with a battlefield mentality. Consequently, every month or so in some unexplained way he was involved in at least two car accidents – his car would overturn, the body would be bent and crushed, and David would emerge sometimes wounded and sometimes unscathed… until the next time. He turned the highway into a war zone. At home the pain and rage would sometimes bubble up alongside his fear and his compulsion to go on testing fate. It were these feelings which led him to wayward driving and to the slaughterhouse.

"How about a truce?" I asked, astounded by the incredible strength that fighting these battles demanded.

David wasn't prepared to answer that yet.

But at our next session, he stood up suddenly and said: "I'm ready to think about other directions and maybe even consider the possibility of some other kind of work. What do you think?"

I was very glad to hear it. In order not to press too hard on the wound, we promised one another that we'd be satisfied meanwhile with just the thought, stopping short of making a commitment or a choice. Now the time had come to attempt some research.

"What kind of work would suit you right now?" I asked David. His response surprised me.

"What I should be doing now is building a little petting zoo in a corner of my back yard, where children can come and play. That way, I was thinking I could bring children closer to animals and teach them, through play, to care for them, while I would have the most fun of anybody."

This bowled me over. The gap between his childhood dream and his post-war choice of job seemed no mere coincidence, and easily bridgeable. David, too, suddenly saw how far he had come from his soldiering days to get to this place. David the child wanted to play with pets and take care of them. David the wounded, in his pain, sent them to the slaughter. David the adult was ready and willing to instruct children in how to care for animals and play with them.

I thought about how drastically difficult events can blur true desires; how wars slay not only people, but also the true dreams of the people who live through them and their ability to visualize new dreams with a real chance of fulfillment.

"I think I'm going to look into places to study," said David, smiling, as he stood up and bid me farewell.

I was left alone in the room. It wasn't surprising that Jake and the Sidni Ali caves on the Herzliya beach came into my memory. When my children were little, we used to hike along the high cliff overlooking the sea "to be with the waves." It was just at that time that a man named Jake started illegally building his castle on the pebble ridge facing the mountain. At first, he dug a cave, then he added a structure on top, and finished it off with a tower and a moat...

One day Jake allowed us to enter the little zoo he had established. Everything a small boy could dream of was there: strutting peacocks, waddling ducks, red-crowned roosters, cats and dogs of every type and species.

Jake's extraordinary personality fascinated me. He was a man of rare vitality and creativity. Unlike so many of us, Jake wasn't afraid to live out his dreams.

On one of our visits to his little zoo, Jake invited us inside his castle, from there we watched a glorious sunset.

"How did you come to be here?" I asked.

He answered simply but unequivocally: "I knew how to dream, and I wasn't afraid of dreaming. I knew that I'd fulfill my dream. I wanted a house by the sea... so I built one. There's no such thing as people who can't live their dream," he said forcefully. "There are only people who don't dare to dream..."

At my next session with David, I told him about Jake. I asked him to try to connect with this fundamental capacity of his own that had been so damaged – the ability to dream. Although David's ability to dream had been injured, it had not been slain altogether. David took on the challenge.

Movement towards rehabilitation accelerated. At the next session, David told me of his desire to build a restaurant next to the petting zoo.

Within a month, the dream had evolved in the direction of a small business enterprise in the hotel field. "The petting zoo will remain a hobby," he said, "but meanwhile, what I'm choosing to do is to pursue the profession of offering people hospitality."

As David proceeded to address the question of what to study and how to become a professional in the field, the way opened before him. The rehabilitated dream began to take on flesh and blood. Very gradually, he was able to climb out of the killing fields and return to his core needs. He began reconnecting with the person inside him who had always loved to take care of others.

David succeeded in recovering his ability to dream and in learning how to make his wishes come true. "My dream and its fulfillment are modest in scale, and the disability is still there inside me," he said, "but I've started to love life again. Now, I want to live and also to love others. You know what? Nothing gets lost and forgetting is impossible. There's only a vast forgiveness."

Another three years passed… "Hi – it's me, David," announced a pleased voice over the phone one day. "I wanted to tell you that I've finished my degree in Hotel Management. I did it!" After a short silence he asked uncertainly: "It's David, you do remember me, don't you?"

"Now really, David," I wanted to say, "It was thanks to you that I learned about how I'd killed my own memories of pain…," but that would have been too profound. Instead, I just laughed and asked him, "And how's the petting zoo coming along?"

"I didn't give up that idea either," he replied, adding, "but these days it's only a hobby. Something for the soul…"

David reminded me of something a therapist friend of mine had once told me, "Within each of us is a kind of jar. At the brim, there is pain. One layer beneath that lies indifference, and below that, sadness and depression. Lower down lie layers of anger and hatred. When all of these are brought out into the light, friendship and affection are uncovered next, and after that, at the very bottom of the jar, lies love."

David had kept the lid on for so many years. He had loaded the jar full of pain and rage and reinforced these with indifference. He hadn't let love and friendship surface. When he was able to move beyond vocational indifference to rage and pain, he was also able to uncover the affection and reveal the love.

I have never forgotten David's words "Nothing gets lost, and forgetting is impossible. There's only a vast forgiveness." They struck a dissonant chord that has haunted me over years of counseling.

Chapter Seven
An Interlude for Contemplation

Burnout led me to face up to my inner emptiness

In midlife when I moved to the mountains of the Galilee, I left almost everything I knew behind and headed for unknown territory to further explore my life quest. As a workaholic passionately involved with my career, I suddenly found myself sitting for entire days at a time doing absolutely nothing. I felt that I needed this time-out, yet I had no effective means of coping. Sometimes the deafening silence around me was painful, and the noise inside me frightening. I had no idea how to justify my existence. I had no idea what would validate what I was doing when I was no longer on display and subject to approval – my own or someone else's.

The days passed and nothing happened. I had left the world of productive activity behind, but had not yet arrived at the realm of creation. This was scary. It reminded me of my fear when I went rock climbing for the first time. The jumping-off point was clear to me – a narrow black boulder, slippery-smooth, but still solid and real. The landing spot was an enigma: a dark abyss, an unclear distance away. How was I supposed to leap out into space and let go of the only place I had a grip on, without knowing if I'd land again, or where? It was the closest I'd ever come to fearing death. But it was also a starting point, the point where my self-confidence began to grow significantly. I sensed that it was all right to let go of the supposedly safe and sure... and leap into the unknown, enjoying the sensation of freedom and daring. These feelings were new to me; I had never experienced such release. After learning to let go, suddenly all the initiatives I'd always been afraid to contemplate seemed possible to accomplish.

As this critical stage in my life was unfolding, I was simultaneously sharing a journey with Henry. Henry, too, needed to learn to deal with the inner void, and with the unknown. Possibly because we went through this experience of survival together, we were able to stay the course successfully. We came to realize that without that leap into the unknown, it is very hard to undergo change and extract the hidden treasures that lie within.

Together, we learned how crucial it is to find the strength and the tools to intentionally make space for a time-out. We discovered how critical it is to hear and properly interpret our own distress signals that ultimately symbolize burn out. If we don't listen and don't understand, we become increasingly exhausted until eventually we find ourselves – by default – in a place of nothingness. But that restricts our choices and deepens our fears. Still, in the end, even a time-out that occurs accidentally owing to unacknowledged overload can generate new possibilities and interesting new directions for development.

Henry reached that inner void after recognizing that he was stuck. Together, we realized that the situation was a result of his work. After we had pinpointed the nature of his impasse, he was able to go on to the next stage – movement within the void.

Many times, feelings such as sadness and a sort of nothingness, a not-being, are part of the sojourn into the void. The experience is a difficult one emotionally. It's an intermediate stage, a kind of limbo – you are no longer connected to the previous life, yet the new phase of your life is still taking shape just around the corner.

The sojourn in that inner space of emptiness inevitably involves feelings of loneliness and loss of control. Sometimes the emptiness is so frightening that a person will fill the void by busying himself with "noise" and excess activity, simply to stave off self-confrontation.

People engage in a struggle with themselves so as not to take time-out from the known and familiar. Self-examination, with everything stripped bare and nothing veiled, is difficult and cuts deep. The question is – without lifting away the veil that separates us from the world – can there be any real change in ourselves?

Henry came to me by chance. A colleague at his office suggested that he call me: "Under the circumstances, you have nothing to lose," she told him.

Eventually Henry decided to take her advice. At his first session, he made sure to create an impression of perfect order – Armani suit, gold Rolex, and of course, a well-planned smile. He was tense and alert, spoke as was expected of him, and made an effort to project an image of business as usual.

Henry the star, the wunderkind, a man who had risen rapidly to dizzying heights, who had impressed the elite of the nation's capital markets, suddenly started to forget things.

The signs appeared gradually. At first he was a bit confused at the office, and official memos disappeared with no logical explanation. After that, his fantastic memory began to fail and he began to miss board meetings. His memory simply betrayed him. At his wife's urging, Henry underwent a series of comprehensive medical tests but to no avail. The doctors identified no physical problem and pronounced him healthy. Henry tried hanging on for dear life to his usual routine, but his professional functioning was rapidly cascading downhill.

The man was simply worn out. He suffered from severe accumulated fatigue. Over the years, he had always done exactly what everyone expected of him – his parents, his army buddies, his superiors, his colleagues and staff. He went to the right plays and concerts, saw the right films, and was one of the first to go on the now-customary backpacker's odyssey to far-flung sites in India, Africa, and South America.

Henry's life seemed like a TV mini-series, starring handsome men who were strong and sensitive. He was the most successful boy in primary school, a star athlete in high school, a combat soldier in the army's top unit. He had graduated with honors, married the right woman, and rapidly made a niche for himself at a successful and well-known firm.

Henry was truly "perfect" – and then, somehow, suddenly, he began forgetting things. He forgot names, assignments, and numbers. He couldn't remember where he had been planning to go, or why. This absentmindedness descended on him viciously. It forced him to stop his life in its tracks and take time-out in the middle of life.

At our first session, Henry and I understood that he had hardly ever done anything that was born out of a true desire of his own. Henry did things because he was supposed to do them. He read the right books, but never really enjoyed them. He studied accounting, but dreamed of painting and designing houses.

Henry the Superstar was busy proving himself even on holidays when the idea was to relax. He always took on the chief executive role, right from the planning stages. He'd organize a dozen families who would get together and follow the itinerary he'd set up for them. On the trip itself, while his friends were lounging around after long miles of challenging hiking, Henry would be taking care of logistics. He was the compulsive organizer who never rested. This was his life in a microcosm.

He excelled at organization and management, but didn't know how to relax and enjoy the fruits of his labor. He didn't know how to simply be – just as he was, for himself. The mountain top was never the goal for him; it was merely another stage on the road to reaching the next peak of the next mountain.

Applying the brakes was terribly problematic for Henry. He had trouble accepting the simple diagnosis that he was so saturated that he had no room for anything more. And especially not for himself. He had no room for Henry. Whatever he tried to pour in, simply overflowed.

"Why me? Why is everyone else fine?" he raged, during our session. "It sounds like something's wrong with me. Maybe I'm going nuts?"

"I don't think so," I said, smiling. "Other people start to slip up, from overload, too. Possibly it could even be beneficial. Maybe deep inside you, you have stored a lot of anger and an inner voice is trying to tell you something. Maybe you are fed up with excelling and always being a good boy. Your soul wants time for itself. It wants to get close to the real Henry."

"That all sounds like psychological mumbo jumbo – maybe you're even correct!" shouted Henry, "But what am I supposed to do about it?" His outburst seemed to me to be part anger, part cry for help, reflecting his anxiety at not understanding what was happening to him and his fear of losing control.

"What am I supposed to do?" he asked again.

"That's exactly the point," I replied, smiling. "Nothing."

Henry glared at me in astonishment. "With all your expertise, that's all you can suggest?" he asked.

What else could I say at that point? Henry was in that classic place where moving from transitional emptiness to reaching a turning point would bring him to a fresh chapter in his life. As yet, he didn't know that.

It's worth remembering that even a person who is ostensibly stopped in their tracks still has powerful inner energies that continue to drive them forward. Bubbling under the surface, tremendous upheaval and significant activity are taking place – painful and new, yet constructive and creative. This is the point from which a person can and must curb his activities, in favor of inward listening that is so crucial to his future. Listening to one's self is critically important in figuring out whether our lives are truly fulfilling and really making us happy, or whether changes need to be introduced. Certain questions come into play here. What should be changed, how should it be changed, and what direction should the change take? It's only natural that often the process involves strong feelings of anxiety and confusion.

What appears to be in neutral may actually be a transitional stage – a time to apply the brakes, get rid of excess clutter, and make plans on how to move on successfully in life. We clear out new spaces and create a new place for love, choice, and new ideas better suited to the lives we are leading at present.

Executive managers and businesspeople are quite familiar with this situation. There are chapters in their lives, as in the life cycle of the organizations they are running, when they would like to be initiating and moving things forward; yet everything seems stuck. The more impatient among them are in a hurry to move ahead nonetheless, and do so, with business transactions or organizational changes that fail later on. Others try to identify new channels for investment, but in vain. Some try to fill the void with a new lover, although they may have been perfectly happy with the married lives they were leading. Others will rush into switching careers, only to discover in short order that their new choice had been a mistake and that the root of the problem wasn't in their selection of a career. In contrast to all these, there are however some people who do understand the message and try to pay attention to it.

As noted, the inner void, crucial as it is, can be misapprehended as a disaster threatening to ruin our lives. Women who find it hard to deal with this void may get pregnant in order to fill the space that suddenly looms inwardly. Couples who experience the void may move to a new flat despite not really needing one. Others sign up for expensive, long, sophisticated courses of study that do not really interest them. And of course there are those who become ill or create unnecessary conflicts at work.

Then there was Henry, sinking under his overload, so afraid of change that he began forgetting.

"You must understand," I told him at one of our sessions, "nature has its own pace, and loathes shortcuts. The path is wiser than the one who travels it ..."

I decided to tell Henry about a chapter in a wonderful book, *Work and Love* (Jay Rohrlich, 1980), which tells the story of a successful CEO whose wife surprises him on the occasion of his fortieth birthday with a holiday on an enchanted island.

Two hours before they leave for the airport, the CEO is still working at his elegantly appointed office. When he finally decides enough is enough, he rushes home, hastens to the airport with his wife, gets on the plane for a long flight, arrives at the island, and at the end of his first day of vacation has a massive heart attack and dies.

"You understand," I said to Henry, "this was the first holiday that this executive had ever taken in his entire life! The sudden transition from "forward" to "neutral" was too fast and too acute for him. Possibly if he had made a few intermediate stops on the way, he might still be alive."

"So then what do people do in order to stop?" asked Henry.

"Some, like you, begin forgetting. Others create family crises, some are hospitalized; others get depressed and stop functioning and some stop and actually begin to listen."

Henry gazed at me skeptically. I decided to tell him about the private void I had experienced on moving to the Galilee. "Right after a series of impressive achievements, when I could finally lean back and relax, I suddenly started to feel that the fullness of my life threatened to blow me away from the inside," I told him. "I couldn't create any more. Anything I tried to add in, just flowed out again, spilling over. Even in my role as a mother, I couldn't go on. 'You're faking it,' my children informed me, 'even when you're here, you're not with us.' 'What do you mean, I'm not with you?' I cried. 'You just aren't,' said my children, not giving an inch. 'You don't listen, you don't see, you're just running around from one place to another. Maybe you need to get a grip on yourself?'"

Henry smiled slightly, and I went on: "Without a doubt, that was the beginning of my time-out. It happened gradually, accompanied by confusion, wondering, and a lot of anxiety. In the end, I decided to pick up and move to the countryside. My children agreed to come along for the ride. They, who stood to suffer the most from being separated from their friends at adolescence, understood that their mother was struggling toward new challenges and that they were likely be better off for it. Even now, I am amazed at their understanding of something that many adults, myself included, found so difficult to explain."

"Just as I wasn't really present with myself or my family, you aren't really there with yourself," I wound up, gazing at Henry. "Maybe that's why your memory stopped working," I added.

Total silence followed. Henry, the forceful and dynamic businessman, who ran his life like a never-ending marathon, finally stopped and tried to digest the messages his body was sending him. He had to consider whether he wanted to go on running at all, and whether he wanted to go on running in the same direction.

"Even my son has given up on me... we have no common language," said Henry quietly.

The two of us agreed that it was best to strike while the iron was hot. First of all, we decided not to consign Henry to that fearsome inner void that would demand that he refrained from any activity whatsoever. The first goal was to shift him toward some other activity, as a kind of intermediate phase. We added fitness training to Henry's calendar. The next phase required him to divert from his routine activities by taking up something new. For example, he no longer had to read the "right" books, but books that would be fun to read. He discovered that even the daily newspaper could be opened first to the arts and culture section, and not directly to the financial section...

Instead of going to "must-see" films, he began watching action movies, films by various directors he'd always wanted to see but had never allowed himself. Sometimes it was a concert rather than a play, and he began coming home from the office at six instead of at midnight. Henry didn't merely change his agenda, he began making space for himself and choosing his priorities. After tossing out the dead weight, suddenly there was room for a great many new things.

Change prompted more change. At our first sessions, Henry looked every inch the well-groomed yuppie. This changed gradually – first the tie went, then the dark jacket, and then lo and behold sometimes this polished businessman showed up looking superb in blue jeans and a T-shirt.

Henry was gripped by panic in the wake of the changes churning around inside him, but he didn't blink. He began, for the first time in his life, to drive the children to their evening activities, which demanded him to remember when his wife was out of the house at her exercise class.

In time, his memory began working again.

At our seventh meeting, when Henry reported that his forgetfulness was gradually receding, I told him about a formal tea ceremony conducted by a Tibetan priest for a younger priest who was a candidate to become his student. The student, who had labored at intensive training for years, was invited to the tea ceremony conducted by his master teacher to be. When the designated day finally arrived, the young priest entered the teacher's small dwelling, bowed low and reverently, and observed for several hours how the master conducted the tea ceremony. He patiently spread a silk cloth on the table and carefully arranged the tea leaves. Then he brewed the tea kettle and slowly set the porcelain tea cups in place on the table, all the while remaining silent as he faithfully fulfilled the traditions of the ceremony.

The young priest watched his teacher's actions, admiringly.

He had waited so many years for this event and now he feared that any superfluous movement on his part would upset the order of things.

Awed, the student continued to follow the teacher's every move until finally, the elderly man began pouring the steaming tea into one of the delicate porcelain cups. The teacher poured, and poured, and poured. The cup filled to the brim. But even when the tea began overflowing from the cup, the teacher continued to pour....

The young priest knew that he was bound to silence, but at this point his nerves were shattered. He didn't understand what was happening, or why the teacher had decided to ruin the ceremony. Something snapped: "But, revered master," the student burst out loudly, "the tea is spilling!" The old priest smiled and stopped pouring. He leaned down to the student and told him almost in a whisper: "You are like this cup. You are too full of yourself, so whatever I pour into you, will overflow and spill out again. Come back for the next ceremony when you are emptier and able to absorb new things that you have not yet learned."

Henry loved my story. "Apropos new things," he said with enthusiasm, "I was approached by a voluntary association that helps disabled children, asking me to contribute my talents to help them raise funds."

"And is that what you'd really like to do?" I asked, pointedly.

"That's what I'm good at," he answered quickly.

Though I was glad that Henry was beginning to work on identifying his true needs and desires, I put two and two together and said: "But maybe this isn't what you would have chosen to begin with? Lots of people automatically choose to do what they know they're good at, rather than what they would have really liked to do. Perhaps this choice reflects a desire that you may have had at one time, but not your real passion and dreams for tomorrow. And, conceivably, you aren't yet practiced enough at identifying what you really want. In fact, maybe you'd like to do something vastly different, but you're still afraid to go public with such an initiative, to people who know you as an expert in some other field entirely."

Henry was silent. He was working on giving himself permission to continue to ask questions and consider alternatives.

The more rapidly things changed, the more Henry needed silence to digest and understand the transitions taking place.

In the same way that music is made up not only of tones, but also of the silences between the notes, our lives are created not only from periods of activity, but also from the spaces between them.

In the same way, a woman preparing her womb to receive a pregnancy in the near future needs a time-out. Many women have trouble conceiving when they are tense, when they don't permit themselves to relax and move into a state of nothingness as preparation for receiving the fetus. Their urgency does not allow them to create, just as it does not allow others to choose a fruitful path of activity to impregnate their lives with newly born ideas.

"So what are you saying?" asked Henry with a smile, at our next session. "I have to drop everything and open myself to changes? Do you know what they'll say about me at work? Do you realize how my family will look at me?"

"It's true that you can get into countless pressurized situations at work," I added. "But things can also be different. You can try to look at everything from different perspectives, to think things through clearly in peace and quiet, and possibly arrive at new conclusions. Pressure is bad for intuitive thinkers like you."

Henry was again taken aback. "And what am I supposed to do in the meantime?" he asked.

"I would recommend that you take some form of time-out, and open yourself up to new experiences," I suggested. "See life with new eyes. Give yourself a little space."

Henry thought a minute, then nodded, "Okay, decision taken."

Daily, Henry took a half-hour time-out. Even in the middle of a tense day crammed with meetings, and "despite that it was virtually impossible," as he put it, Henry would stop what he was doing and leave his office, which was close to the Tel Aviv shorefront, and head for the beach. He'd sit himself down on a bench near the breakwater parallel to the shore, turn off his cellular phone and do some thinking. Alternatively, he would simply close his office door and listen to music he loved. Occasionally, he would go out and walk around the busy alleys of the outdoor market, and sometimes he strolled down the streets of downtown Tel Aviv. Gradually, the void within ceased to be an enemy and became a trusted friend. Eventually his photographic memory, which had begun to return, became sharper than ever.

The change in Henry was clearly discernible. People began complimenting him on his appearance, on the change in how he talked and laughed. He began his new activities by raising funds for a disabled children's association. After winding up that assignment successfully, he became the mentor for a twelve-year-old boy whose legs were disabled. This is how it happened that a businessman, who for years had rarely found time for his own children, immersed himself in a comprehensive get-well plan designed to give his protégé a better chance in life.

"You won't believe it," Henry related with enthusiasm, "One meeting with this kid gives me more inspirational ideas than a whole management workshop. For some reason it's when I'm there, away from the daily frenzy, that the best ideas come to me. It's really amazing, but I'm still afraid to tell my wife about it."

"What are you afraid of? That she'll be jealous?" I asked cautiously.

"Maybe," he said. "What I've done with that child is still hard for me to do with my own."

"Why don't you try sharing this paradox with your wife," I suggested.

Henry just needed permission because he already knew how

to go about it. We both knew that deep down, he'd already made up his mind. Some inner part of him was changing right in front of me. The process began with me, and went on successfully without me, during the time he thought of as "Henry's time with Henry." Suddenly, he discovered things in himself that he would never have guessed existed.

"To think that I could have lived my whole life without really getting to know Henry at all," he said at our last session, "That sounds really awful."

Henry's understanding expanded. He saw that taking time out was important not just for himself, but for those around him at work, too. He realized that these thinking breaks also served him well in coming up with ideas on how to outsmart his competitors.

"The inner void lets me see myself as I really am," he concluded. "It lets me think differently, ask questions, and allow new ideas to surface. Sometimes I still use intensive activity as a way of running away. But then I quickly realize that I miss the time with myself. I've undertaken to stick with these time-outs, and you know that I'm good at keeping commitments."

There are people who can pull themselves out of their inner void by reconnecting to long forgotten hobbies such as painting, acting, community activities, and so on. For these people, self-expression takes on the role of a time-out which can help to confront and heal a person's inner void.

Henry represents but a small part of what each of us has inside ourselves; the part of us that is afraid to confront components of the inner void, where often emptiness and silence dwell.

It is well to remember that the void is merely an intermediate phase and sometimes even serves as an incubation stage. In this period of our lives, we are called on to look deeply into ourselves and to wait patiently for the growth and new vigor that comes with spring. After all, spring always follows a period of winter hibernation.

Chapter Eight
Personal Vision Is a Craft

What do I want to be when I grow up?

When my daughter Natalie was five, I used to take her to play with her friend Melissa. One day, when I came to fetch her, the two were in the middle of a heated argument. Melissa was immersed in a Wall Street game using play money for various transactions via banks, cashier stations, and the stock exchange, all made from empty shoe boxes. Natalie, my daughter, was trying to explain to Melissa why her way was better... "But all I want is to make a lot of money," Melissa said. "Uh-uh, money isn't everything" claimed Natalie, "With my way you can make a profit and also have fun..."

Melissa's father and I observed this dialogue with amusement. Melissa's father, a globally known financier, remarked in an apologetic tone mixed with pride: "She must have got that from me."

"And my daughter," I replied frankly, "Got her views from me..."

I don't know who raises the question first, the parent or the child. Somewhere around a child's fifth birthday, an intense dialogue on the subject begins: "What will I be when I grow up?" Most children have very clear answers, even if very oversimplified.

Sometimes it turns out that the core of these responses can hint at future vocational patterns that the child will in fact undertake as an adult.

Evidently, as the typical five-year-old begins asking basic identity questions (of gender for instance), he or she is already taking first steps not only to the fundamental question of "Who am I?" but also to questions like: "Who am I, in terms of how that is reflected in what I do?" The child, like the adult, aspires to fuse uniquely within him or herself, the various inner seeds of identity that he or she has internalized and inherited.

In all my years of experience, I have generally discovered that the majority of people, after a committed search process, achieve some vision of what they ought to be doing and know in their heart of hearts what profession or mission would bring them meaning. However, the road to discovering this knowledge and then actualizing it is both complicated and full of obstacles.

Rachel, an art teacher, came to me when she was on sabbatical leave from her job. She was suffering from depression and a sense of having missed out on life. Though she had come to request my advice, she herself noted, "I do actually know what I want to do."

"What?" I asked.

"I very much want to be an artist," she answered and a few moments later, added quietly, "I hate teaching art."

"Well, okay, so what's the problem?"

"I can't actually manage to do it. I feel as if there's some part of me that needs the teaching profession. Teaching is what keeps me on track. Do you have any idea what it means for me to become an artist? It means changing my entire world – maybe even being married to another man, wearing completely different clothes, living another culture, thinking and dreaming differently... having new friends... changing my house... my daily life... my passion, my craziness. Today everything in my life is organized and orderly. Everything is in balance. The only thing missing is the desire to live. It's driving me crazy."

I know from experience that people who have identified their dream yet refrained from fulfilling it are more accepting of their lives than those who don't dare to identify their dream.

Rachel was one of those people who chose not to follow her dream and gave up taking a journey that she felt would ultimately be too risky for her.

Similarly, the children of parents who've identified their dream have an easier time choosing a profession, too. They generally don't take upon themselves the weight of that bitter sense of having missed out that so typifies those who have given up without even knowing what their dreams were.

A dream or a calling is not always something "big." It could be a desire to express one's thoughts in writing, even if the results go in a desk drawer. It could be the desire to help a youngster prepare for a religious rite of passage. It could be a wish to grow one's own special herbs and spices at home. But so long as our heart's desire has not been identified and sketched out, it can take on unreal dimensions that may at times be fearsome.

Ben was one of those people who felt the urge for self-actualization, and he was also ready to set out on a journey to achieve it. I met him at several key crossroads over a number of years.

He arrived at our first session confused and worried. His appearance suggested carelessness. He wore tattered jeans and an old, brightly colored shirt. He had long curly hair and I was immediately struck by his sad, sensitive eyes. Twenty-two years old, Ben's neck and arms were festooned with beads and bracelets; trendy reminders of his latest visit to India, the Mecca for so many young people in search of answers.

"I came here," he said in a quiet voice, "because I want something but I don't know what it is. I know that I probably look ridiculously mixed-up. A friend of mine came to you for counseling, and he recommended that I come too. I'm at the end of my tether, but he inspired me with his optimism that there are solutions to my problems."

Ben resembled a broken bell. I knew that my approach had to be gentle and thoughtful if I wanted to help produce a delicate resonance. Ben's hesitant undertone made me fear at first that he might be on drugs or affected by some kind of hallucinogenic mushroom from his last trip to the East. But when his pain erupted, I realized that he was totally there with me. He was present, and had traveled a long way, but he didn't know how to move on.

"The truth is," he said sadly, "it doesn't really matter what goes on here today. Whatever happens, I'll go to university this year, and I'll study accounting. That's my dad's field, and that's what I'm going to do in life."

"And is that also what you would like to do?" I asked. The self-contempt was perceptible in his tone, and I felt his anger at the choice forced upon him.

"It doesn't matter what I want," he replied impatiently, "it's what my dad wants and does, it's what my successful genius of a brother does; and the way things look now, it's what I'm going to do, too."

"And what about you? Are you a genius too?" I queried.

"Me? I was never a good student," Ben said almost proudly yet rather defiantly.

I wondered whether this might be his way of setting himself apart. Was this how he was building his uniqueness?

"Perhaps you didn't want to be a good student?" I suggested. "Maybe you were your mother's child?"

Something in him thawed. "That's right. How did you know?" he asked, surprised.

I smiled. "Sometimes," I told him, "nature dictates its laws and that can influence our entire life. When the first-born son chooses the same professional route as his father, which happens frequently, the second son is likely to take the mother's path. Similarly, when the first born daughter chooses the same profession as her mother, the second daughter is likely to take the father's vocational path."

"And does this non-choice alternative also apply to a five-year-old child whose parents are divorced?" asked Ben derisively.

"Yes, even at age five, " I said, "because though it might seem too early, age five is particularly significant in shaping our primary vocational choices. 'What are you going to be when you grow up?' is a question that comes up precisely at that time, together with questions about sexual identity. And with great importance we announce to one and all: 'When I grow up, I'm going to be like Daddy' (or like Mommy); or: 'When I grow up, I'm going to be a pilot.' The replies, even if they are stereotyped and drawn from the proverbial world of headlines or stories, are amazingly precise in terms of the activity the child favors or eventually undertakes as an adult. Some children will change direction over the years or will miss their calling. For many children, the occupational choice will not be significantly different from that announced at age five, even if then their descriptions were not classic professional titles per se – researcher, retailer, teacher, artist, etc."

Ben smiled. "At five," he told me, "I was told that I would manage people and businesses, yet I also loved to listen to people and write stories in my imagination. I thought that since I was a leader among my friends, but also loved to create alone, that it was possible to combine these things. Now I'm not so sure…"

It would seem that in some fashion we always "know," yet something goes awry – some circumstance of life – like parents divorcing for instance. When parents divorce, our two most significant figures blast away our cushioned world of security in one shattering blow. Such an occurrence can certainly place tremendous stress on our inner attachments and make vocational fulfillment far more difficult.

When choosing a gratifying career or satisfying path in life, a person tends to forge inner connections between elements of work and activity that have significance for him or her. People are particularly influenced by their parents' activities and sometimes even those of their significant others, such as an older sister, brother, or grandparent and so on.

Schematically, if the mother was a computer programmer and the father a graphic artist, the son may likely choose computer animation or software development for a living while doing photography, a kind of hybrid interest, as a hobby. This occupational integration is almost like the psycho-genetic emotional integration inherited from two parents. The content bequeathed by each of the two genders comes together in the child within the adult, creating a new whole.

There is, however, a downside. When the two "halves," the two parents, have trouble uniting in a stable attachment or in a happy, satisfying married life, the children will typically have trouble internalizing their legacy of content and emotions. Frequently, each part will be assimilated separately but the connection between them will be missing.

Beyond that, in order to be a "good child," the child of separated parents may feel forbidden to "choose" between the father and mother. Thus he or she may not be able to pursue either the father's or the mother's field. "I'd better watch out," such a child thinks to himself, "because if I become an artist like Mom, and not a computer expert like Dad, it will be as if I've betrayed Dad." This dilemma is a derivative of the eternal question, "Whom do you love more, child – Daddy or Mommy?"

Thus the choice of profession has critical implications. In my experience, this conflict exists for both the children and the parents.

Parents are not always aware of the fact that their children are torn between them, not only emotionally but also vocationally. This very difficult conflict has a crucial influence on career decisions even during adulthood. If the issue persists over many years as a power struggle between the parents, the children are liable to be drawn to the profession of the preferred parent or the parent who favors them, rather than making their own original choices.

In Ben's case, the reality of his life and apparently of his vocation was split apart at age five when his parents separated.

Ben had been a delicate child who was viewed as his mother's son.

"My mother showed artistic tendencies," Ben related at our second session, "and so did I. The two of us – I, at age five, and she at the age of thirty, were both at the very beginning from a vocational standpoint."

After pausing, he added: "Even then, I felt like an artist. I used to sit in the room with my mother and draw. Maybe I was always trying in that way to ease her loneliness. Now, my mother shows her paintings and photographs in prestigious galleries in New York and Paris; but back then, no one looked at her work. She sat at home, working now and then, taking care of the house, and she focused on her health problems. The house and I were her whole world. She almost didn't go out at all. My father in any case was hardly ever home, even before they were divorced."

"But you stayed with her," I added gently.

"Right," he said.

I was reminded of a story about Henry Moore. When Henry was little, he was at home with his mother, who had arthritis, and Henry was supposed to have massaged her aching back. Maybe the sculptor was already sculpting his first works, based on the curves of her back…

"You stayed with your mother to take care of her," I suggested.

Ben sat quietly for a little while, thinking about this. After a few minutes, he said hesitantly: "I didn't think of it in that way, but I guess that's what happened. Even then, two camps were forming in our house. In the winners' camp, there was my father and my big brother, Jim. In the losers' camp, there was my mother and me."

Ben paid a heavy price for "protecting" his mother, for not wanting to leave her alone in this situation.

In many families, the roles of the children and those of the parents are fixed in accordance with the family's situation and the dominant qualities with which the children identify.

In Ben's family, his father played the "strong role" and his mother was relegated to the "weak role." Her choice involved more than herself, however. It was also automatically forced on Ben, her second son, whose older brother was his powerful father's son.

The story of Ben's and his mother's difficulties brought me back to my own story and to the emotional whirlpool of my mother's marriage. A multi-talented and extremely energetic woman, my mother was clearly meant for the arts, but she wasn't able to find fulfillment in tandem with my father. Between my father and me there was a kind of covenant of the wise. My mother was the intuitive one, weak, and sick. She was sometimes an artist and sometimes just "crazy." Who would want to be like her or be in her camp? It wasn't for nothing that I turned into "a smart woman with a profession," one of those women who is not expected to cook or undertake the traditional duties of an ordinary housewife. I could not, of course, become someone who writes... That was too close to the arts, and would also have been like waving a red flag in my father's face... I was Daddy's successful, masculine woman. This was unquestioned. Sometimes, I was even his son. I paid a high price for avoiding the realization of my feminine, artistic qualities at an early age, and I was reluctant to admit that I had inherited artistic talent from my mother.

I didn't allow myself to connect with my mother's weakness, just as Ben had trouble connecting with his mother's. Both of us lost out – Ben by not pursuing his artistic inclinations, and I, by not entering a high school of the arts as I had dreamed of doing, and didn't dare to express myself through writing.

I wanted to share with Ben the complicated things I was feeling. "Have you ever tried to connect to your father's power or identify with him?"

Ben was surprised. "With his power? His power scares me. That was never even an option."

"Did your father ever tell you about what kind of a child he was?" I asked.

"He was the oldest son who was also the most talented and successful," Ben responded.

"What about his brothers and sisters?"

Ben paused, trying to remember the story of his father's childhood.

"My father had a younger brother who was always indecisive," he said finally. "My uncle suffered from juvenile diabetes. He was chronically ill and fragile. When he grew up, he did odd jobs – painting, fix-it jobs and plumbing repairs. He never matured or settled down."

"Maybe he was an artist like you, and through those manual, physical occupations was searching for his way to art?" I asked.

Ben listened silently.

I decided to take a shot in the dark, relying on my faith in the way things tend to interconnect on the vocational family tree. "Is there any way," I asked, "in which art and weakness always go together in your family...?"

"How could I not have thought of that?" said Ben suddenly. "We never acknowledged him, his uniqueness, his talents..."

I told Ben about Salim, a repairman from a small Arab village in the Galilee. Salim had always wanted to study art, and to draw and sculpt, but the harsh realities of his life had dictated otherwise. Nonetheless, Salim had tried to fulfill his dream through building renovations, seeing each project as an artistic endeavor deserving of creative inspiration. He was highly respected in his field and his work was in great demand.

"If I don't enjoy renovating a home," Salim once told me, while working on mine, "if I feel that there's nothing unique in the job and no special talent is required of me to do it, I don't take the project."

"Heredity is a devious thing," I told Ben. "Perhaps your uncle the repairman was a closet artist like Salim, who had found his calling, but never received recognition from his family?"

"It's really moving to hear that people do things because of their mother or their father," Ben said bitterly. "As pop psychology, it's not bad. But do you honestly believe that it works like that in real life?"

"That is my impression," I told him. "We do a great many things to be loved and accepted by at least one of our parents. We are also ready to pay a heavy personal price to avoid rejection. You were pushed onto your mother's side, especially when you felt that your father preferred your older brother to you. That may have happened because, as the first-born, he was given automatic preference, or possibly you reminded him of his younger brother."

Ben scratched his head with seeming indifference, and said: "The truth is that my father was always very busy but, in spite of that, everyone knew that he preferred Jim."

This was another characteristic of Ben's family; a clear division of territory and authority. Perhaps his father wanted to be what he considered "fair" and leave his wife a child of her own, so that she could raise him. He took the oldest son for himself and left her the spare boy, so that there would be someone to watch out for her. The father was unconsciously replicating the pattern of his own birth family.

"Did you ever go to work with your father?" I asked. I wanted to know more about Ben's relationship with his father.

"Almost never. Jim went there a lot. I didn't like the office," Ben said.

"Why not?"

"I don't know," he retorted heatedly.

I wondered whether Ben didn't like to go to his father's office or whether he was simply never really invited. In families where the distance between parents has already widened passed the point where it can be bridged, and where there's a tendency for the children to be on different sides, the parents sometimes make a kind of "family property" settlement. The children, unfortunately, serve as one of the resources to be split up. That appears to have been what happened in Ben's family.

Yet, although the family was torn in two, this represented an excellent opportunity for Ben and his mother. The separation from Ben's very powerful father enabled his mother to begin growing on her own. After their divorce, bolstered by generous monthly child support, Ben's mother made a daring leap to freedom embarking on a new learning curve. Gradually, the novice photographer began selling her work to well-connected acquaintances. Over time, her friends introduced her to gallery owners in New York who came to see her work, and eventually exhibited it. That was how it began. After New York she had her first show in London, which paved the way for further exhibitions around the world.

"Those were good years," Ben summed up. "I also felt as if I were getting stronger, and that the world was starting to be more balanced. I was with Mom, Jim was with Dad. I believed that everything would be okay. During those years, I started to write poetry. You know, the kind you put away in a drawer."

"No one saw your poems?" I asked.

"Are you kidding?"

"Even your mom?"

"Not even my mom, and definitely not Dad or Jim."

"Apropos Jim, what happened with him over the years?"

"What could have happened? My big brother did what we always knew he would do. He was an officer in the army, graduated from university with distinction, and after four years began working for Dad at the office."

"And what about you?"

"Me!" he said with emotion. "With me, it was a totally different story. I started working as a youth counselor in the army and I was pretty good at it. I knew it and my mother knew it. Even my dad was encouraging."

"Finally you had joined the men's world."

"Evidently."

The man facing me smiled. I thought that, for the first time in his life, far from his mother and his authoritarian father, Ben was able to connect with the qualities that the world of men valued: power, success, and the ability to influence others. Of course he didn't become an officer like his brother, but the respect he received from his commanding officers became his calling card in the masculine world of achievement and success, notions that had always been so foreign to him. At the same time, however, exposure to that world threw his internal compass wildly out of kilter. The delicate, intelligent, artistic child was now a prisoner of success.

"Don't you understand?" he queried at our next meeting. "After my army service, I felt smart, successful, like a man. I thought that to hold on to all of this, I had to be accepted at any price. I had to study accounting."

"Like your father and Jim," I noted.

"Right."

"But that's not what you really want to be!" I burst out, as if speaking for him.

Ben gazed at me with that uncomprehending look of his. "You really don't understand that what I want is irrelevant? For me and my family, art and photography are for women and people who don't matter. Accounting is for real, successful men. So that's what I've made up my mind to study."

With that statement, in effect, the first chapter of our journey was over. Ben understood that, like his success in the army, going on to study in the family's "successful" field of accounting was for him a prerequisite in his developmental journey, even if he already knew that his vocational vision directed him elsewhere.

After that meeting, Ben disappeared as if the earth had swallowed him up. When I tried reaching him at his apartment, a woman's voice answered, saying that Ben didn't live there anymore. At his mother's house, a voice answered aggressively: "My son has an unlisted number and doesn't wish to be disturbed." I understood that Ben had decided to cut himself off and I respected his decision.

Another five years passed. One day Ben – that Ben – simply walked into my room and sat down opposite me. Only after a few seconds was I able to identify the handsome and stylish man who had just walked in. Gone was the long hair, gone was the confused, perplexed child I'd met years before. In his place, or so it seemed, was this successful businessman, steering his way decisively through life. It actually seemed as if there was no connection between the two; the one from then and the one from now. The only thing that linked them was the smile that leaned sideways to the left, and that same feeling he still projected of carrying a heavy burden. It looked as though the businessman had dug a very deep hole somewhere and buried his inner child forever.

"I've come to clarify my calling in life, and this time, I won't give up!" declared Ben.

"I don't think you ever did give up!" I countered, seeing the light in his eyes.

"I'm not sure," he said, and waited until I was calm. "Do you remember that I broke contact some years back? It wasn't easy. I took the entrance exams for business school, and failed. Then I understood that I didn't really want to be accepted. Only when I realized that it was really my own choice, only then did I make the decision that I would succeed after all. And in fact, the next time I took the exams, I passed. Studying wasn't a great pleasure, but it wasn't a big deal either."

Ben didn't actually know why he had to suffer through a long course of study that he didn't like, but evidently his soul knew what it was doing. Studying accounting for him was like a training course in growing up – almost like an initiation rite of manhood. As a way of toughening himself up and creating a solid foundation of masculinity to support his quest for success, he set out to study the family profession pursued by the successful men in his family. "I knew," he said, "that from there I could build up my capacity to reach for different choices for myself. Accounting is not my real choice. It's only a socially accepted platform to give me legitimacy and provide me with the money to choose my true profession later on – my calling."

"And then?" I asked, impatiently, as I surveyed the trappings of luxury – the expensive leather case, the Breitling watch, and the Waterman pen – which broadcast his success and prestige.

"Now I'm a successful accountant in my father's and Jim's firm, earning well, living in a yuppie apartment – and still, I know that this isn't it," he said, his familiar smile widening. "I think you're the first one who knew, a long time ago, that this wasn't going to be it. You knew even before I did. Now really, why are you always smiling?"

"Because of your tone of voice. You've turned into such a businessman. So matter-of-fact…"

"Look, one could say that Stage One has been successfully accomplished. The question is what's going to happen in Stage Two?" said Ben, trying to curb my enthusiasm.

"Before we begin, and although I am dying of curiosity, maybe you could fill me in a little on what I've missed. What has happened to your inner being during the last five years?"

Ben almost permitted me to see the child again, the one

who had come to me years earlier, but suddenly the softness disappeared and he seemed to come to his senses.

"Really," he laughed bitterly, "I haven't the faintest idea where that child is."

"You didn't come back here, by any chance, to find him again?" I asked.

"Maybe," he said, and the sadness was back in his eyes.

I understood that Ben had not come back to me solely to find his inner child. He had also come back seeking to broaden the arc of his vocation and continue defining it, so that he could come to it whole. Like many others, Ben knew the direction of his inclinations and was in need of focusing. He needed hand-holding and the ability to define the new skills that his chosen route would require of him.

This was no easy mission. Ben, a man of many talents and abilities, had already met with impressive success, yet his next mission was to go back to his inner child and his dreams. In that way, using the power he had accumulated for himself in the business world, he would be able to forge the inner connection between his two "vocational parents" – link the popular photographer-artist-mother with the successful-businessman-father. At the same time, Ben needed to connect the two poles of the myth: the "strong" father and the "weak" mother. He felt that his vocation lay within this connection. And the connection was in no way an easy one.

Long minutes passed in silence.

"Does your father have a partner, a girlfriend?" I asked, going back to the point of connection.

"No," he replied, "Though now and then he has romantic interludes. Nothing serious. The same goes for my mother."

I realized how Ben still felt the need to create balance between his parents and added: "It's still impossible to relate to one without mentioning the other."

A pause. "What about Jim?" I asked, deciding to broaden the

circle of connection and relationship possibilities.

"Jim has all kinds of trophy girlfriends... but his true love is money and business," he declared.

"And you? Do you have anyone?"

"I didn't find anyone either... but let's remember the constructive changes," Ben smiled. "Look at Mom, for instance. You may remember that she used to lie in bed for entire days, doing nothing. If you saw her now, you wouldn't believe it. After she became famous, she threw all her pills away, and now she uses every possible moment for creative work."

"And are you still her defender?"

"Yes, but a lot less...," he replied.

He paused briefly and then added: "I still don't really know why I came to you today. Perhaps, you can tell me why I'm here," he ended, in a cynical, executive tone of voice.

I smiled. Clearly, he already knew.

"You psychologists," Ben continued defiantly, "never talk. You always smile, and give away half-clues at most."

"Nonetheless," I said, "I think you've come to close a circle. You said it yourself, didn't you?"

His smile disappeared. "Tell me the truth," he spit out, "do you believe that there are a lot of people in this world who work in a profession they really love?"

Ben evidently had known where to go and to whom. I strongly believe that there is a growing number of persons who are determined to find work that fulfills them. Increasingly, people seem unwilling to relinquish their right to work at something they really love.

"The number of such people," I said, sharing my thoughts with Ben, "is increasing all the time. Granted, the road is not an easy one, but those who are brave enough to persevere, reap fulfillment down the line. Meanwhile, those who miss out are having a harder and harder time. We are living in an age when it has become possible to make a living and find satisfaction, too;

to find success doing work that taps into one's inner sources… one's soul. It may be that one day only that kind of work will lead to advancement and success in the most competitive markets."

Ben went on gradually opening up, "If we're talking about success," he said, clutching the straw I held out to him, "then outwardly everything is fine. I have a comfortable income, a great jeep, lots of friends, trips abroad. I dine out regularly in one fashionable restaurant after another. Everything seems to be fine, but nothing is really fine at all. I come home at night to my apartment, but I still feel that I haven't done anything that I was actually meant to be doing."

I told Ben about Yuppie Disease, the core of which is a debilitating physical and mental fatigue. I believe that for some people who suffer from it this is a syndrome linked to vocational impasse and emotional dissatisfaction, often striking people who don't listen to their bodies or have gotten lost in their own success. Some, thanks to the illness, are obliged to take a time-out and set out on a journey of deep inner listening. Some report feeling inwardly enriched thanks to this disorder!

Ben dedicated himself anew to his vision quest. Slowly but surely, he freed himself from the constricting business suit. At this stage, I could see in him both the child and the successful businessman. I probed a little further in that direction.

"You have several worlds in you. Try to connect them," I suggested to him.

"I have always had many inner worlds," Ben stated, with growing confidence.

"Maybe that's why you're here," I went on. "You're here because you are ready to connect the powerful businessman with the weak, ill child who didn't get good grades at school. Maybe now is the time to link inwardly between your mother, who stayed home in bed and dreamed of the arts, and your father, the practical, talented man, who was a financial success. And maybe now is also the time to connect your successful mother with your strong father, getting in touch with her essence. Now you are ready to connect all the components."

An oppressive air returned to the room, but this time it came from the force of a very significant question. I could feel that this time, in our renewed encounter, Ben was finally able to give himself the permission his mother and father had never given him. I thought that precisely now, after his mother's success, Ben too, could link the arts – where his main talents and strongest desires lay – with his career success, and thereby find his way to self-actualization in his work.

Ben still couldn't see the end of the road, nor could he say how long a way lay ahead of him. He was bogged down somewhere, right on the verge of finding his way out of that vast void, moving towards a state of readiness. It seemed that the inner process was drawing to a close and would end with maturity and flourishing. These invisible processes convey a feeling that nothing is happening, when in fact, significant growth and development are taking place within. When the time is ripe, a vision will suddenly present itself like an embryo that's spent nine months in its mother's womb. We can't see it, but we can definitely feel that it's there. Trying to do without or bypassing this maturity phase only prolongs the journey.

"It appears that your twilight time is nearing its end," I told Ben, "although the way ahead isn't clear yet. You're still willing to go to the office every day, to rub shoulders with your successful father and career-minded brother. That fulfills your need to be in touch with your inner male model of success. This connection is helping you finish building your foundations and will help you later on to pave your own unique way. You still have a stage of confusion and perplexity to go through before you finish making all the necessary inward connections. There's no rush."

Ben continued to undergo all kinds of change outside the work sphere. At one of his mother's photography exhibitions,

Ben met a news photographer several years his senior and they exchanged business cards. The professional collaboration led to romance. Contrary to Ben's previous brief liaisons, this relationship developed slowly, with patience, tolerance, and love. Later, Ben even joined his new girlfriend at a creative writing workshop at a small studio in the Artists Quarter in Jaffa. When she asked him to write a short story for the autistic children's home she was photographing, Ben was happy to oblige. This loving relationship with a woman who wanted and accepted him facilitated his growth and development, enabling him to move forward. Ben chose well when choosing his partners on the journey.

We lost touch again. Ben continued working at his father's firm, but in the evenings he began studying social work. A few years later, he began working with disabled young people. Gradually, he integrated creative writing into his work. The business projects and wise investments he initiated enabled him to devote himself full-time to caring for people. Simultaneously, he began writing a well-received weekly column for a daily newspaper, about the youngsters he was counseling and their successful business initiatives.

About five years later, Ben returned for another short session. This time, he looked at peace with himself. He smiled a lot and talked about his children.

"Wait, let me understand – you're telling me about your biological children?"

"Them too, but mainly about the ones I do therapy with," Ben said, smiling.

"You're their therapist, as you were your mother's?"

"Yes, in that field I've acquired considerable expertise and had no small success."

"And a lot of love," I added. "How is your mother?"

"Great!"

"Well of course, she had a good therapist. Care that comes

from such great love can't help but succeed. And how is your father? And Jim?"

"The same as always. Dedicated to their work, and dedicated playboys."

"And you – are you okay?"

"I'm fine, really fine. My mother can't get over her surprise at my weekly column, and my father is very proud of my successful investments in the market and in real estate. And sometimes I think he's a little jealous of my writing. Recently he even wrote a very impressive professional article. After all these years, I feel that I've finally integrated both Dad and Mom within me. To borrow your words – I have their will and their wishes, their admiration and their encouragement inside me. I don't have to wonder any more whether I love art best or prefer financial success. I don't have to worry about whom I prefer, my mother or my father. I simply feel connected to both of them as one great whole. You see? Just choose Dad, then choose Mom... then connect them... then add a little, subtract a little... and then... choose a profession."

We both knew that Ben had been on a complicated journey... a journey of choices.

The drama of Ben and his family is but one example of how much energy it takes to build a personal vision and what a huge role it plays in the entire family system. The family with all its various components provides the starting point from where one begins a committed quest to self-actualization.

Ben's journey taught me yet again the extent to which a person's development lies within his family system. It is extremely difficult to set out on a journey of fulfillment when meaningful family systems are stuck in a rut. Often, we discover that what we needed was to draw in the people close to us and make them part of our process of vocational self-actualization. When we do, we are likely to find that they become a central part of the entire journey... all the way to its end.

Chapter Nine
Better Relationships, Better Careers

I was blind to my own faults

When I was in kindergarten, I was often surprised and frustrated that I had to learn to do seemingly marginal things to be able to later on perform various other tasks. For instance, before we could draw pictures, we all had to wash our hands, straighten up our tables, choose the colors we wanted to use, pick suitable paper, listen to instructions, select a child to sit next to, decide if the picture was going to be serious or just a scribble… and only then, finally, could we start drawing.

When I grew up, I discovered that the world of adult activity has similar rules and that in order to pursue one's calling, a large amount of training and preparation are required. Once people have decided on their next steps towards their career or life goal, they need to outline them and select the right "course of training" to achieve their goals. What sort of "course" do we need and where does it take place? Who trains or coaches the traveler? Who else journeys on the "course" with us? We have to figure out the context and the system that will enable our flow of development and progress on the trip.

For Sylvia, this context was marriage.

The secret key to her success lay in developing her ability to differentiate between herself and her spouse and to be a separate personality, without losing him. A process like this typically resembles the process of adolescence, during which we were compelled to separate ourselves from the loving, beloved parent figure without losing him or her. Such a process often turns out to be a necessary precondition for arriving at inner permission to do meaningful work.

Sylvia knew exactly what her vision was. She was, in fact, poised on the point of achieving it. Yet, something else was required of her before she could proceed.

We first met over the telephone. "My name is Sylvia," she announced. "I'd like to make an appointment with you, but not at your clinic." She spoke hastily, yet with the confidence of those who know how to get what they want.

"Where would you like to meet?" I asked her, unwittingly giving my full cooperation. She chose a restaurant on the beach, and I agreed.

Sylvia's tremendous distress was immediately evident. Even from that initial phone conversation, I sensed the clamor of her many inner voices. I also got the impression that Sylvia knew how to use her strengths, and that I wasn't the first to acquiesce with one of her requests.

I was not surprised when I saw her coming along the path leading to the restaurant where we had arranged to meet. Sylvia was one of those women in whom fragility and strength simultaneously coexist.

As she made her way through the tables, it was impossible to ignore her presence, yet she projected a strange elusiveness, as if she weren't really there. True, she was present, looking at you, listening with her calm, penetrating gaze. Yet it seemed that a part of her maintained a distance, observing from the side or rather from the outside – there was something cautious and extremely vulnerable about Sylvia.

Sylvia was the composite of a wounded child and a strong,

mature woman. Her polarization fascinated me and was probably the reason why I had agreed to make an exception and accede to her seemingly impudent request to meet her for a professional consultation at a location of her convenience.

The session began with no hint of what was to come later. She sipped her coffee and nibbled on an apple strudel. Suddenly, with no advance warning whatsoever, there was an outburst of confused statements. Some of what she said was clear and articulate, yet most was rather vague and incoherent.

Sylvia was an attorney and words were her primary working tool. She had come to me to find out why she had panicked when she was proposed as a candidate to become a judge. She knew she wanted the job, yet something was holding her back.

"For years now, I've had this inexhaustible yearning in me to find a way to express my inner world," began Sylvia. "I have no problems with writing legal documents or expressing a professional opinion. When I'm faced with a statement that innovates or sets a precedent, I suddenly become anxious and can't find the right words. It's like I'm struck dumb. My speech comes out technically, precise, yet dry and soulless, not at all the way I want to sound."

Sylvia had tried for years to suppress her need for self-expression. She tried to make do with the prestige conferred on her as a successful and well-known professional in the legal field, but in vain. She struggled with herself until she understood that she would have to find an outlet for the internal pressure that kept relentlessly accumulating. She knew that only by being named a judge could she work toward the fulfillment of her vision.

I was newly struck by the contrast Sylvia projected between confusion and order, giving in and holding firm, resignation and struggle – contrasts that popped up repeatedly and conspicuously in her speech.

When I shared my thoughts with her, she burst out crying.

I couldn't help but be moved by her profound pain and the difficulty she was facing, obstacles so very familiar to me.

Sylvia had trouble connecting the different parts of herself. The woman facing me had delved deep into herself and discovered alarming feelings of being torn between different desires and different dimensions of being. Mainly, what stood out was her desperate need to bring order to her inner chaos – the need to try to climb out of the well of her inner worlds with something definite in her hands.

We sat in silence. Sylvia calmed down and finally turned to me, smiling, "You probably want to ask me about my history. After all, you are a psychologist."

My intuition suggested that Sylvia was a woman of inner journeys. I felt that she was the type of woman who tends to do things the hard way, while analyzing every obstacle in her path and demanding personal attention for herself. It was also clear to me that during the meetings ahead of us, Sylvia was going to explore some very deep places inside me, without realizing how this would touch my life.

She was born to parents who were "professional orphans," who both had no parental models of their own. Due to circumstances at the time, and the hardships of earning a living, her parents were unavailable to their children when Sylvia was growing up. The children, curious and bright, stopped asking questions at an early age, and learned to deal with life on their own. By the time Sylvia, the family's third child, was born, it was a foregone conclusion that she would find herself in a state of emotional abandonment.

Her parents, like all others, could give their children only what they had to give. The problem was that their emotional resources were very limited. They had so little and, thus, had never managed to build an emotional foundation adequate to enable their daughter to grow with sufficient confidence. Over the years, I have learned to identify people like Sylvia. I can do this mainly by the copious sense of confusion they emanate during my sessions with them. They have their own special mix of maturity and common sense alongside a certain innocence and vulnerability.

Sylvia was a child of nature. She was her father's little soul mate and her mother's little doll. Her entire life, her house had been full of books. Her father, who worked as an inventory clerk, would closet himself in his room before a festive event for several days and write. The ten lines or so that he was able to read aloud in a quivering voice on the day of the event were never good enough for him, even if his audience thought them wonderful. Years later, his daughter told me about how it used to pain her to see her beloved father so hurt and disappointed.

"And when you grew up," I said, "were you able to talk to your father about this?"

"No. I never talked to him about it. This is the first time, I think, that I've allowed myself to feel how much I was carrying his pain around with me."

My father was back in the dialogue again, and I returned to the drama that has preoccupied me for years - father daughter relationships. There are fathers who "give" permission for fulfillment and fathers who "withhold" it. I found out once again how difficult it is for parents who as children themselves did not receive the inner permission to fully grow and develop. Sylvia was one of those children who would have to learn to seize that "permission" for herself.

"You know," she said, cutting short my musing, "when I was in second grade, and I had homework to do, I used to come to my dad and ask him to write it for me."

Only twenty years later could Sylvia look back for the first time at what had happened. "My father also suggested which girls it was worthwhile for me to be friends with, and which not. When I read books or novels, he would get angry: 'That's a waste of time, that literature. You need to be practical... to do things... not get sidetracked with stories.' I did as he said... I thought the way he recommended I should think, and felt the way he recommended I should feel…"

Sylvia was by now drowning in emotion, and I thought to myself how tough it must have been for Sylvia the little girl to live on two planes, and how hard it was for her now as a successful, grown woman.

I've learned over the years that people who live with profound internal conflicts like Sylvia often tend to be paralyzed, mainly in emotional situations that require a choice and a commitment to action. This paralysis blunts the pain, but also stunts their natural abilities and talents – dampening their spontaneous joy in living and their inner passion to perform.

I decided to concentrate on what was causing her current inner paralysis and to find out why she had come to me just at that crossroads.

"What else is going on in your life apart from work?" I asked. "How does work fit in with your other worlds?"

Her face fell. Clearly, my question had touched on her pain.

"Do I have to answer?" she asked, eyes narrowing. "You psychologists, you link everything up to something else, even if there's no connection. Well, so… where shall I start?" asked Sylvia, a bit childishly, hoping I would make allowances.

"Tell me about your husband," I asked adamantly.

"All right, I'll tell you, but what does he have to do with this?" replied the woman-child, not budging.

I decided to relate to Sylvia the adult and ignore the fragile child.

"Often the bond one has with work is no less intense than the bond with one's life partners." I said. "A person often brings the same set of tools to both relationships."

"Excuse me," said Sylvia quickly, waving her hand in the air sharply as if in negation, "but I didn't come here for that. I need advice about my professional life. I didn't come here to get marriage counseling."

I saw that I'd gone too fast. I was going to have to relate to Sylvia the child, after all; hold her hand and move her along cautiously, step by step.

"I understand that you loved your father very much," I said, deciding to backtrack to her relationship with her father.

"More than anything. He was my whole world. I wanted to give him everything I had, and everything he didn't have," she said quietly.

"That's a difficult task for one little girl," I replied gently.

Sylvia's body trembled, and she began crying softly. "My father passed away a while ago," she said.

Neither of us cared about the other people looking at us curiously or the seascape sun setting behind us.

I was drifting down into my depths like an undersea diver, towards my father's great love for me, and mine for him, and towards our loneliness. I revisited our struggle over the right to fulfillment and the right to be separate from each other. I remembered so well how much pain can follow when one sets off on a new path.

These memories drew my thoughts to my diving adventure that summer. I had gone swimming alone with a mask and snorkel at the Coral Reef in the Sinai Desert. Until then I had always seen the reef through the glass bottom of a tour boat. I am nearsighted, and I never would have believed that I'd be able to see what was happening in the deep sea without some kind of special preparation. I don't know what pushed me to try it anyway. Maybe it was my age, maybe the heat. Maybe it was some kind of special moment of self-indulgence, whatever. I took off my glasses – the screen between the world and me – put on the mask and went exploring in the clear blue waters. I found a domain of incredible beauty inhabited by radiantly colored fish and infinite quiet. I don't know what moved me more, the beauty of nature or the simplicity of suddenly being able to connect with it. I was so emotionally involved that I didn't notice myself treading on sea-urchins, scratching myself until I was dripping blood on the sharp corals. Later that night, all three of my children sat with me, taking turns changing the wet towels laid against the soles of my lacerated feet.

"Mom," they reprimanded me, "why weren't you more careful? Why do you always have to suffer so much when you try new stuff?"

my diving experience and the pain connected me again with Sylvia and the long journey into the depths of which she was only just beginning. As I shared my diving story with Sylvia, I wondered: Does she know how to connect with herself in solitude? Will she be able to dive down alone into her inner resources and find the coral beauty within herself, despite the pain mixed with the joy of discovery?

"To understand where you are in relation to things you want to do but can't, we must understand your other relationships; they will give us..."

"Okay," she cut me off, "I'm in your hands. Now I'm ready to tell you about my husband, Matty. The thing is, I can't talk to him about emotional stuff. When I begin talking to him, he falls asleep. The more I try to wake him up, the deeper he sleeps. It makes me feel so helpless and frustrated."

Sylvia had surprised me yet again. With no prior indication, she suddenly dove recklessly into the water.

Pain engulfed me. I thought how often we women, especially those of us who are overly verbal, become flooded with feelings that deluge our men with too many words that unwittingly block the dialogue that could lead to intimacy. We are so sophisticated in presenting ourselves as the side that is capable of talking; yet at the same time, we are partners in the inability to create intimate communication as a couple. It seemed to me that Sylvia was likewise under the illusion that she was better at communication and intimacy than her spouse was.

Sylvia seemed to read my mind as she said, "I always

take responsibility for other people's lives, especially for my husband's. I think I'm responsible for his appearance, for what he does, for how his career develops... Sometimes I forget that I have my own life and my own career."

Sylvia was only one typical example. Often women – and sometimes even men – avoid taking care of their own business and behave as if their entire purpose in life comes down to raising others – their children, their spouse, etc. These needs also provide a marvelous all-purpose excuse not to grow and develop.

"It was always important to me that my husband will do meaningful things," Sylvia went on. "I thought he was a very special man destined for a top job, and a grand calling, just like my father. I, after all, had spent long hours in discussion with my father about his career and his seeming inability to fulfill himself. Maybe I provoke this intimacy with my husband because I miss that special closeness I felt when listening to my father's problems. It seems to me that I've never actually listened to my husband..."

"I think," she added, "that maybe I really came here because of him. This past week, he disappeared for hours at a time and only came home the next morning, without any sort of explanation. We could both see clearly that it was a declaration of war. We've passed the stage of rebellious declarations and moved on to the phase of an open power struggle. Apparently he's fed up with my demands. I came here feeling like someone who's been wronged, whose husband falls asleep when she wants to talk, and suddenly I discover that actually I'm the one who's been pulling the strings in a rather nasty way. Evidently he understood what was happening better than I did. He's the one who sent me for counseling, to learn how to be less demanding of him."

"All that time," I said, "that you saw yourself as the victim, you were actually dumping all your childhood pain on your husband."

Sylvia was upset. She needed some time to digest all of this.

"So my husband's not so bad, then?" she finally said.

"Let's cut your husband some slack here. Apparently he loves you enough that he led you to come here," I said. Inwardly I was already preparing for takeoff, like a copilot starting on a preflight checklist. I wanted to cautiously propose that she began connecting with herself. This would probably require continual massaging of the muscles of her soul and the nerves of her will, all of which had almost surely gone numb when she was married, and possibly even before that.

I could not help thinking that Sylvia, like many other women, had learned in childhood to keep busy on behalf of others but had never really been trained to listen to herself.

All this reminded me of Ron, who unlike Sylvia's husband had upped and left the house because his wife wouldn't allow him to do what he really loved, which in his case was carpentry. She wanted him to be a businessman. Even when he failed over and over again, and lost their money, she wouldn't give up her dream for him. Only when he found another woman who accepted him as a carpenter did his ex-wife begin a long, difficult journey of her own. She needed not only to look at him from a different angle, but also at herself, her work, and the question of her own self-actualization. Until her husband left her, she never dared ask herself what she wanted to do with her life and how she could fulfill herself. She also didn't want to acknowledge that her blindness to his needs was paralleled by her blindness to her own.

Sylvia had better luck. Her husband knew he had to travel his own path. He pushed her in the only useful direction – towards herself, towards her own path, towards her own vocational self-expression. And in some way, she also accepted it. Moreover, she was able to seize the opportunity and leverage the crisis as a steppingstone to success.

As Sylvia went on talking about her husband, she began touching on that special and sometimes inseparable link between marriage and career. "This week, for the first time, I asked him to come home at seven," Sylvia said, incredulously. "I was always so afraid to tell him when to come home. I was afraid to admit to having needs. I was afraid to demand his presence..."

"This week, too, for the first time," she went on, absentmindedly, "I started to think about what I really want to say when I'll be appointed as a judge. I was so scared. Suddenly I thought that maybe I don't have anything to say. Do you think these two things are related? Maybe during all those years when I was busy with my father and my husband, I was running away from myself? It's interesting that I'm not overly occupied with what my daughter does. I'm sure she'll be fine, and she really is fine."

Evening had fallen. A cool breeze was blowing, and a quick glance showed that the view was changing as dusk deepened.

"Maybe," said Sylvia suddenly, "I have to ask myself whether I want to be a judge at all. Maybe that's the most desirable career promotion, but not what I actually want. Maybe it's really my father's desire for 'real' achievements that I'm carrying around with me? Maybe all I have to do is get out from under this burden and go on my way. And then again, maybe not..."

Sylvia was very confused. She was searching for a new path to follow.

"It sounds like you've set out on a new path," I smiled at her, "where all questions are legitimate. Most important is that you know how to recognize when the questions are 'yours' and when they are 'inherited.' Generally," I said, "the clearest sign that you've missed your way and may be walking someone else's path is when you've lost clarity about whose path belongs to whom. When you experience your significant others as clearly separate from you, and their paths as separate from yours, then that is the sign that you've started walking your own way. When your father's envy of your success begins appearing in your dreams, you'll know that you have begun to separate from him.

"After that, as you experience your father or your husband

as ordinary people, as separate human beings in their own right, with their own set of problems, you will know that you are continuing to walk your own path. Consciously or unconsciously, people want to blaze their own trail. They are prepared to accept help, but only when they ask for it. If by way of self-defense they try to misrepresent their calling, the paths get mixed up and the wires get crossed – between a parent and child, a husband and wife, and so on. After the confusion comes anger and blame. At the same time, if we try to help someone who hasn't asked for it, they more than likely try to evade us or fall asleep like Matty. I'm sure you'll be able to learn to recognize the signs of this kind of behavior. They have to be learned slowly. It is possible, I promise you that."

Sylvia was looking tired but excited. "Will you meet with me again?" she asked, like a spoiled child who knows ahead of time that her request will be granted. "Now I can come to your office, like everyone else," she wound up. She already wasn't calling my office a "clinic" as she had at first. Perhaps she had already stopped relating to herself as "ill."

"I'll be glad to meet with you in my office," I said.

Sylvia left; yet I found myself unable to go. I wanted to get up from my chair right away – after all, the time was up! Suddenly, I was flooded with anger and frustration. I didn't want to leave that place, the sea, that permission to feel. When lately had I allowed myself to feel the void, the empty space, the encounter with myself? Why was only Sylvia allowed to, and not me? What gave her the courage to pick up the phone and demand a special meeting with a perfect stranger? A mixture of feelings welled up within me – envy and yearning, together with an old familiar desire – to learn from others and be inspired by them. I wanted to learn from her. In counterpoint, another inner voice was remembering my old, long-drawn-out, demanding struggle to give up being so needy.

Our next meeting began in a way I had not anticipated. "I had a dream," Sylvia began, speaking rapidly; "I dreamt that I went to a fortune-teller. The room was heavy with the scent of her flowery perfume. I had come to ask her about my terrible migraines. The fortune-teller, Flora, was a very fat woman lounging in front of brightly colored wallpaper. 'Your headaches...' she began while closing her eyes and baring her toothless mouth, 'are not the real problem.' Her voice suddenly became deep and masculine as she repeated, 'Your headaches are not the problem. Something else is worrying you. You are in terrible danger. Someone... a man is calling you from the other world ... he needs you. Do you know who it is?' Taken aback, I shook my head.

'Think hard,' Flora said.

'Maybe my dead father? Maybe my father-in-law, I don't know. I know so many dead people,' I said, frantically trying to answer.

'Who is it? You have to tell me who it is!' shouted Flora. 'Now! Otherwise I'll have to light candles at midnight... I'll have to pray to the spirits. This struggle has worn you out. You want to stay here, but he won't let you. Someone has to help you. No no no, not your husband. You need a woman to help you. A husband can't help with this sort of thing. Find a woman you can talk to. Look out only for yourself. There's no one else who will.'

"That's exactly what Flora said," related Sylvia. "So what do you think she meant? Do you believe in stuff like that?" Sylvia was very upset by the time she finished telling me her dream.

Evidently both of us felt that the reprimand to "look out for yourself" was the key to finding the way, not only on our shared journey, but also on our respective individual paths.

After Sylvia calmed down she began telling me another story as if it had no connection with the previous one. "About a week before that dream," she remembered, "I went on holiday with my husband. I spent more than an hour getting myself ready to go out the first night. We went with another couple, friends of ours. As we were about to leave with them I was very upset by my husband's long, ugly toenails sticking out of his worn leather sandals. Those ridiculous toenails and his unshaven cheeks looked so awful next to the Italian leather loafers my friend Lily's husband wore. I tried to catch Matty's attention and thought silently: 'Why is he doing this to me?' I was convinced he was doing it to me on purpose. He knows how much his appearance matters to me. It was probably one more little rebellion he had against his mother, who's been dead for decades. I felt this really deep, violent wave of rage rising and swelling up inside of me. I decided, no way was I going to keep quiet. But another voice inside me insisted that the game was already over, and I knew that this huge wave was already rolling along, growing higher and stronger, and that it would eventually break with a terrible crash. That's what happens to waves. That's what happened to me...

"So we arrived at the restaurant and sat down," she continued after a long silence, "with Matty's sandals screeching on the gravel path in the courtyard. I took a chance and turned to him with a smile: 'Nice place, huh?' And then, I noticed a stubborn crease in his shirt, and two missing buttons. Next to the coordinated shirt and tie Lily's husband wore, Matty's sloppiness was almost provocative. I tried to persuade myself to show some empathy, but I knew it was no use.

"That big wave went ominously rolling on. I drew farther and farther into myself, when suddenly Lily turned and asked me: 'Sylvia, what's the matter with you?' That was the last straw! I knew I couldn't fight a war on two fronts at once. I couldn't start shouting at her as well. Surely she must have known what was going on with me, I mean, she was there, wasn't she?

"'You always ruin a good time for me,' I shouted at Matty my dear, beloved husband, 'You make absolutely no effort to dress the way I like and you had to go and wear those disgusting sandals. You leave all the clothes I buy you in the closet and wear old rags like these. I know you're doing this to me on purpose. If you really wanted to consider my feelings, at least tonight you could have made a little effort. Is it too much to ask that you just wear normal shoes and a pressed shirt?'"

Sylvia smiled bitterly. "My husband looked shocked," she went on. "Yet all he said was: 'Get a hold of yourself. You're losing it.' The embarrassment was awful, and my husband went on in this cold, hard-edged tone: 'When are you going to get off my back already? When are you going to see that this whining self-pity of yours doesn't help?! When will you understand that when you ask me to do things to show you that I love you, it drives me crazy? Do you think you're my mother? When are you going to learn that if you want something from me, you have to negotiate like an adult?'

"I was choking back the tears, but I knew I had nothing to lose. 'I'm ready to negotiate,' I told him quickly, completely ignoring the embarrassed couple sitting there with us. 'So what do you want?'

"'What do I want? Just be yourself. I don't need you to do stuff for me all the time,' Matty said, angrily, 'I don't need anything from you.' It was almost like he was trying to provoke me. The words hit me so hard. I felt insulted: 'I don't need anything from you... I have everything.'

"I said to him, 'So now that I've given you everything, don't you need me for anything else?'"

Sylvia stopped. Tears were streaming down her cheeks and I wanted to comfort her.

"Sylvia," I said hesitantly, "I know it hurts, but maybe all the same, this pain is necessary in order to get in touch with your strengths. Maybe you have inner resources that you're afraid to touch, realizing that discovering them commits you to independence and to your own identity."

I felt that the words were too sophisticated for her, but needed to be heard for Sylvia to focus on herself, rather than on her need to be busy with her husband and all that "look what he's doing to me" stuff.

"You really are very tired, Sylvia," I said. "Maybe you could take a break and stop worrying about your husband and your father. In reality, your man, whom you've reincarnated into your forbidding father has actually given you a gift. Maybe that's what Flora sensed in your dream. Matty wants you to lay off him, but you keep on nagging him. Maybe it's time to let go of things that chain you to the past and pave yourself a new road to independence. Maybe it's time to take care of yourself, and invest in your new and satisfying career."

Sylvia wasn't happy with my comments, but she remained silent as she sank down further into the armchair.

"You're so tired, Sylvia," I said again. A heavy silence stretched between us.

Then a soft weeping made her tremble, her shoulders and hands shaking, her body shrinking. "Do you think I shouldn't have said those things? Do you think that it's not really important what he wore, and how he..." Sylvia didn't finish. She broke down, but her crying was less despairing. It seemed to me that she was crying because of her fear of the long and lonely road she could see stretching out ahead of her...

I didn't tell her then, but I thought that in her dream and in the restaurant, Sylvia had been confronting her existential dilemma and the feeling that she was going to have to become her own person. She was going to have to let go of the people around her and stop trying to mold them in her design. Even if the feeling of being alone was frightening, it's the being alone that was going to enable her to finally make room for herself.

"And furthermore," I told her, "I know that every time you let go of your husband, you die a little, but you are also reborn a little..."

Sylvia understood that I was on that same road, but she doubted her own ability to move forward on and conclude the journey.

Six months passed after Sylvia cancelled our third meeting. Though she didn't make an appearance during all those months, I knew that she was walking her path equipped with the provisions and marching orders she'd taken from our two sessions together. She needed to find herself and continue her journey.

Finally, when she called and asked to meet again, I was curious and excited. This time, like the first time I'd seen her, a real surprise was in store. Sylvia came into the room, looking radiant. There was something new in her that hadn't been there before. Her step was lighter, her body slimmer, and she projected a heightened determination.

"I wrote something. I want to show it to you," she said. She fished around in her bag and produced a notebook that was already half out, ready to hand over to me.

"You know," she said, "I started to write a diary. I write down all kinds of simple things; thoughts, meetings I had with people, meetings I didn't have. The more I've written, the more I've felt the simplicity of things. I could have done this a long time ago."

She told me that she had been appointed a judge, and that she was enjoying every moment, including the hard work of composing legal precedents. She also spoke of a screenwriting course she was taking, and her pleasure in "doing things I love."

"The main thing is that I've started to become really interested in my life," she added. "And you know what's the most surprising of all? My husband made a huge leap forward in his career as well. An opportunity for a new business venture arose out of the blue, and he grabbed it with both hands. He's doing marvelously and is really happy. It's amazing how everything is so fluid. Now we are so good together. For sure, we went through a process that wasn't at all simple, but there's no doubt we've come through it stronger."

"It's interesting to notice," I responded, "the parallel processes that go on between the development of the marriage and the careers of both partners. There is so much similarity in how far and how high they reach." This is something I've learned from my experience with couples and their careers. "Maybe," I mused, "it's because the growth of each spouse is so intertwined with the vocational development of the other. Where there is emotional growth, there is also vocational growth… But It seems something is still bothering you,"

"You're right," said Sylvia, "I'm always anxious that everything could suddenly disappear, that some terrible catastrophe could happen…"

"Do you mean that you're not allowed to enjoy doing what you like?" I asked.

"I guess… Would you be willing to walk along with me on another journey, so I can learn to cope with the anxieties that come with self-fulfillment?"

I promised Sylvia that I'd be with her as long as she needed me.

Chapter Ten
Torn between Work and Family

Instead of finding a new job, I found a lover

For years, I learned to relate to work and profession, love and marriage, as expressing different aspects of the same source; the well of passion or the life force that Freud called libido. When Anita Rodick, founder of The Body Shop chain, was asked how she'd succeeded, she replied with one word: "Passion!"

According to the mystic Jewish traditions of the Kabbala, passion has godly attributes, and in the Hebrew language is the combination of "desire" and God. When children are at play, their games often stem from a core passion. These early childhood activities evolve into mature adult work. Through adult activity, we continue to develop our uniqueness as people who perform, and as individuals who create and seek activity that has meaning and expresses our identity. When these activities are defined and experienced as a vision or a calling, it's as if we have found our connection with the primal work of the Creation of the Universe.

Our loving, like our careers, does not take place in a vacuum. Love develops from within our life systems. The First System, which is the foundation for all the other systems in our lives, is our family of origin. This is the first organization in which we live and learn how to function in a developing, ever-changing system. Throughout our lives, we continue to create various other functional contexts in terms of love and work. In fact, over the course of our lives we build other "families." Our second family is the one we build with our chosen partners, the family into which our children are born and grow up with us, and where our most intimate dramas are played out. At the same time, our other systems from within our "working family" evolve to serve as the context in which our career or vocation are defined.

Thus, even after defining our vision and setting our goals, our work is never finished. We still have to search for the particular context that can provide the working conditions most suitable for fulfilling our vision and achieving our goals.

For my husband Dov and me, our professional partnership served as a training ground for both our personal and professional development. Moreover, we realized gradually that for other people, too, the process is a similar one.

Building our vocational partnership, and building our relationship in terms of love and marriage, is very closely bound up with the work each of us does.

During the course of my work I have met a number of people who maintained they'd chosen a particular partner because they somehow knew that with that partner by their side, their career would take off. Other people felt that their partner was their main source of inspiration, and often only through their partners could they express themselves and fulfill their dreams.

The late Daniela Kedar, a wonderful psychologist with whom I once worked, told me during the period she was looking for a life partner: "If I don't find the one I'm looking for, I'll just become that person…"

There are people who, though busy supporting a family, still invest deeply in their partners' creative activities as a way of expressing their own creative energies. By doing so they are meeting a creative need that they may never have permitted themselves to realize or fulfilling a dream that they themselves would never have dared to pursue.

If profession and personality are connected with one another, then choosing (or choosing to leave) a partner is connected with the partner's choice of work and is possibly even a way of identifying with that profession.

Paula came to me looking for vocational direction. She wanted to consult with me about where her professional life was heading. But in real life, vocational direction is often the story of a person's life. Dealing with Paula's career require understanding her life story and her frustrations within her career. Her love, and her betrayal of love, mandated changes in a life and a career that until then had appeared organized and orderly.

"It was a regular day that began with the regular routine of cooking, serving a meal, and doing laundry," began Paula, as though moving back into a past life. "It was a Tuesday... a month after my daughter was born. I was still weak and depressed; I remember it as if it was this morning. I went out for a little air, found myself walking down bohemian Shenkin Street in Tel Aviv, and entered a jewelry store. The moment I entered the store, it was as if I had been struck by lightning. I saw Martin, and somehow – don't ask me how – I knew that this was the man meant for me. Now you must understand that I was a married woman, with a newly born baby."

Paula never returned home that day, nor did she ever return to her editing job. "I remember myself going to a pay phone later that evening," she told me, "trembling all over and dialing the number of what until that morning had been my home, my husband, my family. I announced to my astonished husband that I had found my true love and that I was never coming home again. Since that day, during the twelve years that have passed, I've been with Martin, who is the love of my life. For me it was as if I had immigrated to another country…"

I had no intention of accepting Paula's story just like that. I asked her to tell me a bit more about her marriage and work prior to that time, and since that time. It was important to compare the two worlds. The fact that she'd begun her narrative with a love story only reinforced this for me.

"What does that have to do with it?" she asked surprised.

"I believe that a person has at least two 'partners,' and people sometimes get confused and mix them up. One is the romantic partner. The other is the vocational partner. Frequently, the vocational partnership is the one that complicates matters. The vocational relationship is such a mentally intimate one that sometimes it distorts our vision; because vocational partnerships also involve stories of love and passion and sometimes have elements of hurt and betrayal," I explained.

Paula preferred to talk about the other love. "Look," she said, "my work is a really complicated thing."

"And is your love life any simpler?" I asked with a smile. "Often, our work life and our love life go together…"

"What's the big deal?" said Paula, unmoved. "I loved one guy, and then I fell in love with another guy."

"If only it were that simple," I said aiming to explore the whole complicated array of relationships between a woman, her husband, her lover, and her work.

I asked Paula to tell me more about her husband and the choices she had made – how she had chosen her profession and how she had suddenly left her job and her family. I asked her to describe her family and her vocational history. I wanted to know what dormant emotional volcano had suddenly erupted one day, spewing hot lava everywhere, after years of "calm."

"Wherever this kind of volcanic eruption occurs," I shared my thoughts, "you'll find an immensely powerful emotional obstacle blocking the person's natural development. Perhaps this is what happened in your case…"

"I'm the only child of Holocaust survivors," Paula began. "My parents were never able to realize their professional potential. They invested all their energy into me, their only daughter. It was a second marriage for both of them. Both had survived, but had witnessed their families and children murdered. We never talked about it. Maybe because of all that, they never allowed themselves to behave naturally as parents with me, the child of their second marriage. They were haunted by guilt and worked from morning till night, while I, their little girl, was left alone with the voices of the dead for company."

Paula was a good little girl who helped clean the house and brought home good grades. She was especially outstanding in the arts, and her prize winning paintings were hung on the school walls.

"Isn't it interesting," said Paula, angrily, "that during all those years, they didn't hang even one of my paintings at home. Not even one."

Paula grew up and completed a university degree in the arts. But this talented young woman for whom well-known teachers predicted a bright future, never became a great artist. Initially, she tried to exhibit at a small Tel Aviv gallery but met little success. Later, she rented a studio apartment by the sea and tried to fill empty white canvases with drawings. At a certain point it became clear to everyone that her great promise had become a great disappointment. Paula faded from the scene because something inside her had brought her to a dead end. She gave up the studio, tore up the canvases, threw out her paints, took a certificate course in teaching, and became a teacher. When teaching became too frustrating and the students too aggravating, she switched to editing. Until that morning when she met Martin, she had worked as a newspaper editor.

"I wasn't able to discipline the students," she explained. "They drove me nuts."

Editing – which for Paula had been a way out, not a choice – was predictably unfulfilling. She hadn't solved her vocational dilemma.

The pain was so great that, at a certain point, she decided to have nothing to do with art anymore. She stopped thinking about her career, and so the years passed, filled with frustration.

"I wanted so badly to paint," she said. "I wanted to be able to express something meaningful, but nothing happened. Nothing came out."

"Well, it seems I wasn't mistaken," I told her. "What we have here is an impasse in self-expression – in your work and in your career."

"My husband and my parents were glad to see me work in a stable field," Paula went on. "But how could I steer my students to creativity when I couldn't steer myself? How could editing eventually be creative? I felt blocked, and that I was causing other people to be stymied as well."

"How long did all this go on for?" I asked. I wanted to inject a time dimension, which can often be a yardstick of cumulative suffering and frustration.

"Too long," she said, "in the first few years, it was somehow okay. Later, the suffering gradually got worse. I took a year's leave and tried to break the grip of this thing that was choking me. I tried to do something – to paint, to write. Nothing happened. I tried changing the kind of editing I was doing, but things only got worse. That's how I felt until I fell pregnant. When I discovered that I was pregnant, I said to myself: 'Okay, that's it, now you have to get out of this space.'"

"Get out of this space?" I echoed.

"From the killing field," answered Paula immediately. The harshness of the phrase took us both by surprise.

"What do you mean?" I asked.

"I felt like I was dying from within. Like I had a terminal illness..." replied Paula hastily.

Paula was a beautiful woman, yet didn't take care of herself. I was struck by her agile understanding and harsh idiom. Her chillingly empty eyes gave me the feeling that I was staring into the infinite blackness of two endless chimneys.

"I don't know why inspiration abandoned me," said Paula.

"Maybe it was blocked somehow and didn't develop?" I ventured. I was thinking to myself about how love and marriage can be destroyed when vocational satisfaction and the desire for self-expression is frustrated.

"What was your husband's profession?" I went on, referring her thoughts to the aspect of relationships that is often a factor when self-actualization is frustrated.

"My ex-husband was a very successful and creative man. He was a senior computer consultant. He didn't really understand what I wanted... and I didn't really know how to explain it to him. I tried to be a good wife and I wanted us to be good together... I didn't make a big deal out of my problems..."

Experience had taught me that vocational frustration is so much harder to deal with when there is a lack of dialogue. I had already begun to realize that Paula's perception of vocational success was not necessarily in accordance with her husband's since poor communication seemed to exist between the two.

"And what was it like, living with a partner who was so successful?" I asked.

"To tell you the truth, we never talked about it," replied Paula. "It was convenient that he supported me. It was easier for me that only I had a problem."

"And did he understand you?" I asked carefully.

Experience has taught me that in marriages with vocational issues, there's more chance of success for the marriage if both partners discuss their careers openly. When one partner is fulfilled and the other not, the former may have trouble listening to the latter, who may wrongly deduce that their problems are being ignored, thus widening the gap. In other cases, the problems really are being ignored – not from a lack of concern on the spouse's part, but rather because one partner avoids dealing with some work-related problem of their own. This is especially likely when one partner's work is seemingly secure. That partner then prefers to keep his distance, rather than risk the consequences of opening a vocational Pandora's box of his own.

The immediate danger in not dealing with things is of a festering explosion. In fact, it is virtually inevitable, though it can have useful results if the couple works through their issues. The explosion may even lead to new understanding on both sides. On the other hand, when problems are denied, the situation may deteriorate and the crisis intensify, with mutual distancing taking place until finally the couple separates for the wrong reasons. No matter what the scenario, when one partner's vocational dilemma is not addressed, it becomes a ticking time bomb.

The upheaval in Paula's life and the dramatic step she had taken may have been preceded by a long and slow process of self-destruction, whereas her daughter's birth had merely pushed her to the edge. I suggested that her "peaceful" marriage may actually have served as a fig leaf that concealed her problems of identity, her vocational dilemma, and her pain at never having fulfilled herself as an artist.

Paula thought over what I had said, her brow furrowed.

"That's interesting," she finally ventured. "In fact, after my mad dash out of there, my husband did go through a crisis at work. So what everyone explained as a reaction to the crisis of my having left him may have actually been the inevitable outcome of being freed from his connection with me…"

"Possibly one of the cornerstones of your marriage may have been protecting your husband's status as the one who knew what he wanted, and who was satisfied with what he was doing," I said, after a long silence. "It turns out that it wasn't only your problem but also his. Only when you abandoned him could he 'abandon' his role as the strong and successful partner in the marriage. Only when his family fell apart did his vocational problems surface. When his marriage unraveled, so did the veneer of his pseudo-satisfactory career."

Paula needed some time to think things over.

At our next session, she began talking energetically: "The source of the problem was a lack of love. It's a fact that when I had love my vocational problem disappeared."

I said nothing. I wanted her to go on exploring her journey.

"What happened to me anyhow?" Paula asked out aloud, resuming the slower pace of our previous meeting.

"Perhaps we can take another look into how it happened?" I pressed.

"I loved Martin so much, I adored him," she said, going back to the story she preferred to stick with and wanted to sell. "I didn't want to work or do anything; I just wanted to be with him all the time…"

"And how was married life with him?" I asked.

"It was one big act of giving on my part," she said. "Martin had no profession. He was an artist. One day he became ill and it turned out that he had a serious kidney problem. I began taking care of him, and I identified with his pain that came mainly from how hard it had become for him to paint. There he was, having succeeded in expressing himself fully, and suddenly his illness had cut off his creativity…"

"And so life acquired new meaning for you?" I persevered.

Paula affirmed my words with a tired smile, but kept silent.

"Only this time, he was the one who was terminally ill; not you," I went on relentlessly. "Or maybe both of you, together, were 'the terminally ill patient'?"

Paula gazed at me in astonishment, but immediately understood.

"I never thought about it that way, but that marriage was a lot more egalitarian," she said. Her voice held no bitterness, only compassion.

"And then?" I asked her.

"After years of caring for Martin and a wonderful marriage, he died. I was left having to work and support myself," said Paula resolutely.

"How did you support yourselves before?"

"From loans my parents gave me," she replied. "I really milked them dry, and now it's over. All the money my parents left me is gone. Martin and I didn't work for years. I gave him the best possible life. He needed me and I took care of him. I grew organic vegetables in a greenhouse I built on the roof and I cooked special food for him. Sometimes giving to him in this really big way was a kind of compensation. I gave my beloved, with my parents' money, everything that they didn't give me. Often he was me and I was his parents, who could make his every wish come true…"

"As if you and Martin were one…"

"Yes… When he was in pain, I suffered. When he wanted something, fulfilling his wish became my greatest satisfaction."

"And now, are you ready to find work that will meet your needs? You'll have to learn new skills; identify your own needs and desires," I noted.

"Yes, I have to, and I want to though I've never done it. No one ever did that for me…" said Paula.

"Do you have to work?" I asked.

"Yes. I have to support myself, and I have to do something with myself."

Again I repeated insistently, "Are you looking for work only in order to support yourself, or are you looking for something more? What about your long-dormant need to connect with some kind of personal statement of your own?"

Paula didn't reply.

"Maybe now you can allow yourself to connect with your yearning to paint?" I went on. "You've finished taking care of the sick artist. Maybe now, you're ready to develop the artist within, who also 'got sick' or was held back somehow by something. Maybe now is the time to put together a program to heal yourself?"

Paula evaded my questions, and stuck stubbornly to immediate material needs, "But I have to earn a living. I was left with nothing."

"If it's only about earning a living," I insisted, purposefully, "would you think about going back to teaching or editing?"

Paula looked at me incredulously. Her eyes held mine with a look of tremendous disappointment. "After all this discussion, are you still suggesting that as a possibility?"

"Then I gather that you're not going back to teaching or editing," I stated for her.

Paula's look confirmed what I'd said. Now it was clear to both of us that we were discussing more than just earning a living here. Evidently Paula felt that she had paid her debt. She was prepared to finally deal with her place in the world, with the work she would do, and accept herself for who she truly was.

"Apparently I needed those twelve years of 'rehabilitation,'" said Paula at our next session. She seemed somewhat pacified.

"And what now? Are you planning to be the Good Samaritan?" I joked.

"Why not?" she joked back, smiling at me for the first time as the atmosphere in the room lightened.

A few weeks later, Paula surprised me: "Now I'm starting to understand," she said with a new found assertiveness, "that love, however passionate, can sometimes serve as armor against pain, as a kind of spiritual buffer."

Paula and I spent many hours together looking into the hypothesis that Paula had fled her home and family as a result, above all, of existential distress stemming from deep career frustration.

"I ran away from that lack of fulfillment. My marital problems grew in the wake of my vocational frustration. The distancing and the misunderstanding were direct results," she said. "Taking care of Martin and loving him was like taking care of Paula. Martin and I were like one; I was him and he was me," she repeated over and over.

Only later on did Paula articulate her profound yearning to break through the barriers to her creativity. This time, she had made up her mind to find the wellsprings of her inspiration. One of the new needs she identified was the need to care for children...

Thus, down the line, Paula chose to become a teacher-therapist. This work allowed her to integrate creativity with her strong desire to care for people in need, and thereby continue to nurture herself. Only later on, artistic fulfillment once again became a significant part of her life. She never went back to painting as a self-declared artist, but her love of art gave her unending nourishment through art lessons she had begun taking.

A good career and personal satisfaction are fertile ground for romance. Thus it was no surprise that shortly after she began finding real work satisfaction, she also found a new love.

I was certainly not surprised. Clearly Paula had no emotional problem in finding a loving partner. She did, however, have a problem in terms of finding herself, and recognizing that she was entitled to self-expression. The moment she was able to connect with her creative self, the rest of the puzzle fell into place in the most natural way.

Often people who don't find creative satisfaction in their work, "create" crises in their married lives, which, it often turns out, are in the nature of a diversion. After work-related problems are resolved, a marital crisis often disappears.

Women very typically may be caught for years in a frustrating round of domestic chores or working at some unfulfilling job to supplement their husband's income in order to enable him to develop professionally. When a woman in such circumstances wants to begin a more fulfilling career, she may feel that the only way to gain her freedom is by breaking all the rules.

In such cases, the marital and career systems should be clearly distinguished from each other and dealt with separately, even if they are clearly related. Typically, I often receive phone calls from a husband who stammers: "My wife is really getting to me. She's threatening divorce, but I'm not sure that we have a problem with our marriage. I think it might be worth checking what's going on at work... hers, or mine..."

Looking at even a few of these cases proves him right. The source of what appears to be marital problems is often a vocational or calling issue. When the source of a longstanding frustration is difficult to pinpoint, the aggravation from the two disparate sources becomes confusingly mixed up.

I thought of Todd, a senior police officer, a married man with a family, who messed up at work and was fired. One day he was simply told to leave the organization he had worked in for so long and which was like a second family to him. Shocked and despairing, Todd met another woman within a week, fell in love with her, left home, and started a new chapter in his life. Only when a couple of years had passed did he realize what a mistake he'd made. He separated from his girlfriend and tried, cautiously, to find a way back to his family, but it was very difficult at that point to restore things to the way they had been.

Todd's example brings us to the question: How can a man, who is committed to his family, shatter the family framework they have spent years building, in a matter of days or even months?

On close scrutiny we can see that being fired was like an earthquake for Todd. In his distress, he flailed out at everything. It took two years before he was capable of dealing with each realm of his life separately and making a clear distinction between them. This came about only after he had understood that his firing had been the outcome of a crisis with his superior, and not a crisis with the organization itself nor with his wife.

Don's story was the opposite of Todd's. He came to me in a state of great confusion, seeking counseling. Shortly before that he had left, on his own initiative, a top CEO position, and started a new company with a partner.

When I first met him, he looked as though he'd just awakened from a stressful nightmare. With his disheveled hair, bloodshot eyes, and careless dress, he looked like a fugitive from a battleground.

"I'm totally not suited to be self-employed," he said to me in a panic, "and really not cut out to have a business partner. I picked a really messed-up guy to be partners with – unreliable, uncommitted to the business... what the hell came over me?"

Don was sure that he'd made a dreadful mistake. He could only now understand that his former position as head of a large company in the food sector was, after all, his natural niche for success. He missed the people, the environment, the way of doing things. "What came over me?" he asked again.

"Maybe you really did want to be self-employed, in the sense of being independent?" I asked him.

"I had all the independence in the world at my last job. They respected me, and they needed me. The board couldn't heap enough praise on my work," he retorted.

"So maybe you wanted to be independent in some other context?" I asked him, thinking of home and hearth.

Don looked at me, shocked, "What does that have to do with it?" he muttered, not actually asking the question.

"Sometimes things get interconnected and it can be confusing," I said.

Don looked at me again for a moment and immediately lowered his eyes. In that instant of eye contact, I understood that all of this upheaval was coming from his home, and his marriage.

Don needed a little time to digest this new thought. "I guess," he finally admitted, "I realized on some level that my marriage was over. I don't know when exactly. Maybe when my daughter left home to go to school. Suddenly, I saw that my wife and I no longer had much in common. We had this huge void between us. Everything was empty."

"And you panicked?" I said, more as a comment than as a query.

"So it would seem," he replied. "When I faced up to the recognition that my marriage maybe had ended years ago, it threw me..."

The problem was that Don had left the wrong "family" – his work family – the organization to which he belonged, and his fantastic job.

"But why? How could that have happened?" he demanded angrily.

"It's like having an accident. You simply got onto the wrong track."

"Okay, but look," he said, "my parents were divorced when I was four. Even while I was little, I remember how awful it was – splitting up the family, living without my father, who left the country... I made a vow then that this would never happen to me. I would never get divorced. My marriage vows were forever."

"Possibly it was precisely this vow," I suggested, "that made it hard for you to accept the fact that you were having marriage problems, and that you needed to cope with a crisis there."

"For sure," he said, "it was much easier for me, however absurd it may sound, to leave my job where I felt secure and successful, rather than to leave my family where I felt like a stranger who didn't belong."

Understanding such an action may be hard, but identifying with it is easier.

"Sometimes," I carried on, "it's easier to do something shocking in a situation where we are in control and know we have the tools to put things right one day. It's far more threatening to face our weakness and vulnerability in a situation that's painful to us and already showing the cracks."

In Don's case, his marriage and his family were his more vulnerable side.

When he understood and accepted this, he left his new business venture and found a new job, similar to the one he'd resigned from, as a salaried CEO. We both agreed that he was now completely satisfied with his position and self development in his worklife. Now we came to the real training ground and the tough repair job – his marriage.

Don proceeded to spend a lot of time and emotional energy trying to work through his marital crisis. In the end, he realized that nothing could be salvaged – it was too late for that. Sadly, Don's marriage ended in divorce.

Joan's story offers a different perspective on the complex area of marriage, family, and work.

Joan came to me for counseling because she wanted to stop working in the family jewelry business, where she had been an employee for many years. She was considering starting her own business.

At our first session, she said she wanted to bring some order to her life.

"Right after high school, I began working in the jewelry manufacturing business answering phonecalls." she told me. "After the army, I went back, and while I was studying at university, I continued working there, in the production department. After graduating with a BA in Economics and Management, the owners – a husband and wife – offered me a chance at marketing and I happily agreed. At that time I was about to be married. The family business was like a home to me. Gradually, I developed new markets domestically and later on abroad. A year ago, I requested a promotion. I wanted to be a partner in the business or leave for somewhere else where I could develop further. But this was a family business and they didn't want partners from outside of the family, and I had no other way to advance there. So after fifteen years, I decided to leave and open a business of my own. My husband supported my vision, and I knew I had the passion and the ability to succeed. Yet something held me back. The months passed, and it was as though I had lost interest in work. I didn't leave my job, but neither did I begin planning my own business.

"Then, on one of my trips abroad, I met Amos. I fell desperately in love with him. He was also married. He was in communications, two years younger than I, and went on lots of business trips and had numerous love affairs... I gave myself passionately to this relationship... I started smiling again... The plans to open my own business and to leave the jewelry company faded... Surprisingly, this didn't affect my married life at all. My relationship with my husband remained as good as ever. I did feel guilty and mixed up, but in a strange way my love for my husband didn't change, really... it was an odd sort of betrayal..."

Joan was confronting this paradox with the innocence of a woman having her first affair, and she surprised even herself when suddenly, she decided to tell her husband about her affair.

"Don't ask me why," she continued, "because it happened suddenly; without any planning..."

"And then?"

"My husband said nothing. He was in shock. It didn't make sense to him. The next morning he left the house without saying a word. I was in shock, too. I realized very clearly how much I loved him. Suddenly it dawned on me that the affair and Amos weren't very significant for me. I wanted more than anything to rebuild my life with my husband. Two months passed, and I still had no rational explanation. I had no idea why I'd started having an affair, or why I'd chosen to confess it... Maybe I wanted to be stopped..."

Joan sounded exhausted and the pain in her eyes was profound.

"And you came to me because…" I queried gingerly.

"Look, I really have no idea why I told you that story. I came for counseling because I'm stuck in this family business and haven't been able to get out of there and move on… Now, when it looks as though I've gone and destroyed my marriage for no reason, I have to weigh my plans very carefully."

Joan sounded really confused. This confusion did not match the logical, confident person she had been on the surface all these years. There certainly were gaps, which at first were perplexing.

"It's really hard to leave a job where you've been for fifteen years, especially when it's the first and only place you ever worked at," I said.

"Leaving that business, even though it wasn't mine, would have been like leaving my family. Leaving to go elsewhere – it was like cheating on them …" said Joan, speaking rapidly. Our eyes met and we understood, in unison, that Joan had found an explanation; maybe the only logical explanation for her odd sort of betrayal.

"Perhaps, instead of 'betraying' your work family, you cheated on your own family – your husband – with another 'family' via your love affair. It may be that, for you, leaving your job – and especially the people who were almost like your own family – was more of a betrayal than taking a lover."

"You're saying that maybe cheating on my husband was in place of cheating on my workplace, which didn't fill my needs any longer?" Joan was visibly angry.

"Only you, inside, felt that this would be a betrayal," emphasized. "You couldn't give it a rational explanation, especially since they 'permitted' you to leave…"

Leaving a family is so very difficult. It's so hard to acknowledge our dependence, to face up to the way we are bound by our need to belong.

Joan understood fairly quickly that the fear of separation and the fear of becoming independent were also part of her story. She especially realized that with her new understanding she could forgive herself and be forgiven, and challenge her vision to build her own business.

Before we parted, she told me, "I never really took stock of how much love and dependence were bound up in my relationship with my job... between people in general and their work. It's so powerful... it's really frightening."

Indeed, that's the source of the power wielded by work – a mighty wellspring of passion and love that can become either a path to destruction or an inspirational source of growth.

Chapter Eleven
Where do Visions grow

Exploring the work context that enables fulfillment

At the age of thirty-two, my husband and I became business partners when we established the Adam Institute, an Institute for Applied Psychology. Nothing in the course of my life up to that point had suggested that I wanted to or ever would be the owner of a business, even though it was crystal clear that working for someone else was not for me.

The entrepreneurs that I have counseled and with whom I have shared journeys of discovery have taught me to view the process differently. Over the years I have learned that people, who grow up in family environments with chaotic, non-authoritative parenting, often have trouble working in a regulated system and tend to build "systems" of their own. People who come from families with clear levels of authority and well-defined rules tend to join "clear-cut" organizations and gravitate to positions that correspond to roles they had played within their families.

When I was nine years old my parents wanted to buy a new apartment. Before signing the contract they asked me to have a look at it. They explained how moving to a new dwelling involved me, too, and that I had a one-third share in the decision. I took their proposal very seriously and walked around the apartment, surveying it carefully. Within a few minutes I returned to my parents and asked them three questions: Did this apartment cost more than the one we already had? Why was it more suitable than the old one? What were they looking for in the new apartment?

My parents responded that both apartments cost approximately the same. After some unpersuasive dialogue and argument, they agreed that in fact they were not really sure why the new apartment was more suitable, and that actually it was not what they were really looking for. After I had listened to all this with due seriousness, I told them, "The deal is no good." My parents were astounded at this authoritative pronouncement, and my father pounced on me, "Who gave you the right to decide that, young lady? You're out of line!" Although I knew my suggestion was going to be adopted, the hurt and confusion I felt remained with me for a long time.

For years afterward I was afraid to make important decisions.

I came to understand that it's not enough to be born or grow up in an atmosphere of entrepreneurship. Beyond being endowed with the appropriate personal profile and an inner enterprising quality, the would-be entrepreneur has to master many skills. But these can most definitely be learned.

My impression is that the ranking of people in various organizations tends to correlate with a person's birth-order rank and with the quality of his or her sibling relationships. Professional literature documents this phenomenon exhaustively. In his book *Born to Rebel* (1997), Frank Sulloway details hundreds of biographical sketches about people in politics, the arts, the sciences, and the clergy. In all cases he found that firstborn children identify with authority while younger siblings rebel against it. He presents findings from thousands of cases showing the links between birth order and family dynamics, management style, and creative endeavor in general.

Sulloway addresses additional important variables linked with choice of organizational framework and an individual's niche within it – how authoritarian the father was, how rigid the system is, how that person experiences management, how highly the individual respects management and vice versa. All these factors influence not only work style but also the organizations a person chooses to join or to build, and their satisfaction in belonging to them.

Most entrepreneurial activity is built around an entrepreneur's personality and not the other way around. The people around them do not always understand just what they are striving for. They themselves know very well where they are going, even if their road traverses complicated and unknown territory. Entrepreneurs often fuse different fields or professions to suit their own needs.

My journey with a businessman named André was training for me in identifying the skills entrepreneurs require and in recognizing the pitfalls they encounter along the way. When I first met him I didn't know precisely how to pinpoint the problem. André was then in his forties. He had an unusual combination of qualities that should have paved his way along the fast track and brought him rapidly to the top. He had a pleasant, disarming appearance and a well-honed sense of marketing communications. He had extensive knowledge in the field of pharmaceuticals and a prophetic sense of where the global pharmaceuticals market was headed. A classic entrepreneur, he constantly came up with original solutions fusing market demands with innovative products.

Though André ought to have been assured of success, in practice he went through one failure after another. In the local pharmaceutical industry he had a notorious reputation. He would devise some outstanding new idea and move quickly to implementation but, at some unclear point later in the development process, production would somehow crash. The enterprise would quickly go under; the business would go into receivership, then the rights to his innovative product would be sold to some other smart entrepreneur who would reap the rewards of André's innovation and make a financial killing.

Poised on the verge of throwing in the towel, André somehow mustered the strength necessary to ask for professional guidance.

"I'm at the end of my tether," he said at the start of our first session. "I've been setting up great business ventures for over twenty years, implementing infrastructure and logistics, recruiting teams and first-round financing, working night and day – and then, for some reason I can't figure out – everything collapses."

"And why did you come here now, at this particular point?" I asked. There is always special importance and timing attached to the circumstances that cause someone to request help.

"I came because I've lost hope. I felt that if I didn't go for professional counseling, I would simply die."

I looked at him. I felt as if I were gazing at the merest flicker of a candle that was on the verge of being extinguished.

André gazed at me vacantly, and I thought about the immense variety of talents an entrepreneur needs on the difficult road to success. Some of the skills required – curiosity, know-how, a clear vision, financial acumen, an ability to exploit business opportunities – are obvious. The stumbling block for someone with the typical entrepreneur's wealth of talents is generally rooted in some hidden corner of their emotional world. This emotional block can cause the whole growth process to be derailed, almost as if some fragile greenhouse flower were deprived of the special condition necessary to bloom.

"In my opinion," I told André, "your awareness of your repeated failures at several key crossroads hold the key to change. Once you have identified these, you'll be able to transform any situation and control it."

I advised André to think like a farmer who, having found a diseased plant, takes a good look at the roots. André knew there was a problem, and now he needed to explore what was going on at root level. What happened to him time after time whenever success was just around the next corner?

André was relieved to know that he had a choice and that there were in fact tools that could help him diagnose the problem and facilitate its prompt resolution. When he left that day, I caught a glimmer of hope in his eyes.

At our next meeting André told me of his happy childhood in Morocco.

"My father had a successful leather-processing factory," he recalled smiling. "He was full of original ideas and incredibly industrious. He knew how to assess market needs, and was always a little ahead of the competition. We lacked for nothing at home. Although I was only three at the time, I understood that the big leather workshop next to the textile market was what provided my food and all the toys and nice clothes I had. Observing my father taught me in the most natural way how to run a business, how to identify market needs and how to negotiate. And my father taught me how to relate to workers and to know my way around the business community. I was immensely proud of him."

The big crisis came at the beginning of the fifties. André and his family were part of a massive wave of emigration that found themselves torn from their palatial marble villa in Casablanca and dumped in a humble tent in a transit camp for new immigrants in Israel. "This," reminisced André sadly, "was something my father found impossible to cope with. Overnight he turned into a shadow of his former self. In Morocco, everything he touched had turned to gold, while in his new home everything he tried to do ended up in total failure. Still, he wasn't one to give in easily. After he'd recovered somewhat from the trauma of the transition, and mastered a new language, he gathered up the meager savings he'd been able to spirit out of Morocco, enlisted a partner, and set up a business that completely bombed. He was in shock.

"Nonetheless," André continued, "he wasn't completely beaten. Since he had no money left, he tried to find work as a manager in a leather enterprise, but that didn't work out well either. My father wasn't cut out to be an employee. Entrepreneurship is a personality, not a profession. I, who was six at the time, understood that he was almost fading away right in front of us. To save him, my mother sold all her valuable jewelry and precious family heirlooms. She gave the money to my father and told him to go start a new business for the family."

"And did he succeed with that?" I asked, nearly whispering.

"It was almost too late, but he gathered up the strength and managed to open a new factory. However, after a few months we realized that the jewelry so close to my mother's heart was never coming back to us. My father had wonderful ideas and he knew the leather business like I know myself, but he didn't know how to run a factory in this new business environment. My father was connected to his plant like someone kept alive by intravenous feeding; as the business declined, so did he. In the end, the business went bankrupt, and a few months later my father had a massive heart attack and died en route to the hospital. If you ask me, he simply died of a broken heart."

André, a little ten-year-old entrepreneur by nature, and orphaned only a week, now made himself a vow. "I saw the empty refrigerator at home, my mother crying, her hands devoid of her diamond rings, and the picture of my father on the sideboard. I decided that my family would never go hungry and I swore to continue my father's legacy."

"You took on some tough goals forged in great pain," I remarked.

André smiled sadly, and looked at me with an expression of bitter irony. "When I grew up," he said, "I chose pharmaceuticals which is a field involving chemistry and chemical substances. Pharmaceuticals have a lot of scope and good money can be made; if you're lucky enough to have one of your drugs succeed in the global market, you can make a fortune. I teamed up with the best pharmaceutical people in the country and created a network of connections. Yet somehow, somewhere, I always fail."

A little warning bell began to ring somewhere in my head and its sound was becoming familiar.

In subsequent sessions we figured out that André had succumbed to a classic and well-known trap that causes the downfall of many outstanding entrepreneurs – a problem in making the transition from the entrepreneurial phase of a start-up to the more institutional phase of an established business. The institutionalization stage demands new and different skills appropriate for managing and building a business. André was not able to cope successfully with this. He could not let go of the reins and delegate someone with the requisite management skills and expertise. Being an orphan had petrified him in survival mode; he was simply unable to move into institutionalization mode.

Many entrepreneurs are easily confused when it comes to the extent of their skills. They wrongly assume that their ability to invent an outstandingly original product and put it on the market implies an ability to manage the process.

"The business is my baby," many entrepreneurs tend to say with pride. "Who can know an infant's needs better than its mother?" They tend to forget that the ability to give birth to a baby doesn't guarantee parenting skills – even when a young mother is assisted by caregivers, parents, or older siblings.

Managing a business is a profession at which very few entrepreneurs excel, nor are many interested in doing so. However, at the same time, they find it hard to relinquish control over the business by transferring its management to a professional. They also find it difficult to commit themselves to the sort of personal development process that would teach them how to assume ownership of the business while maintaining clear distinction between ownership and day-to-day management.

Most entrepreneurs I've known have fallen into one of two categories – born entrepreneurs, who are generally offspring of entrepreneurs – and those who take on the role owing to specific circumstances in their lives. Both types are the kind of people who, at least in the context of their work, aspire to "be their own father or boss." They want to run the business themselves. They don't merely own the business, they become the business.

That, generally, is the story of their lives. They are unprepared, unwilling, and sometimes unable to work in a situation where someone has managerial authority over them. Some are able to learn, through great effort and investment in the process, how to manage their business. Others hire a professional manager and move on as successful entrepreneurs. All the rest simply fail – they cannot manage themselves, they won't let anyone else manage them or their business, and they are not able to work for anyone else.

It is almost impossible to tame entrepreneurs and turn them into successful employees. It is preferable for the entrepreneur to undertake a journey of personal development and learn self-management, or else install a manager in his place and learn to direct his energy as owner into nurturing the manager he has hired. To be a good owner also requires a learning process.

André was an entrepreneur who grew up without a father. Sitting there across from him I thought about my father, who was orphaned in infancy. All his life he had worked for someone else. His attitude to authority was a fatal combination of pain, rage, covert rebellion, and fear. He needed to be told what to do by someone in authority, yet was unable to come to terms with the essential nature of authority.

On the experiential level, I thought of how my own father

had abdicated the authoritarian role that he should have played for me. Just like André I taught myself to take the initiative and manage my own life, and in the most natural way I constructed a work environment for myself wherein I functioned as my own parent and boss. Nonetheless, since I had no inner model of the authoritative parent, I left a lot to be desired as a manager. My breakthrough came only at the end of a long process, when I was finally able to see that just as an infant needs a skilled caregiver with suitable training, my own company required a professional manager.

Making that leap required a tremendous effort of inward development on my part. Beyond acknowledging my inability to manage, I needed to transform our Mom & Pop Company into an organization, enable a professional to run it successfully, and build my role as owner.

This is what led me to a further personal breakthrough. The moment that the weight of management was lifted from my shoulders, I was able to turn to more natural skills in areas where I was far more productive. The entire process required a kind of incubation period and a readiness to move on to new activities.

André reached impasse because he had trouble distinguishing between his abilities and his limitations as an entrepreneur.

Aside from his failed management attempts, André did not yet have a fully developed capacity for mature entrepreneurship that encompassed an ability to recruit assistance from others and take full responsibility for his own challenges.

Although he had twenty years of botched entrepreneurship behind him, André did not find it easy to understand that, at this point, he needed to stop trying to build new business ventures. He needed first of all to build himself up. Coming up with great ideas was not a problem; André was always bursting with inspiring ideas. His problem was that he wanted to implement them himself!

After André had more accurately defined his goals for self-actualization, he needed to focus on the learning process he was about to undertake, the gist of which would be to develop his ability to be successful at a business he chose to pursue. He understood that he needed to expand his emotional range and acquire new skills while learning how to build stronger organizational and business infrastructures. Now he would have to define goals and timetables. He would also need to prioritize outcomes and decide which routes to follow in achieving them.

By analyzing his past failures, André realized that he lacked the skills for building an organizational-family structure to nurture goals, products, and work teams and unify them within a structure reflecting professionalism and a set of relevant values.

"It's like building a family," André said at one point, when he had lost his way and profitability was down. "Step by step, with love, and constant communication. And mainly, I have to take complete parental responsibility for my business, not just for having invented it."

The learning process took five years. André learned to run his business, and when he became more successful he learned how to delegate work to the professional managers working under him. Chiefly he learned how to parent himself responsibly, and succeeded in overcoming the circumstances of his childhood events.

As already noted, the family is the first organization we encounter. The character of this organization, our place in it vis-à-vis our parents, siblings, and grandparents – and sometimes even aunts and uncles – is likely to influence the choice of organizations in which we choose to work in the future. That initial organizational conception and the experiences involving our place in the family are the foundation of the way we relate as mature adults to our work environment. An organizational climate, like a family climate, has a special "aroma." This aroma can become either magnetically attractive for us, or a guaranteed recipe for failure.

Grace came to me for vocational counseling in the context of her disability. Even though Grace had been struck with a degenerative muscle disease, she was the kind of person who refused to accept or even acknowledge her limitations.

Most of the time Grace didn't stop long enough to catch her breath. Her disability and the fact that she could move only by using a wheelchair didn't prevent her from being in a constant state of hyperactivity. She talked rapidly, and periodically looked at her watch. It was obvious to me that Grace was an entrepreneur to her very fingertips.

At sixteen, together with a friend, she had set up a sandwich-making business that she later sold at a substantial profit. While others her age were spending the bulk of their free time going out and having fun, Grace set up her next business, a convenience store that turned into a neighborhood fixture and was constantly packed with customers. She never rested and was completely devoted to the business. She had no concept of time. "I lost myself fairly quickly," she told me. "I was so busy, I ceased to exist. I was drunk with success and high on achievement."

The turning point came when she was twenty-seven. She began suffering unexplained pain and weakness. The doctors found that her muscles were highly atrophied. Grace called it "an electric short circuit due to system overload." For a brief period she became depressed but in due time fell back into her regular routine. She preferred to ignore her illness. She was still able to work for two or three days nonstop, paying little attention to efficiency or to results, always racing on ahead, spinning the wheels of her sporty wheelchair. When she eventually weakened, she came to me for advice about adjusting to this new reality. We both laughed. We knew this wasn't a matter of merely adjusting; it was clear that we were going to be dealing with her workaholic nature.

Grace was a classic case of the entrepreneur without borders. Typically, people like her use up all their energy reserves in a relatively short period of time until they collapse. They get stuck because they are incapable of setting limits for themselves and are often unable to be parented even by a therapist. Generally, they do not set exact timetables for work and rest, for home or office. Most set ever-changing goals or objectives and don't pay enough attention to their working conditions and their effectiveness. They see only one thing – the next peak to be conquered. Mountaineers of this type know that they have, for one brief moment, conquered a worthy summit, and cannot rest until they have conquered the next one, and the next one and the next one.

Perhaps because Grace could not stop, we had a problem identifying alternative objectives. We knew that only a change in her entrepreneurial style was likely to help her. We needed to look at whether she would be able to accept the message her body was sending her and do something about her addiction to work.

Grace sensed that she wasn't capable of undergoing such a process. "I'm already a total loss. Why should I waste the time?" she said, at our final meeting. "I can't behave in any other way, I can't start changing now. I've gone too far. It's too painful, and I'm totally exhausted."

"So what will happen?" I asked anxiously.

"I'll keep running till I drop – till I'm completely dried up."

Grace was unable to tame her entrepreneurial spirit and commit to a painful rehabilitation process that would wean her off her work addiction. She let the muscular deterioration serve as brakes that gradually brought her impossible, crazy rat race of a life to a cruel halt.

Indeed, weaning oneself from an addiction can be a lonely and terrifying business. As a professional, I had to respect her choices, however sad it made me feel.

Along with born entrepreneurs, there are people who are not cut out to be entrepreneurs, yet find themselves on that path for the wrong reasons. As difficult as it may be, such people, must become conscious of their poor choices and change their entrepreneurial role, which is completely wrong for them.

Sammy came to me for counseling when he was thirty-eight. A self-employed man, he had started all kinds of businesses and owned several small factories, mainly in printing and publishing – none of which were successful.

"I have the feeling that maybe I never really wanted to be self-employed," replied Sammy hesitantly to my question about why success had eluded him.

His brow was furrowed with wrinkles as he thought about what he'd said.

"Deep down I guess I've always wanted stability, yet I was afraid of my desire to be a salaried employee, to be part of a system. I don't know why I've never been able to fit in as an employee, nor as a businessman. I've failed repeatedly. Small time failures. I made a living. But that's about it."

Sammy was the son of Holocaust survivors whose lives' had been saved by their own efforts. After the war they were both employed: his mother as a bookkeeper and his father as a clerk. Their dream for their son was of something different. They wanted him to be a gutsy entrepreneur or a daring businessman. They may have made an unconscious connection between vocational initiative and the survival initiatives that saw them safely through the Holocaust. They mistook entrepreneurship as a sure way of making life safe for their son and providing him with the tools to survive any obstacles.

"And do you have that?" I asked him.

"I'm afraid not," he replied, immediately adding, "That's it. I said it. And you know what? That's the first time I've admitted it out loud!"

His face softened; he looked happier.

Sammy, unfit for entrepreneurship, had been stifled the wrong way around so that his natural need to be an employee had been repressed.

Deep down, he had always known that he was not a born entrepreneur. At the same time, to confess that was almost like a death sentence for his career, and he'd been struggling against it for years. Aside from that, he was afraid of disappointing his mother and father. "It hurt me, but I accepted their almost unspoken message," said Sammy, with pain. "Now I feel I can choose what suits me best. Now I can finally break through the walls of the concentration camp."

With this revelation, things seemed simpler and easier to Sammy. He closed his small businesses and found work as a salesperson in a young company that appreciated his experience. He now understood that he belonged to that group of people who need structure, and who are happiest as part of a team. As an employee, Sammy felt he had a family; he felt at home.

"Being on my own," he concluded, summing up the brief process we'd undergone together, "battling it out with the authorities and the bureaucrats, the income tax guys; I couldn't handle that stuff."

Once Sammy identified the environment that suited him, he was able to make a choice.

Many people have very similar feelings to Sammy's regarding affiliation with a large system versus joining a small one. Some people feel lost in a large organization and prefer to develop and create within a narrower framework. These folks need an organization where personal attention and intimacy exist. Other people derive tremendous strength from belonging to a large organization. They are proud to be part of a large corporation and do not seek to rub shoulders intimately with their colleagues.

Sammy came from an "orderly" family where the hierarchy was clear and the style of parenting and family life provided security and defense against the outside world. He felt safe and energized within a small organization.

What's important is to become conscious of one's entrepreneurial needs and identify the kind of organizational frame wherein one functions best. Although, entrepreneurship is an existential need for some people, it is critical to pay attention to one's inner needs. Once a diagnosis had been clearly defined, the rest of the journey becomes easy.

Chapter Twelve
Sibling Rivalry is Good for Business

Our childhood spats were a great training ground for life

Along with the special love I felt for my little brother Zorik, I was also jealous of him. His death at the age of two didn't blunt these feelings. Sometimes I think his death even gave them an enduring timelessness. I went on missing him; and that special sense of sibling solidarity, that united front against parents, was reinforced over the years. Some of these emotions were invested in the partnerships I developed as time went by. Experience taught me that even though I could perform more efficiently when working alone, a partnership somehow still draws out the best in me. When working with a partner, I am in some way living out that richly intense power of sibling togetherness that I so yearned for and that was so utterly lost to me. I realized that this factor is also the source of the tremendous power of other people's partnerships, for better or for worse.

The immense influence of my brother's death on my life and work also taught me that we don't pay enough attention to the special relationships that exist between siblings. Our sibling relationships contribute to shaping our basic relationships in general and our work, careers, and vocations in particular.

Jenny was a war widow who came to me for counseling

when she was thirty-two. Before being widowed, she had been a frustrated teacher. The Ministry of Defense, who took responsibility for her after her husband's death, sent her to me for vocational placement in response to her frustration with teaching. She arrived at our first session reflecting rigidity and a lack of spontaneity, meticulously dressed, almost like a mummy wrapped in a blue and white pinstriped suit; with pearl earrings and a matching pearl necklace. Jenny had come for counseling, but was frozen solid, almost impossible to get through to. In our first few minutes together, I asked myself, who wrapped her in these shrouds, and why?

Jenny immediately provided an official answer. "I was sent by the Ministry of Defense to examine options for vocational placement," she said laconically. "It's included in my widow's benefits." I sensed that she was on her guard, and I sought an opening that would allow a point of contact.

Despite my impatience to reach out to her, I decided that a slow pace with gradual progress, was also fine and I should respect that. All we did at our first session was exchange information and check each other out. At our next meeting, I was thoroughly prepared. I didn't want to continue in such an alienated fashion. I wanted to try to arouse Jenny's curiosity and find some other path that would lead me to her. I felt we had little to lose, and shared a few options with her. "We can look at lists of vocational possibilities and discuss them on a functional level," I told her, "or we can try to understand your life story in vocational terms."

Although Jenny was a bit surprised, she made sure to remain aloof. "All right... I haven't really prepared myself to get into a process like that," she said, "but if you tell me what to do, I'll do it."

I felt a bit like a novice equestrian about to ride his first horse.

In the beginning we talked about the significance of life and death choices: the choice of self-fulfillment or its relinquishment. We also talked about how choice can be handcuffed, about the price to be paid when we choose one road or another. In this way we sharpened our swords, gradually yet cautiously moving to a more profound dialogue. This round, too, despite our mutual efforts, ended without noticeable results.

I came to our third meeting feeling tired. This had nothing to do with Jenny, apparently, but perhaps as a consequence of my fatigue and passivity, Jenny began taking the initiative.

"I hate teaching," she said after ten minutes of silence. "I didn't choose to go into it, and I don't want to teach anymore. I've had it with education."

My fatigue vanished. Jenny had opened a window through which I could see that she had seized permission to ask herself questions about what she was permitted to desire and to do. She had given me enormous hope.

"How did you become a teacher?" I asked carefully.

"My mother died when I was twelve. My father decided that his children, or I should say his sons, would follow in his footsteps, study pharmacology or chemistry and work with him in the family drugstore. My father sent me, his only daughter, to study languages so that later on I could be a teacher. Do you understand? The father is the one who decides, and daughters are not sons. I always envied my brothers and wanted to be with them. I was something of a tomboy, always outdoors, climbing trees, getting cuts and scratches. However, when I grew up, my father sent me to study piano and learn languages. So I did it, but it gave me no joy."

"Your father decided that you would be a good girl, a good daughter, and so you were. Afterwards, you went on doing what was expected of you – you became a teacher, got married and made a lovely home." I said emphasizing the closed, passive nature of the path Jenny had traveled.

"That's irrelevant," said Jenny, annoyed. "I could have done that and still been like my brothers."

We were going to have to go into Jenny's deep-seated jealousy of her brothers. There was no avoiding it. From there, we moved on to her anger towards her father, who had relegated her to the position of the little woman. Her father only gave his sons permission to study fields useful for the family pharmacy business. Despite Jenny's urgent wish to study pharmacology, she was obliged to stick within the traditional woman's role. Furthermore, she had to deal with the pain generated by the thought that her father had preferred to have his male heirs at his side.

Sibling rivalry has preoccupied humanity since the beginning of time. The Holy Bible distinguishes between Cain and Abel on the basis of their respective vocations and order of birth and thus evaluates their personalities differently. It describes the difference between Cain and Abel in terms of God's preferences as the ultimate parent who favored one son's occupation over the others – the shepherd over the farmer. The resulting envy was so powerful that it led to murder.

Today it is known that parental preference for a particular child has a direct influence on all the siblings' development and their mutual relationships. I've learned that there's also a considerable impact on their vocational choices and the way they function within their professions. Children are profoundly influenced by being favored as well as by being rejected.

Frank Sulloway, in Born to Rebel (1997), reports that first-born children prefer occupations devoted mainly to conserving the status quo and maintaining ascendancy. Younger siblings, by contrast, confront an entirely different developmental challenge oriented toward change, revolution, and entrepreneurial initiative. While firstborns need to defend their rank and territory from incursion by younger siblings, the younger ones confront a need to find themselves a distinct niche that is valued within the family.

Younger siblings want and need to excel in some way that is not related to the elder sibling's supremacy. Thus the younger ones develop openness to change, to new experiences, and to taking more risks.

Sulloway theorized that children never stop competing for parental attention and seek to reinforce the approval they get from their parents beyond the leftovers of the eldest. Sulloway maintains that parents generally invest more in the first-born child.

In a sense, then, each sibling is born to a different family, figuratively speaking, and not only to a different place in the birth order. It's not for nothing that we hear parents query: "How is it that both these children grew up in the same house, and turned out so differently?"

In the working world, it is relatively easy to discern the type of person who is a classic first-born child. Often, such people are Number One in an organization – responsible, conscientious, and conservative. They coordinate people and tasks, and demand a great deal of themselves. By contrast, classic Number Two people, tend to fill deputy positions, and are either second-born, "sandwich children," or their parent's favorite. We're used to seeing them as the Number One's right hand. Younger siblings are often rebels.

Sometimes, personalities are shaped according to this vocational rank order, and when a successful Number Two does really well and is moved into the Number One spot, they are liable to fail due to a lack of psychological suitability for their new rank. For a second-in-command making the transition and succeeding as a Number One, requires a thorough developmental change process. One is also influenced by the gender mix of one's siblings from the childhood playground.

Jenny felt as equally qualified as her brothers were to study pharmacology. As the only girl in a family of boys, she had learned to work in an all-male team, yet in her traditional family, it wasn't acceptable for a girl to study pharmacology. It went against tradition and it went against her father. Jenny, as a daughter, was forbidden to choose her own path in life. To change this situation, she had to undergo an emotional upheaval. She had to permit the rebellious girl-child within her to stand up and express herself.

Generally, a family exhibits a kind of division of property of the sibling's psycho-genes passed down through the generations. This division is designed to moderate and, if possible, to prevent jealousy and competition among siblings, and perhaps also to enable them to selectively develop different psycho-genes. Thus it happens that one brother is assigned the role of "the good-looking one," and another the role of "the talented one" or "the science-oriented one," as opposed to his "humanities-oriented" sister, etc. This categorization, intended to channel development in one direction or another, can be a two-edged sword. In some families, one child may be labeled "the successful one" while another sibling may be branded "the unsuccessful one." For some people, this may be a heavy burden to bear.

Sometimes this kind of situation arises when the parents themselves are carrying around their individual sibling rivalry which is often continued down the generations. In some families, the first-born's crown can be stolen by a younger sibling and unless decoded, this can also continue through the generations. (see *Genograms in Family Assessment,* McGoldrik et al.). In other families, the second child may "steal" the birthright and be the more successful sibling. Such venerable old patterns can be altered, but to do so, one must first detect them and discover their roots, and then one must learn new behavioral patterns.

Channeling someone's talents in a given direction is a complex matter. Labels like "the smart brother" or "the science-oriented sister" don't always hold up on close examination of reality. In fact, it would seem that children send messages regarding their personalities and talents in one direction or another, yet they respond to what is expected of them rather than what they desire to express. Only objective assessment or intensive study of vocational Genograms can reveal whether these choices were made in order to prevent sibling rivalry or authentic choices. It's very common for people to suddenly realize that they are equally as smart or science-oriented or art-oriented as all their other siblings were considered to be.

Indeed, there is tough competition within the family over the selection of vocational fields. In my experience, the initial vocational distribution among siblings is by gender. Generally, brothers choose fields that men in the family have pursued, and sisters choose fields pursued by the women.

When there are two boys in a family, typically one of them, generally the elder, will select the father's primary occupation while the other will choose a complementary vocation or a hobby that had been pursued by the father. In other cases, the second son will choose his mother's vocation or some occupation engaged in by a valued male member of his family. In any case, the second son takes from what's left over.

And the girls? The first daughter generally chooses whatever her mother did or does. When there are two girls, the other will choose from among her father's activities. In some families, all the sons and or daughters choose the same vocations and compete among themselves. This can happen in families where parents raise their children with a dose of healthy competition. Over time, a differentiation process occurs so that even if all the siblings have chosen art or business, one will become an entrepreneur, one a manager, and one will take responsibility for communication between the others.

It's astounding how closely linked we are with our siblings in the realm of achievement and career development. Over the years I have observed changes in the careers of siblings and have learned that a change undergone by one sibling, be it progress or regression in their lives, can influence and affect the other siblings.

Furthermore, if the so-called "non-intelligent" sibling succeeds in altering this label and gets relabeled as the "smart" one, this will greatly impact the other, so-called "successful," sibling.

For Jenny, the loss of her husband represented the shattering of a very special relationship in which she had invested tremendous energy in preserving her role as "the little woman." Once she recovered from the first shock of her loss, she was ready to relate differently to her brothers.

"Maybe now," I said, "now you can finally study pharmacology as your two brothers have done, and still be Daddy's girl. Your aptitude tests affirm that your skills and inclinations are clearly science-oriented which confirms that you inherited the family genes."

Her face lit up, "Does that mean I can be like my brothers?"

"Of course you can," I said, "this field belongs equally to you as to them, and teaching is clearly not your forte."

A short time later, Jenny registered for degree studies in pharmacology. "They accepted me, in spite of my age!" she exulted.

"And what did your brothers say?" I asked.

"I haven't told them yet. I decided to tell them only after I was accepted. I was afraid they'd laugh at me. Anyhow, if you ask me, I think that although they were the ones who received Dad's blessing to be in the profession, they were always envious of my great grades, and of the special way Dad treated me." Only now was Jenny able to see the jealousy from her sibling's eyes.

"Jealousy is hard as hell," claims the Bible. There are parents who have trouble dealing with their children's sibling rivalry that can sometimes become extremely aggressive as the siblings endeavor to outperform each other on the path to success. In one way or another, some parents may conspire with one of the children, metaphorically sacrificing the other child and minimizing his or her achievements. Sometimes only a part of the other child's personality is sacrificed in this manner.

Over years of counseling, I have found that there is a parallel between envy and competition in sibling behavioral patterns and their peer relationships at work. People whose sibling relationships facilitated shared enjoyment succeed in becoming happy and successful team players, and vice versa. That's why I advise self-employed people with difficult sibling relationships not to take on business partners. First, they have to tie up loose ends and come to terms with their unresolved sibling rivalries. A person who brings unresolved sibling issues to a partnership will constantly recreate destructive patterns, even though they may not be based in reality.

Some people invest most of their energy in sibling-style battles and some repeatedly seek partnerships, only to be repeatedly hurt by them. This goes on despite the fact that these tortuous experiences can cause terrible fights, financial losses, and even physical illness. Often people with troubling and emotional relationships are driven to search for family patterns in the hope of repairing and healing them.

Sibling rivalry, we should note, also has its constructive aspects. Competition between siblings is what first prompts us to measure our strength against an equal. Through such competition, we learn about social order: who's bigger and who's smaller, who's stronger and who's weaker, and so forth. The bond with a brother or sister is one wherein we have not chosen the partner, and there are few possibilities for cutting our ties. This connection is also one that comforts, asserts a sense of belonging, and pushes threatening buttons at our most sensitive points – love, territory, ability, parental attention, respect, and so on.

Rick, a senior manager in an advertising firm, told me how the trivial and unnecessary bickering between him and a long-time work colleague resembled what used to go on between him and his eldest brother, and how he found it difficult to wean himself from this type of negative exchange.

Competition between siblings who love one another may indeed be frightening and difficult. Moreover, for the most part it is suppressed and thus is liable to break out, sometimes years later, in completely different contexts.

Sibling rivalry can also be a spur to achievement, prompting the choice of particular goals and the quest for vocational uniqueness. One sibling in a family business expressed it this way: "In our family, you have to get good grades, and it doesn't matter in what. So I got good grades in the sciences and my brother, in sports. That's the way it is."

Sibling relationships are not just for a lifetime; they go on even after death. The death of a sibling can torpedo a career, even a life.

Loss of an adult brother or sister has a profound influence on the surviving siblings. Timothy's story comes to mind. Timothy was an exceptional manager, and a phenomenal success story in his field, until his brother was killed in a car accident. "Since the day he died," Timothy told me, "I've felt as if I wasn't supposed to go on living. I wanted to die in his place. In retrospect, it seems that instead of 'killing' myself, I 'killed' my career. I ask myself all the time: 'How can I continue living and being a success, when my brother failed to survive?'"

Losing a sibling in infancy or childhood typically drives people to want to do something extraordinary with their lives, or to make a special contribution to humanity. They are often burdened with feelings like: "What I do is never enough" or "I know that I have to do more, but I don't know what," and so forth.

The story of Guy and John is an inspiring example of a partnership that repeats earlier asymmetrical sibling relationships and seeks to repair and heal them. Guy and John worked in hi-tech and were curious to check their suitability as partners.

Guy struck me as an experienced professional. He had clear market insight, came with impressive credentials, and was something of a Renaissance man, hard-working and businesslike. John was different. I wasn't certain of his communication skills. He came across as needy and not grounded in reality. He was distracted, sometimes brilliant, but had trouble even detailing his work history, which was full of serious breakdowns, despite promising beginnings.

Past experience has taught me to rely on the people who come to me for counseling, no less than on myself, concerning all aspects of their suitability for partnership. Still, this time I faced a tough call. When I shared my reservations concerning their potential partnership, they disagreed with me. Guy and John insisted with surprising persistence that they believed in their partnership. At that same meeting, the idea came to me to have them try doing something separately and then doing something together, as a test. The first task, which each of them was to do alone, was to draw a diagram of their future joint activities. As I expected, Guy drew his in a very impressive way. John's was sketchy, confused, and disjointed. The second task was a shared one. The result was spectacular. Guy in fact "connected" the disjointed points and lines that John had drawn. The product of their combined effort was astounding in its complexity and precision, and yet equally so in its simplicity. The outcome of their cooperation left no room for doubt. All three of us saw clearly that a potentially successful partnership was possible for Guy and John.

Only later did the real surprise come to light. As always, I looked into the "vocational genetics" of both of them, and learned that one of Guy's brothers, Richard, a genius, had fallen ill with schizophrenia when Guy was sixteen. "I was never able to accept my older brother's illness," he told me. "I loved him so much. He was so sensitive and vulnerable, and I always looked after him. Together, we thought up new inventions and actually made them. We had a wonderful time together, even after he got sick."

John, by contrast, was the child of his parents' old age; both of whom had been refugees. When his parents went to work in the morning, they left him with his older brother. "He took care of whatever I needed. He raised me," John explained.

John and Guy came from special kinds of relationships, full of love and mutual respect between brothers. They had experienced no painful sibling competition. Each, in his inner being, felt certain that they could grow and be creative in a partnership with a sibling. Later, when Guy and John's empire took shape, it was clear that their partnership was both opportunity and repair for each of them. They were able to develop their partnership concurrently with their respective individual development. Each of them broadened their range of skills while helping the other to heal.

Sometimes, people feel the need for a business partner for all the wrong reasons. This was so in Howard's case. Only in his early forties did Howard begin to understand that for twenty years or so he had basically been supporting his partner because he was so afraid of not being able to succeed on his own. Half of all the profits were given to a passive partner, solely on account of Howard's belief that, without his partner, he wouldn't be able to earn even twenty percent of current profits.

"I felt as if he had to be there for me to succeed," he told me. "He was my good-luck charm."

Only at the age of forty did Howard feel ready to try making it on his own. He wanted to retire his good-luck charm.

How did Howard get into this situation? Why only at forty did he recognize that he could manage on his own? It turned out that when Howard was six, his brother was run over and became an invalid. His father put Howard in charge of watching over his disabled brother. Even when his brother became independent, studied graphics, and became successful, Howard still felt responsible for him. Over the years, the boundaries became blurred in terms of who was taking care of whom, and who needed whom.

Howard came to me about six months after his father had passed away. With his father's death, Howard began to feel that he now had permission to let go of his responsibility as a guardian. Only now could he break out of his old framework and build a new one, without the partner who had, as it were, always watched over him, or vice versa.

The high point of this drama came when Howard was able to feel that even when he finally separated from his brother or business partner, no one was to blame and no one was helpless. Howard began building a new inner experience of things. He began feeling capable of acting without a partner. The capacity to mature, to feel independent and separate, enables us to be unique and independent and brings all the significant figures in our lives together in a loving way.

"Perhaps your business partner will also find it preferable to stand on his own two feet?" I pressed. "Maybe, though less successful with you, he could be more successful on his own or with some other partner?"

Howard didn't deny the possibility. Later on, we created a phased end to the partnership, based on mature, businesslike negotiations. After that, Howard and his partner went their separate ways. Each of them saw their parting as the start of a new journey towards sovereignty and personal development. Sometimes separation – as difficult as it may seem – is a necessary stage when walking along the path toward fulfilling one's vision.

Chapter Thirteen

Every Family is a Family Business

I had no idea that my family tree held so many apples

In my family, the distinctions between parents and daughter were always a little vague. My father, my mother, and I, all lived together with equal rights. The difference between us was in our duties. My father worked at a job, my mother ran the house and did her artwork, and I went to school.

At home, we had one "bank account" with everyone's money in it. I could "withdraw" as much money as I liked whenever I wanted. My parents trusted me completely. As a child, I was a full partner in family decisions, and hence I never really internalized what "organizational discipline" was about. I never got used to having someone in authority over me, neither did I learn to be a proper foot soldier that simply did as she was told.

My brother's death stunted my learning curve on how to behave with my peers and become part of the club within organizational systems and corporate contexts. This naturally led me to build my own organizational contexts.

In my thirties, I left my academic career and went into partnership with my husband. I was yet to discover that our successful business venture would eventually become a fertile training ground for us both as a couple and as a family. Later on in my career, after gaining wide experience working with entrepreneurs and family business owners, an interesting concept began to slowly form in my mind.

Every family can be defined as a unique type of "Family Business." A family, like a business, can experience profit and loss, promote growth or stagnation, create synergy via teamwork, and offer a warm place of creativity and partnership, or it can become a chaotic organization where misery and inefficiency prevail.

In retrospect, our family business offered me years of training ground on how to transform my confused childhood experiences into positive growth. It gave me the tools to accompany people on their corporate career journeys through generations of their families' vocations and leadership roles as well as understanding their patterns of coping within family organizations.

As the partnership with my husband grew and developed both personally and professionally, we encountered unimaginable difficulties that took us through the full range of pain and anger, threats and arguments, all the way to repressed envy and a disturbing feeling of competition between us. This demanded a great deal of emotional investment and intensive learning of our mutual needs and different personalities. Ultimately, this enhanced our relationship while intensifying our friendship and improving our work. Our journey as a couple, on the job and at home, was also significant in helping us optimize our parenting skills.

Over the years I began to understand that my calling lay in helping people make career breakthroughs by decoding their intergenerational family vocational DNA or psycho-genes. My own family business which had helped me shape my vision and develop my quest further, now led me to set up a separate consultancy with a long-time colleague, Dr. Tamar Milo, an experienced and renowned organizational consultant. We named our new venture "AMI", a unique company offering consulting focusing on the special challenges facing family businesses.

The Gafni family was one of the first families I worked with who understood the importance of investing in each family member's personal vision from a business perspective. The family came to us initially for organizational consulting. Every time we attempted to put their house in order, organizationally speaking, the family confusion would throw us back to their chaotic structures.

"As a father," Mark, the head of the family explained, "I never knew what to do with my kids when they were little. That was my wife's area of responsibility. She was never directly involved with the business, and I never interfered with the business of the children."

When Mark's children grew up, he felt that through the business, he would be able to get a second chance at parenting them. The first transformation he underwent was in guiding his children in how to manage a business, something at which he was a certified expert.

"As a father, I wasn't so successful, but as a business mentor, I knew my odds were better," he said. His children understood the opportunity of learning from their father who was considered a master in the industry and enthusiastically got down to work.

As the business grew and developed, the second generation family members were by now in their thirties. The talented siblings, who had learned so much from their father, now looked to examine their personal visions and discover how they related to the future vision of the business. Mark, who couldn't understand their need for a personal vision, felt threatened and betrayed, both as a father and a mentor.

My work with Mark included explaining to him how he had never received permission to choose because he had joined the family business at his father's insistence.

Once Mark began to accept the existential human need for freedom of choice, of which he had been denied, he began to free himself of his hostile feelings towards his children's requests. This subsequently enabled an opening for his children to conduct a responsible assessment of their respective individual visions.

The process culminated in two of the children remaining happily ensconced within the family business. One son went on to become the CEO, and the other became a vice president of business development and took charge of the family's future vision. Their sister, the third sibling, took time out to earn a Ph.D. in economics. The family had undergone a constructive process whereby not only the business and the family were enriched but each individual within the family business.

Similar issues exist in all families, yet in families that don't own family businesses such problems can be glossed over, sometimes indefinitely. Conflicts between work and family are heightened in a family business, where all the family's assets may be riding on a risky enterprise.

The feelings revolving around a family business are intense. Its members are forced to cope in a special way with both family and career, because it demands they confront individual and team development within the family/business systems. Family issues and conflicts – from which there is no escaping in a family business – demand effective coping tools.

"Do you know anyone who ran away from a family business and lived to tell the tale?" asked Bob, owner of a construction supply business. "It's like a prison. You can be released, but you can't escape. When I wanted to study play writing at university," he continued, "I had to request permission from my family for leave, even though it was more like probation. Don't think they were in any hurry. It took a year or two before they really started discussing it. Another year went by, during which I was required to work in the business, before I could begin studying. But even now that I'm an established writer, it's clear to me that if some day they wave the flag and duty calls, I'll go…" Bob sighed.

"That's how it is with a family business."

"But," I persisted, "the option to choose, despite how confusing it may be, grants you freedom. You can be a writer and learn to be a business owner on the side, even if you don't actually work in the business on a daily basis."

"That's true," he said, "but it took us seven years to internalize the difference between being an owner and being a manager. Between being a family member and a private individual, no one has time to actualize their vocational vision. The hard work we did together certainly helped me get my life in order. It made certain questions more urgent: What do I want? How do I feel about what I have? And how do I relate to what I want to create from scratch? These are all questions that my friends postponed dealing with until they were much older."

An outsider may not comprehend the degree to which a family business inevitably evokes extreme surrogate personifications such as "enemy," "lover," "competitor," "child," and so on. These passionately intense feelings necessitate the acquisition of conflict-solving mechanisms as well as clear family protocols. Such processes enrich the family, the business, and the individuals, demanding their courage and self-discipline. It trains them to work in teams, identify common values, build respectful partnerships, and formulate fair partners' agreements. A family business that survives the stage of chaos, implements protocols, and continues healthy growth inevitably becomes an attractive market proposition and a company of choice that attracts quality people.

Nancy was thirty-five when she came to me for counseling. She had been appointed CEO of her family's communications business. Assailed by tremendous anxiety, she felt that she was being drawn into work the same way her father had before her and that it was causing her to lose her bond with her husband and children.

"Sometimes the business was like my father's lover," said Nancy. "My mother hated it, pure and simple; my father needed it. He couldn't live with it, and he couldn't live without it. We, the kids, understood Dad, but we wanted to protect Mom. We found ourselves growing up 'against' the business."

Through my experience, I consistently found that in a family business, the family finds itself eternally performing on stage. That certainly explains why a great many of the daily conflicts that occur in any workplace take on a unique intensity in a family business. Competition and success tend to become over exaggerated.

Nancy, who was haunted by outperforming her father, was tormented by questions such as: "Now that I have succeeded in transforming my father's little business into a flourishing commercial empire, maybe in some way I've actually humiliated him! On the other hand, maybe I've actually fulfilled his most precious life dream."

As my work with Nancy progressed, we realized that what had been blocking her next stage of success was her inner fear of competing with her father and showing up his limitations. I have found that daughters have far more difficulty competing with their fathers as compared to sons to whom a male duel comes far more naturally.

Both Nancy and her father shared a strong passion and a mutual vision which played to their advantage. Nancy was able to openly discuss her fears with her father, which led them to build a far more fruitful and respectful relationship. They teamed up not only as father and daughter but also as partners. When their company eventually went public, they led the offering together and were able to celebrate their mutual achievements.

I'll never forget my first meeting with Jacob, owner of a leading family business. Jacob had two sons, both in their twenties at the time; and he wanted their vocational aptitude evaluated. At the culmination of the process, despite the fact that both sons were equally talented in both business and music, they both chose to pursue their passion – careers in music. Their father was enraged and demanded a meeting with me.

Jacob sat opposite me, his face flushed with anger right from the outset. He glared at me fiercely as he banged his fist on my small wooden desk, "And who, in your opinion, will continue managing the business I built up with my two hands? Would you mind telling me why I should go on working so hard alone here when my dear children are studying music at esteemed institutions and winning all kinds of prestigious prizes?"

Silence fell in my consulting room. Charismatic Jacob was a sizeable and impressive man. At that moment however, with his silver hair and the spark missing from his blue eyes, he looked tired and lonely.

I had met with Jacob a few months previously to help him think through his vision for the successful family business his father had inherited from his father. Jacob proudly recalled how he had developed the small factory that his father had left him and turned it into a thriving and successful business. He described the long years of labor, the business triumphs and tribulations. It was only towards the end, almost incidentally, that he told me about his two sons who had flown the nest.

"Don't misunderstand me," he said, almost apologetically, "even though they don't work in the family business, both of them show outstanding business promise. Because I recognized their prodigious musical talent from a young age, I provided them with the best private teachers available and sent them to top conservatories all around the world.

Spurred by their father's overwhelming ambition and their own potential, the boys steered their course through calm waters toward world-class musical careers. In the evenings, their father would shut himself up in his office at the plant, and listen with pleasure, tinged with envy, to his sons' CD recordings; peace offerings sent from New York, London, Paris, and Tokyo. He took pride in their achievements, but his internal dilemma caused him great suffering. He wanted them alongside him in the business, but he also wanted them to follow what appeared to be their true calling.

"Listen," I said to Jacob after some hesitation, "there's nothing to be done; your children are gifted musicians…" He never let me finish the sentence. "How in hell," he thundered, his angry bass voice bouncing off the walls, "can you tell me that they are more suited to music than to business?! What about the family business they're supposed to run when I'm gone? Why are you talking about fulfilling individual dreams? Do you think I wanted to work in that gloomy little gray factory my father passed on to me?"

His fury was terrible to see and even he was surprised by its force. "I wonder where all this anger is coming from?" he asked surprised by his own reaction.

When we have difficulty being supportive of our children's vision quests, it is often necessary to take a good look at what we did with our own.

"Imagine all that energy," I commented, "seething under the surface of your working life."

Jacob smiled reluctantly as the pieces of a complex puzzle suddenly fell into place for him. Deep down inside, he had never really taken full responsibility for choosing to continue the family business. He was drawn inescapably into it by a powerful current. "My grandfather was a popular local singer and played a mean accordion," he said. He was reconstructing the past for me as he sipped from a glass of tea I'd made him after he began, at long last, to comprehend the terrible anger that had simmered inside him for years. "The problem was that he wasn't able to make much money nor earn a living playing at weddings and other community functions. Yet, we all knew that my grandfather had a magic touch and that he was good with his hands."

"And of course we know he had an entrepreneurial mind," I added.

"Of course," Jacob smiled. "Business is in our genes. Grandfather began by repairing household appliances, and when he came to Israel, he opened a small store. He nearly forgot all about being a professional singer because of the difficulty of earning a living from it. When he died at thirty-nine from a sudden heart attack, my father inherited the business. It was always clear to everyone that the business would stay in the family, and that I, as the eldest son, would automatically take over. That's how it came to be my turn."

"Despite your taking violin and singing lessons," I noted quietly, "and even though your father knew that you cherished a dream of studying music abroad. Do you think that maybe that was his dream, too?"

"Definitely!" sighed Jacob, "My father also gave up his dream." Then he was silent, and his shoulders began shaking. The tears from forty years of pain brimmed and overflowed. This was a man who had always been considered an indifferent father and a rigid boss, a man who was focused solely on his business. There, in front of me, he finally connected with his buried yearnings and the pain of never been able to weave the thread of tenderness into his life's tapestry.

"Maybe…" I suggested gently, "that's why you sent your sons to study with the world's best music teachers. Perhaps you wanted to give them permission to realize their dream, which had also been your suppressed dream."

Jacob pulled himself together. "But tell me," he said aloud, "who will run the empire I built? Do you think dreams build factories?"

"Yes indeed," I told him. "Today we know that a business that is built to last is born out of dreams and vision, a vision that is supported by values."

I suggested to Jacob that he should tell his children about his dreams and those of his father and grandfather, about how they had missed out on making their dreams come true, and about a sense of duty and loyalty to the family business. I suggested that he also should try to encourage the entrepreneurial side of the boys' nature and be supportive of their right to fulfill their dreams. Often parents who never managed to work through their youthful dreams remain stuck in that same place... and tend to "compensate" their children by pushing them to fulfill their own youthful dreams rather than letting their children grow beyond these early yearnings.

Jacob adopted my suggestion. He also understood that his children had been pushed, almost unconsciously, into pursuing the dream of musical expression that the men in prior generations of the family had missed out on.

Once Jacob understood that, he was able to communicate directly with his sons. He was able to see that, almost without being aware of it, he had prevented them from integrating into the business. When they were little and wanted to come to work with him during school vacations, he would reprimand them: "First go and practice." Later on he used to tell them, "The business will always be here for you; now is your chance to study music."

When he acknowledged the messages he had sent in the past, he was able to understand and communicate them clearly. We set up family meetings where we discussed needs and parental identification; making choices; how to run a business professionally; and how it's possible to integrate and meet needs when one respects and pays attention to them...

This approach not only helped the members of the family progress in their personal development as individuals, but also greatly influenced their corporate modus operandi and the way they viewed their customers and consumers.

Ten years later, the family business had gone global and executive positions were now filled by professionals. Alongside the trophies and awards for musical excellence filling an entire cabinet in the board room, Jacob's sons sat in key leadership roles. One had become chairman of the board, and the other was responsible for family investments.

The family business was the winner.

"And where are your children?" I asked Jacob's sons. "Are they also musicians, or are they in the family business?"

A shout of laughter filled the room where the three of us were sitting. "They all play instruments and we've got a family ensemble going…" came the reply, "but they are also doing exceptionally well in the business and are very involved in everything that goes on here."

"So you have learned how to integrate all the family talents," I said.

"We hope so," affirmed one, while the other nodded. "You know, they're already the next generation in the business."

"That's right," I said. "They are the generation of integration. Integration of the full range of the family genes comes naturally to them. And how is your father?"

"These days, Dad is working at a far more relaxed pace. He is still president of the company and a source of inspiration in leading critical decision-making forums. You won't believe what else Dad is doing. When he approached his seventy-fifth birthday, he lent his entrepreneurial talent to the music world and he's currently serving as board member of one of the world's top orchestras. Aside from that, he sings at family celebrations and he's even taking voice lessons. He's happy and he's made peace with himself and peace with us. All in all, we are lucky to have been born into a family business. Otherwise, who would have taught us, and what else would have taught us to get along with our father? You should talk with him. Go and see how much fun he's having now, at his age!"

In his later years, Jacob had rekindled his personal development via the family business and his vision. He found a way, using his ability as a successful businessman, to "raise" his children anew.

The whole family journey had been worthwhile for all involved, giving the sons a quintessential opportunity to learn from their dad at his best.

Leaving a family business is often more difficult than staying. It is interesting to note that family members that do leave, often end up building their own family business, which is essentially another way of staying in the "family business." Others that leave the family nest may unfortunately end up becoming the black sheep of the family. Leaving a family business is like giving up a fundamental part of one's heritage, and often parents are not able to give children their blessing to leave. Current family business trends show a tendency of giving children more freedom to explore their roles within, or parallel to, the family business without losing the family heritage.

For some people leaving a family business is worse than cheating on a wife or a husband – an act so inconceivable, akin to slapping one's parents in the face. For some the sense of duty is so deep that it seems almost to be engraved in the family's gene pool.

It is interesting to note how often children of family businesses marry other children of family businesses. It's as if they gaze deep into one another's souls and are drawn together by virtue of their common ground. In many cases, they even set up a new family business of their own. Possibly this feeling of having come from similar organizational-emotional systems draws them to repeat the experience as they discover that they too have inherited the family's entrepreneurial-business talents.

Lisa and Dan got married after a long courtship. A year after their wedding, they decided to realize their romantic dream of starting a business together. Neither anticipated that beneath the surface of their professional aspirations, lay in-depth repair work on family and business matters that had gone awry in previous generations. In the background hovered Lisa's father's nostalgia for his family's bakery business, and the quiet yearnings of Dan's father for his grandfather's leather business. Added to this were their natural talents and their strong entrepreneurship skills, their aversion to working under superiors in hierarchical structures, and their dream of creating something together.

"We were naive and innocent," said Dan, "like two fledgling chicks. We set up a company that was supposed to become a thriving cosmetics business within a few years. However, before we managed to get our feet off the ground, we were already mired in competition. There was competition between the two of us, and sometimes, we even ended up competing over the same customers."

"Being a couple provided a fruitful foundation that enabled the company to quickly develop," agreed Lisa. "Over the years, although the company grew and profited, our emotional space as a couple, and for ourselves, kept on shrinking. Our cozy economic incubator had become too crowded and noisy. Gradually, we began having trouble being supportive of one another. Eventually, we began to realize that deep-seated anger was dividing us, and the business had taken the joy out of our lives. We woke up to find ourselves stuck in roles that we hadn't planned on choosing, in what was, after all our own business.

"We took the competitive issue out of the closet. There was no other way. At first, it didn't help much. Dan distanced himself and shut me out. He worked alone, at night. I was left alone with the kids, and reviewed the balance sheets at home. I knew I was running myself down. Dan and I as a couple had succeeded in building a commercial empire, but we were slowly killing each other. Every day I would ask myself, over and over, why in heaven I needed this business? Was I doomed to go on competing with my husband in the company we'd created together?"

"At the same time," she went on, "as Dan took the trouble to point out, that if it hadn't been for the company, he'd have chucked the marriage long since just like his father had done. When I was at the depths of despair, he reminded me that many couples go through stages of competition and crisis."

'Maybe actually being a couple twice over, in the family and in the business, is keeping us going,' he would say to me, 'you don't go and break up a business in such a hurry...'

"For me, that was the only ray of hope at that point," noted Lisa. "I had no idea what to do. I thought maybe we should get a divorce and sell the business. I even thought about taking a lover. I contemplated leaving the business and starting a new one of my own, or even finding work in another company. I considered trying to stay married and just selling the business, so that each of us could go his own way. I even thought of choosing new vocational directions. Yet in spite of everything I went through, in the end, I always came back to my desire to keep the business. I knew I was in the right place, but I wasn't sure I was with the right partner. It was then, that I understood that our partnership was in desperate need of professional evaluation and direction."

"I felt terrible, too," added Dan. "Yet, despite everything, I still believe in us and in the business. I'm sure that what we have already achieved together is unequivocal proof that we have a great partnership. I am convinced that we're going through a marital crisis, and that everything is intensified because in our work together, we failed to sort out unspoken conflicts and hidden issues. I feel that our commitment to the business can help us solve our problems and keep us from self destruction. Bear in mind that we bear a complex burden – we are parents, business owners, managers, and professional chemists – and we live together."

Most of my work with this couple was carried out by being a facilitator to their dialogue and offering them conflict-solving tools. We defined their strengths and weaknesses in order to create clear role differentiation, and we built professional tools with strict corporate protocols and timetables for board, management, and sales meetings.

All of this eventually enabled a healthy separation of their professional lives from their private ones, and the process led them to clear conclusions. Dan was seriously committed to the business and to his marriage, and Lisa began focusing on rebuilding the business and their emotional life. In this area, marital counseling had proved to be an effective tool for solving their marriage.

As the couple continued working through constructive dialogue regarding their roles within the business, they began defining the changes they wanted to make. Next they redefined their roles – in their marriage, as parents, and on the job. Dan wanted to hire a professional CEO, and Lisa wanted to hire a professional chemist who would be responsible for product development. Lisa was also interested in taking two years off to study business administration, so she could develop her talents in finance and marketing. That suited Dan who also wanted to try investing outside the family business in a start-up with an old friend.

Towards the end of our sessions, Lisa noted, "It's interesting. We underwent a process parallel to what people go through as parents of a grown child who no longer needs them on a daily basis. All the child needs at that point is for someone to keep an eye on him from afar, love him, and give him advice when asked for. That's how it is now with our business… Only through this serious crisis were we able to grow, but it was worth it, and the business gave us a platform that made it possible."

I spent many productive sessions with Lisa and Dan in exploring their respective family Genograms regarding marital relationships and business partnerships. We discovered that on both sides of the families, whenever a set of parents confronted a crisis, it usually ended up in some form of breakup. Dan and

Lisa managed to decode their family DNA patterns and transform their crisis into a growth process. They acquired the fundamental gift of self and mutual respect without which no partnership can survive, and they earned life-saving tools for solving future partnership dilemmas and challenges.

There are cases when a family business provides a training ground for personal development in other spheres. Rachel's journey was about femininity.

Rachel was a leading member of a prestigious family business with a global track record of achievements. A charismatic and attractive woman in the prime of life, Rachel wanted to actualize her personal vision of global management, while preserving her femininity in a male dominated world.

However, there was a frightened little girl trapped inside her who wanted very much to perform on stage but was terrified of the spotlight. She suffered from recurring nightmares and was haunted by childhood memories of absent parents and a sister who had constantly dominated and taunted her.

Although her older sister teased her mercilessly, she had always been there for her, and deep down Rachel both adored and needed her. The sibling bond was so powerful that Rachel felt with or without her sister, she was damned if she did and damned if she didn't.

"When our parents died," Rachel explained patiently, "we literally became the business. The business was the core of our identity. I knew that I was part of a giant corporation that gave us a strong sense of belonging. The sky was the limit, and the bonds of family and business empowered me to believe I could conquer the world."

The business owned by Rachel's family was already a large corporation by the time she reached the age of twenty. The business demanded excessive investment from each of the family members and left little time and space for their individual needs. As Rachel related the whole complex saga, which bore the unmistakable imprint of the strong will and tremendous drive of her family, I felt her inner strength and the tremendous power that comes from growing up in such a family. When she opened up and told me about her stern upbringing, I was struck at how she had inherited the stamina and willpower to survive against all odds.

At the beginning of her career, the path Rachel would follow was clear. She was going to lead the business. Yet, at a certain point she felt the need to make her own decisions and steer her own course in life. She knew something was missing.

"I tried to develop the woman inside me," she remembered twenty years later, "but I couldn't. Originally when I joined the business, I emulated models of masculine aggression, yet I never felt at ease in this role. I wanted to be in the business, but I didn't want to play the role of the protagonist. I had always imagined myself as an intuitive, feminine leader and a valuable team player. I wanted to be different from my mother and father, whose management style was rigid and dictatorial. But in reality, I wasn't able to change my management style; I felt frustrated and unfulfilled and this projected into other areas of my life. After I was divorced, I couldn't go on paying the price any longer. I felt that I needed to distance myself physically and separate from my family legacy for a while, in order to return to the fold."

I empathized with Rachel who had been searching for her own identity and her own way. She had clearly understood that her need to leave the familiar and go far away would facilitate a complete transformation that would eventually enable her to be at ease with herself and allow her final return to the family business. Her words reminded me of a verse from Genesis, "Therefore a man leaves his father and his mother and clings to his wife, and they become one flesh."

"What made you so sure you would return one day?" I asked her.

"I knew all along that being in the family business was my destiny."

So Rachel decided to break out of the gilded family cage and move abroad. She handed over management to her sister and took a time-out from the family business. Distance, a second marriage, and a thriving career in Community Transformations demanded that she examined the reality of her life from outside of the family business.

"I went abroad," she told me, "because I felt that remaining in the same country as my parents would mean having my personality wiped out. The transition itself was difficult. I felt like a little mermaid, who in order to find love, was forced to live on land. I felt confused about what role to play – a child, a woman, a man, a leader. Who was I? I needed to learn to accept my weaknesses as well as my strengths, and the things in me that my mother never loved."

"Do you think that maybe she didn't love the little child in herself either?" I said, trying to get things into focus.

"My mother was part of the generation who considered 'their duty' to be their top priority," said Rachel, having trouble accepting my attempt to soften things. "When she came into the business, side by side with my father, she had to prove herself. She committed herself totally and paid a heavy price for it. She gave up motherhood, femininity, her emotional needs, and maybe even her marriage. She wanted to be a success.

"I, on the other hand wasn't willing to pay the price she had paid. I wanted more, but didn't know how. I felt that if I could achieve success out there in the real world, far from my family's judgmental eyes, only then could I go back. Now, at midlife, after a rewarding career in Community Transformations, I've returned to the family business as a more whole person with an individual operating style that perfectly suits me. Today, I know that only my wider understanding of my true calling brought me home to the family business."

Through our work together, Rachel discovered that for her, returning to the family business was a refreshing path towards new growth. After so many years away from the business, she had acquired a kind of internal mirror that helped her to find her own truth.

"For the first time ever, I have business partners whom I've known all my life. Now I can accept criticism in a professional context because I know that it's not related to a family argument from last night. At last, I'm able to examine the way the business operates objectively. I can also give free rein to new skills and initiatives that I had once considered to be my sister's exclusive domain. I discovered that the family business, which at a certain stage had impeded my development, was as necessary to me as the air I breathe."

A family business can be an excellent framework for self-actualization and a training ground for personal fulfillment, family bonds, and vision quests. A family business is a life drama where family members play their roles nurtured by values and passion, love and hate, jealousy and greed, loyalty and betrayal. Siblings, more than other family members, have a need to divide up the territory and separate roles and areas. Often when they don't, the frustration can ruin all the good aspects of their relationship. But when they do succeed, the reward is generally a more mature and committed partnership. Siblings can capitalize on the fact that they are united by a blood tie that signifies a shared heritage and shared values, in a way that's hard or even impossible for outsiders to recreate.

Based on their intense bonds of sisterhood, Rachel had set out on a long journey to build a new relationship with her sister. They committed themselves to a deep dialogue that only siblings can share. They discussed childhood incidents and adult conflicts openly, and they did it with love, courage, and a growing mutual respect.

"The space I vacated for myself and my sister enabled each of us to shape an individual yet powerful standing in the family business," Rachel related. "Creating a physical distance between us was a necessary blessing yet knowing we had each other provided support for a difficult separation. We were amazed at how the process of dialogue and change we underwent served as both a source of inspiration and as influence on those around us."

Rachel's words brought John Donne's poignant words to mind. "No man is an island, and entire of itself" he wrote," Every man is a piece of the continent…"

Chapter Fourteen

Integrating the Generations

Ongoing dialogue with my parents forged my vocational identity

Love is crucial for vocational self-fulfillment. Anyone who knows what love is, can draw on that passion and inner fire to generate the strength to create.

About a year ago, I met Esther, an eighty-year-old woman, in good health and full of energy, who had never worked outside the home. All her life she had kept herself busy trying to write, paint, and sculpt. Yet, she always managed to get stuck halfway through her creations. Esther was sent to me by her fifty-year old daughter, who was on the verge of key, personal changes. She was about to make a career breakthrough and her marriage seemed to be getting a new lease on life. This was a typical case featuring a daughter who moves beyond career impasse and thereby causes her mother to reevaluate her own vocational impasse.

"My mother wanted to meet you," Esther's daughter told me, "and consult with you about her career." I welcomed this initiative since I am a strong believer in the energy that is transferred from parent to child via intergenerational connections.

"I wanted to ask you something," said eighty-year-old Esther, "even though it may be too late. Could the fact that I never really experienced love be connected to the fact that I never built a career, nor found my true calling?"

I was astounded. The statement displayed such deep wisdom. It had taken me many years of inner work to reach the wisdom that Esther had discovered. "I was born in Poland and left over seventy years ago. About ten years ago," continued Esther, "I went back to Poland for the first time, and one day, I walked into a cathedral garden in the center of Krakow. I sat down on a bench and my attention was caught by an elderly, impressive looking priest, who walked in my direction, holding a huge bunch of white and lilac lilies. All my years of living outside Poland, I yearned for the colors and the smell of my favorite flowers, and suddenly there they were.

"I don't believe it, what beautiful flowers,' I yelled spontaneously, and the priest, as if following my lead, turned around, and gently offered me the flowers. This was the beginning of the closest friendship that I had ever experienced in my life. I had found my soul mate. We only met twice in our lives since that first meeting, but our mutual love of words led to a literary correspondence, that lasted over a decade. It dawned on me that our love was the source that inspired me to connect to my dormant passion for writing. Two months ago he passed away, and now that I'm writing a book of poems, it dawned on me that perhaps this rare friendship had actually been the messenger that finally allowed me to connect with my true passion for writing."

Esther reminded me of Marie, a patient of mine who had been ill with cancer. Although she'd been offered all kinds of treatment, Marie didn't want any of them. "Why not?" I had asked her. "You're not even fifty yet."

Marie gazed at me sadly and said, "I realized that I would never be able to love or let someone love me... I've tried so hard... but I've never known love... There's no point in living that way. Maybe, I'm not equipped to do anything creative..."

Often, fulfillment in love is not only the secret of life, but also the secret of a meaningful career.

Marie was a talented journalist who loved to cook. Her mother had taught her the joy of cooking, but not the art of words. Over the years, Marie stopped cooking. Ironically, it was her success as a journalist that strangled her true calling, the work that connected her to her roots and through which she had been able to express a wide range of feelings and desires. It was only when she became ill with leukemia that she went back to cooking. Through cooking, she reconnected with herself and her sources.

"The words I wrote as a journalist," she told me, "never came from my soul. They came from my head. Only cooking healed me. I went back to selecting ingredients and creating new recipes. I even began competing all over again with my mother via cooking, and reading books on the subject. I returned to the games of my girlhood. You could say that I went back to being healthy. For me, cooking became the quintessential statement of love and life."

Marie understood that journalism was a success story she owed her father, who had been a teacher and a great admirer of the written word. Cooking for her represented the taste of love.

Since the incapacity to find fulfillment in life and work may be traceable to a loving relationship we missed out on, renewing the capacity for fulfillment may sometimes hinge on rehabilitating a love relationship. Sometimes, this can be a repairing a bond with a parent who was stuck somewhere, somehow, and wasn't able to parent lovingly.

Nora came for counseling at the height of a love crisis that was related to both her management career and the way in which she related to herself. Nora was searching for a way towards renewing her relationships. She believed that this was an opportunity to succeed, and she spoke with the self-confidence that came with being her father's favorite daughter. Later on, she was also courageous enough not to give up on her relationship with her mother.

Nora was a well-known executive in a large financial corporation. When we met, Nora came across as tough, yet extremely well cared for; she wore a tailored suit that did little to conceal the excitement gripping her.

"My father wanted a son," she told me in one of our early sessions, "but his first born was a girl. I was born next, so I think, my father decided that I would be 'his special son.'"

I smiled to myself and thought how much power we derive from the knowledge that Daddy or Mommy chose us above the others, making us special and perhaps more loved.

Over four decades of experience, I have found that behind every successful achiever in a particular field, you will often find a supportive parent who chose the child, believed in the child, promoted the child, and offered continuous support.

"I was married once but it's only now, at forty, that I've fallen in love with a man for the first time in my life," Nora told me.

Yet, it was at this stage, that Nora found herself at a career impasse. She didn't want to manage people any more, couldn't get out of bed in the morning, sabotaged her own work, was blind to opportunities, and made bad decisions on critical issues.

Nora was in love, but also very confused. "I don't understand what's happened to me. Suddenly I want to change professions... So what if I fell in love? What the heck is going on here?"

This impeccably dressed woman had a curious expression on her face, a combination of distress alternating with happiness. I could feel how happy she was in her love affair and what a release it was for her, and yet, she projected a sense of pressure and confusion regarding her work.

My intuition warned me to be cautious. This wasn't simply a situation of a woman at forty being in love for the first time. There was something more here.

I have rarely met a serious female executive who had not been

Daddy's favorite girl. Today, although increasingly more female managers in the market have mothers who were also female managers, and for whom being in a management position comes more naturally, they are a different breed. Nora reminded me of the tough female executives who work in conservative male-dominated organizations.

Nora's bright, alert eyes communicated a quiet and self-confident intelligence, yet beneath the surface I could feel the pain of a person at impasse.

"Tell me what you are going through?" I asked her.

"I feel an inner turmoil," she sighed in a tired voice, "that's been with me for ages. I've never completely understood it, because I was always such a winner."

"Was there anyone in your family who wasn't considered successful?"

This intrusive remark was intended to have an impact. In my experience, successful favorite daughters of fathers bear the pain of their mothers who in many cases did not make it in life and lacked a sense of fulfillment. Their pain and disappointment was often unbearable for their daughters. Often these mothers just let go and sacrificed their needs, as if they had given up on their husbands, their marriage, love, and finally on their daughters, too. These mothers find it hard to get through to their daughters; nor is there any great joy in being in their company. On the other hand, the "abandoned husband" and father of these daughters, focuses most of his attention on the favorite daughter, who renounces her mother, even if the loss is painful and the vacuum is vast. Sometimes these daughters can turns into lonely women, regardless of whatever career success they may have achieved.

"In the past, whenever I was stuck, I was able to recognize my impasse and solve it on my own," said Nora. "This time it's different," she continued thoughtfully.

"How is it different this time?" I asked her.

Nora explained to me that now that she had finally fallen in love, her whole perspective had changed. She realized that from an early age, she had always solved major problems together with her father, and it had taken her a long time to figure out that she was still behaving as if she were at Daddy's side. This was reflected at work by her constant searching for a senior male manager to lean on.

"Once I realized that I wasn't actually able to manage on my own," she continued, "I gradually found the strength to enhance my independence and taught myself to take complete responsibility for people and events. I consulted less with others, and stopped requesting permission from my CEO or the Board… Within a year, I became the CEO of the company."

"And did you get your father's permission for that?" I asked.

"Are you serious?" Nora burst into tears. "He never even realized what the problem was… It's so hard to manage alone, to be a grown up and let go of this fatherly protective warmth."

I felt that Nora was recalling the old pain of letting go of her father's strong embrace. Her crying represented the tough struggle necessary in order to achieve permission to grow differently and find her own way.

"It seems to me now," added Nora when she'd calmed down somewhat, "that this was only the beginning of the next struggle. I feel that there's another phase waiting for me."

I wondered whether Nora was ready to move towards a new kind of connection – this time with her mother. I wondered whether this time, she would be able to do it through love and acceptance rather than through frustration.

I sensed that Nora had already begun walking that path, even if she had not yet defined for herself what it entailed and where she was heading.

"Nora," I said, "tell me about your mother."

She gazed at me, her blue eyes clouding over. "My mother came from a good family. A very cultured woman, she was always fashionably dressed and her life revolved around doing what she called 'her duty'. I never knew what really moved her. Deep down, I somehow sensed that she resented 'doing her duties' and that she yearned for something different. I absorbed all of this and knew that I would live my own life differently.

"My mother," Nora continued, recalling the past, "was the daughter of a wealthy textile producer, and she married my father, who was himself a wealthy, respected, textile industry personality. It seemed to me that her marriage was the point where her mission in life had got stuck. Although she didn't work, she was somehow never really with us and we never seemed to please her. Rarely were we able to figure out what she wanted from any of us. I doubt whether she even knew what she wanted from herself," Nora paused, and then continued reflectively, "I think that exploring one's desires is something that also has to be learned, and I think I want to expand my understanding of this concept."

I waited through a brief silence. "You know," said Nora, turning to me again, "my mother lived in a kind of emotional coma. She's still a very bright woman, whose opinion of a book or any other cultural event is a pleasure to hear. But that's it, and beyond that, you can't get much more out of her. What a waste. Maybe only now I'm beginning to grow up, along with my own teenage daughter. Everything is so confusing, yet so interconnected. It's really sad, you know, looking at mom's life. She totally missed out! That's why I'm not willing to live my life like that. You have to help me."

I smiled at her and said: "Even if your mother did miss the boat, that doesn't mean that you can't do things differently. It's definitely possible, although it's not easy. Especially because of the jealousy."

"What jealousy?" retorted Nora loudly.

I was in no rush to give her the answer. Daddy's girls know a lot about jealousy, especially about mothers' jealousy of their daughters. And they also envy other people's ability to love fully and be totally passionate about their vocation. It is my belief that the two are related.

My sessions with Nora continued. Her love affair blossomed and developed into a fulfilling adult relationship. It was impossible not to see the new softness she radiated. At the same time, she began facing up to the painful subject of her mother's boredom and dissatisfaction with life.

Gradually, Nora understood that in some way, her mother had actually allowed her the space for vocational expression. Perhaps she had wanted her to have what she had missed out on in life. From within her closed emotional life, her mother had allowed Nora's father to act as a loving mentor to their daughter. Still, as Nora learned later on, there was always a quiet envy as well, passive yet perceptible. In my experience, mothers who don't take ownership of their own careers are rarely able to support their daughters in their quest for vocational fulfillment. This may lead to some of these daughters ending up missing their true calling in spite of the fact that they have created successful careers. Not every successful career engenders a sense of finding and fulfilling one's calling.

I shared my thoughts with Nora, and we went on exploring the triangular relationship between a father, a mother, and a daughter. Having lived through a similar triangle, it was relatively easy for me to empathize with Nora, and I felt reasonably qualified to walk her all the way to permission.

"I understand that your mother gave up a close relationship with you," I told her, "yet she never gave up on you and it's clear that she took great pride in your accomplishments."

"You're right," she said, smiling at me for the first time, "my mother was very proud of me and of my career accomplishments when talking to other people. However she was unable to convey the message of how to become a fulfilled woman; something she had never succeeded at herself. From her perspective, it was all right for me to have a flourishing career, but to be both satisfied with work and love – that was too much for her, and too much for me…but actually, the dissatisfaction is hers! Not mine! There's no reason for me not to be happily in love."

"The freedom of choice is yours," I quietly concurred

As the weeks passed, Nora was able to become more in touch with her feelings – as a mother, as a woman, as a lover and as a friend – without disrupting her success at work. Her goal was to connect all the elements together into a new triangle: to love and be loved; lead a happy relationship with her lover; and enjoy a thriving career.

At this point, Nora was ready to continue exploring her vocational world. I felt that here the professional management challenges would be easier and clearer for her to deal with. We began to explore how well her management style suited her personality, her individual goals, and the current goals of the company she worked at. Our target was to determine whether Nora was in the right place at the right time. Gradually, she recognized that her inherent management style was not suited to her current position and that she wanted to move on to something new and different. Nora wanted to work in an organization that would be more sophisticated, more team oriented, and more attentive to peoples' needs.

She was ready for the journey. "What path are we going to take?" she asked me.

"You decide," I told her, relieved, "My impression is that you already know…"

A transition from a "masculine" to "feminine" management style is often made by female managers in midlife. Sometimes, they do this while rediscovering their femininity, and often as part of a renewed attachment to their life partner. Others change their work context: from employee to employer; from a local position to a global position; from the government sector to the private sector; and so forth.

Nora was surprised when I shared all of this, "So that means a change in the way I view my position in my own family can also be an opening for changing my position at work. From here I can redirect not only my management style, but also its scope and context."

"They're all interconnected," I said, "If you can manage your relationships with members of your family differently, you can also manage your superiors, your peers and your employees differently. And it works the other way round too – if your chosen training ground is the workplace and a change takes place there, this will also influence your relationships with the people close to you. When you acquire new skills in one particular area of your life, other areas of your life will change as well."

A few months went by and Nora, who had become aware of how much she lacked having a close bond with her mother and with her older sister, now felt ready to contend with these painful feelings. Her older sister was a frustrated housewife, who only a year previously, had finally registered for a local jewelry designing course. More recently, she had even begun selling the jewelry she designed and created. I suggested that Nora consider the possibility that her unfulfilled sister's new vocational development might be nourishing both their yearning for feminine solidarity and the closeness they had lacked in their childhood. They began a dialogue of sharing childhood experiences which improved their capacity for a deeper love and mutual support culminating in the creation of a platform for evoking in both sisters a new need for vocational self-expression.

As their relationship evolved and they grew closer, both experienced improved relationships with their respective partners. After about six months, a period where Nora had begun dressing in a softer manner and looking much happier, she and her boyfriend were ready to tie the knot.

"You're looking lovely these days," I commented, smiling inwardly at how her femininity had blossomed so expressively since she had begun her journey.

Almost incidentally, Nora reflected: "Maybe, like so many women, I'll get involved in fashion? No, no! That's a silly idea. What were we talking about?" she embarrassedly tried to change the subject.

I pricked up my ears. One thing I've learned over the years, from my fellow seekers, is that critical thoughts are often said casually, as an aside or an afterthought, as if the person speaking refuses to acknowledge their importance.

I thought to myself how amazingly the human subconscious works. Sometimes our subconscious knows and indicates in the most subtle ways, what the future holds for us – and knows things long before we actually realize or are prepared to acknowledge and act upon them.

I knew that Nora's comment wasn't by chance. Even she knew that this ostensibly trivial remark would not pass without a response from me.

Still, I was cautious. I knew that the nature of my reaction was important. I dwelt on this silently, waiting for her reaction, and her acknowledgement of her inner truth.

And sure enough Nora obliged, "So what do think about me being in the fashion world?" she asked.

This comment reinforced my gut feeling about what was going on. Perhaps this was the link in the chain connecting her with her fashion-conscious mother; because if Nora's mother had had one passion, it was her passionate interest in fashion. Was this yet another step towards her mother, and her progress on the path towards getting closer to herself, her sister the jewelry designer, and her femininity?

Integrating her love of fashion with her professional talents and her experience was the perfect way for Nora to integrate all of her worlds: she wouldn't have to give up being Daddy's girl, and she could also express her love for her mother.

I answered her simply and precisely: "I will be one of your first and loyal clients! I have no doubt that you are perfectly equipped for the journey. Your mother is passionate about fashion and your father is passionate about the textile industry! You have great fashion sense and highly aesthetic taste," I stressed, encouraging her, "and if I add all your financial experience to the mix, it's a perfect match."

"Actually, now that I come to think of it, I've been going on about working in fashion for ages," said Nora hurriedly, "Did I mention that a few months ago, I renovated my grandmother's old house? She was a well-known seamstress in Vienna and afterwards here in Tel Aviv. After that I went out and bought fabrics and other supplies. It was so much fun. But, you know, just fun; a weekend thing."

I felt that she was a little overwhelmed. I saw joy in her eyes along with her great need for permission. She was bewildered by her buried talents and somewhat surprised that she had the potential to make her mother's and grandmother's dreams come true.

After a few months, Nora's grandmother's apartment became an intimate salon fashion concept, the first store of what was to become a top quality brand. Everything happened so fast – choosing the clothes, purchasing, displaying the goods, hiring saleswoman, and the rapid success at selling all of her designs. In time, Nora – Daddy's girl – was able to connect with her mother's characteristics that were appreciated by the entire family, including her father. At the same time, she was also able to walk her own path. She felt she had it all.

Leaving her job as a top financial executive was not easy for Nora, because a tough struggle still faced her. Making this change was not a simple one. While forging ahead on her new path, she didn't give up loving her father nor relinquish his companionship and help. His acceptance of her new direction and his willingness to stand behind her as a supportive parent, were for Nora part of the basic equipment needed for the journey. At the same time, for the first time in her life she also had her mother as a partner and source of assistance. At certain points, she asked her mother's opinion. Later on they evaluated new directions in design together and Nora delighted at the happiness she saw in her mother's eyes.

"This is a really healthy thing, a family renaissance," said Nora, by way of a thumbnail description of the entire process.

Nora's transformation occurred because she was able to listen to her inner wisdom. She looked inward and was able to reposition her parents, figuratively speaking. Her emotionally estranged mother finally granted her the permission to explore her self-expression. Simultaneously, she was finally able to see her father as an adult and not only as a father. This demanded a not inconsiderable effort on her part, both emotionally and conceptually. Once Nora had opened herself up to self-love and self-expression a new path had opened up simultaneously at work and towards her loved ones.

Folklore and traditions have always taught us that mothers give birth to us and teach us about emotions, relationships, and networking in everyday life. Clearly the mother's share is weightier in the day-to-day education in which the child's basic relationships and work style will be grounded.

Fathers tend to take the role of mentoring our vocational direction and teaching us survival skills. Indeed, we can see an example of this from ancient Rabbinic writings from the Talmud: "A father is obligated to do the following for his son: ... and to teach him a trade" (Kiddushin 29a-30a); "Anyone who does not teach his son a skill or profession may be regarded as if he is teaching him to steal" (Kiddushin 29a).

Of thousands of job evaluations and assessments I researched, about 80% stated that their mother had been the dominant force in their day-to-day education at home!

Indeed, in many cases where I was called in to consult male managers, we discovered that their relationship with their mothers played a key role in their professional development or impasse.

This was so in Neil's case. Neil came to me for counseling after he had experienced management burnout. When we began our journey, he was already at the age of forty, a successful financial maverick. His career was the center of his life and his reputation preceded him in global hi-tech circles. He had spearheaded one of the first Israeli investment offerings on Wall Street. Yet at some point, not as a consequence of any particular event that he could pinpoint, his career had begun to falter, his marriage became a desert, he found himself doing poorly as a father, and his friends disappeared. Suddenly his life was empty and Neil suspected that maybe he needed to reassess his career calling.

I gazed at his empty eyes in his impassive face that hung like a mask above his neck and I sensed that behind the loss of his passion for work was a far bigger loss: his joie de vivre had escaped him.

We discussed his career impasse, and then I asked him to tell me about his family. He reluctantly replied, "They barely influence my life. Why do you psychologists think people always have to go back to where they grew up?"

"Bear with me," I requested persuasively.

Uneasily, Neil agreed to cooperate, and laconically recited, "My father was a businessman. My mother, a housewife. I have an older brother, divorced, and a sister who is ten years younger than I am. My father was always supportive of me. My father didn't exactly miss the boat, but he wasn't exactly what you would call a fulfilled person. My mother is cold and critical. She definitely did not find a way to express her full talents. She looks really amazing, even now, at sixty-five. She is demanding, inflexible, doesn't listen, and gets angry a lot. Most of the time she skims along the surface of things."

Neil talked a lot about his father. All my attempts to talk with him about his mother were to no avail: "Forget my mother; it's a waste of time. There's no one to talk to. She doesn't care about anything; we have nothing in common."

After years of consulting male managers in similar predicaments, there was no mistaking it. Neil, the consummate professional who could solve global challenges of any kind, was a little boy inside yearning for a close bond with his mother. When I tried to explore if other women was an issue in his life, Neil answered: "I'm not interested in other women."

"Neil," I said carefully, "people can't live in a constant state of yearning."

To my surprise, Neil immediately made the connection, "I feel like I'm drying up," he said. "Maybe you're right. Maybe this really does go all the way back."

"You know, I didn't choose my career," he said. "When I was confused about my career direction, my father pushed me in a business management direction and my mother pushed me to accumulate power, money, and control – the conventional tools of successful men."

Neil belonged to a particular category of successful managers: the type, who has a successful manager-father, devoted to his son; and an emotionally inaccessible, though practical mother who is socially ambitious regarding her son. Such a mother is generally cut off from her son's emotional needs, but pushes him to a peak of achievement that demands his infinite investment. Such a mother's hidden message to her son is that only top-level accomplishments can bring her joy and pride.

"So where is my career stuck?" he asked stressfully. "I have the ability, and yet I'm frozen somehow. Something's holding me back. I'm not a nice guy right now. I cannot connect to my feelings. I'm constantly looking for something and I can't get any inner peace."

"Did you, at any point in your life, experience the sort of inner peace you're striving for?" I asked.

Neil was silent for a couple of minutes and then replied: "Yes. In love."

His reply surprised us both.

"And what happened to love?" I asked.

"I let it go. I didn't go all the way..."

"And when did love disappear from your work?"

Neil was able to see that every project he took on, he began with an obsessive commitment, and then would gradually lose his passion for the project by working far too hard.

"You know what I like about a start-up?" he asked rhetorically. "It's like falling in love, it begins with a fire that ignites and burns passionately, and if you don't nurture it with loving care, it begins to slowly burn out..."

Neil talked in terms of love, sex, pregnancy, birth, and parenting. I felt his infinite longing for the source, the beginning, the mother-child bond. Neil yearned for that stage of merging between the mother and the infant – as in pregnancy, or in nursing. He wanted to be with her, to be one with her. Maybe somehow, he even longed to be the mother giving birth... if she wasn't able to be there for him, he would be her... he would take her role...

I dithered and hesitated. I wasn't sure how to go on from there.

"When did you last have a heart-to-heart conversation with your mother?" I said, trying to approach from another angle.

Neil was surprised. "I don't have conversations with my mother," he said furiously, "I fire off two or three words and that's it. Period!"

"Interesting," I said, "you behave just like her, or more accurately, exactly the way you describe her," I said with aggravating decisiveness. Neil was very surprised, even amused.

I didn't budge. "Behaving like an unattainable parent is another way to get close to her. It's also the beginning of your accepting your mother as a woman and maybe also as a person."

Neil reluctantly understood that in recent years, in spite of himself, he had gradually become similar to the image he associated with his mother; distant and cold, alienated and critical, cynical and lonely. Just like her, his contact with the world had become superficial.

Recognizing his need to connect with the tough qualities of his mother's character was an almost impossible mission for him. Yet this recognition embodied his coming to terms with his mother, and with some of her negative traits, that he had consciously rejected, and yet unconsciously imitated in his own behavior.

"Tell me more about your mother," I asked again.

Gradually, Neil agreed to talk about his mother. "My mother is a very talented woman," he said again. "She lost her own mother when she was three, and was raised by a stepmother who largely ignored her. Her stepmother married her off to an older man, and she immediately bore him a son. Evidently she remained fairly immature and after almost ignoring her firstborn, she sort of transformed me, her second son, into the one who'd fulfill her expectations."

Neil began to "get acquainted" with his mother, one adult to another, and not merely through the eyes of an abandoned child yearning for attachment.

He gradually began to notice when he was "behaving like my mother," which of late he had been doing more and more, as if against his will. By learning to accept this kind of behavior on the one hand, and finding alternatives on the other, Neil moved a little closer to her world.

"Recently, I've begun speaking more than two words at a time to her. I ask her about herself, I can even see her fear of loneliness and her inability to be close to people..." related Neil cautiously.

As Neil slowly began to re-experience his work as a source of stability and creativity, he began to explore his other relationships. He was slowly becoming aware of the positive elements his mother had contributed to his life such as his ability to analyze, plan, control and succeed.

"Suddenly a new clarity dawned on me; I had to please my mother all the time," said Neil. "I simply couldn't afford to let her down in any way."

Neil had a lot in common with Nora – the need to connect with the parent that he had rejected. At this point, like Nora, Neil felt that he was fully committed to success and he set up an investment company for seed companies which gained him a renewed reputation as a start-up guru. However, unlike Nora, he was still not ready to fully enjoy love. As far as many of his investments went, he either left at the start-up stage or successfully raised a lot of capital by selling them off.

Neil was only able to bond with himself and with his mother to a certain extent and realized that he still had a longer path to travel. At this stage of our journey, he needed the freedom to walk his path alone. Maybe, it was not yet possible for Neil to take a more profound journey. It was too demanding for him at that time in his life. I often wonder, when I think of him, why despite his immense effort, I had expected so much more from him in terms of love and relationships. Perhaps I, like his mother, had somehow let him down too.

The relationships between parents and children, similarity and individuality, fulfillment and success, are deep and wide. Work gives us the opportunity to comprehensively integrate all the dimensions of our inner worlds – those we come to terms with and those we don't. Those that are complex for us demand a special acceptance and a true inner dialogue in order to get in touch with ourselves. Our identity is built like a pyramid, based on the relationship between our parents, the relationship between each of them and us, and our relationship with significant others in our lives. Once we are able to finally connect our inner worlds in a way that is acceptable to our souls, we will be able to find and shape a more rewarding journey that grants us fulfillment in our love lives, our careers, and our calling.

Appendix: How to Read my Roadmap

....

The journey beyond impasse

At different stages of our lives, many of us may encounter varying degrees of dissatisfaction with our position in life, while feeling clueless about what to do about it. If that description fits you then the first question to consider should always be: If you had no limitations whatsoever to worry about, what would you choose to do? If no obstacles, real or imagined, were placed in your way, what would you dream of accomplishing?

An honest answer to these questions will enable you to take a look at what you would really like to do with your life. Once you rid yourself of pretense, fear, and lack of faith, you will be able to see your real objectives. Furthermore, you will be able to identify what you consider to be your limiting circumstances. These insights are the raw material for the preparatory work of what needs to be changed. Certain elements in your life that you believed to be ongoing, may turn out not to be. You may also uncover fears or expectations that may have been holding you back. New ideas may surface, directly or indirectly, for example when you say things like, "I love philosophy, but being in high-tech – now that's a good profession."

Not every high-tech professional makes money and not every

philosopher is poor. It is the extent of the match between the individual and his/her work that is the determining factor. The more attention you are able to pay to your core needs, the more success you'll have. That is the key to being productive and creative in a fluid, competitive market where a rapid and precise response to changing needs is required.

Generally people know deep down what they really want to do, and thus a person who creates an accommodating environment with a supportive network promotes the ability to develop and create a more focused vocational choice.

Impasse is an evolutionary part of our growth and development as a human being. Vocational impasse is not necessarily a symbol of failure. It can be an opportunity to stop and listen to our inner voice and needs while helping us to recognize crucial patterns of behavior. Being aware of and identifying repetitive patterns may help us to understand what brought us to burnout and what may lead us to new growth. Impasse is an end and a beginning – often painful, confusing and frustrating. However if we face up to it – welcome it and deal with it – it will only leave us enriched.

"I'll never forget," related Fred, a veteran reporter at a leading daily newspaper, "how I used to lie on the grass, looking at the clouds and make up stories. I would lie there like that for hours. In the intervening years, nothing has really changed. I'm still dealing with stories, only now I put them in writing and enjoy every moment. The pleasure hasn't changed in all these years, nor has my profession. But it took me a long time to recognize that this was my choice. Before that, I was always broke and always busy looking for different ways to make a living…"

From my experience, I have noticed that somewhere between the ages of four and six a turning point occurs. At this stage, children begin asking questions about their gender, about whom they resemble, and about what they want to do when they grow up. At that age, however children talk in generalized stereotypes regarding professions: boys want to be policemen, astronauts, or sportsmen, while girls want to be actresses, models, or singers – or both tend to quote their parents' professions. Still, by observing the array of activities a child prefers and enjoys doing – for example, whether it's telling stories, assembling games, bossing/leading other children – we can equip a child to make better choices, even at an early age. In the process of working on their careers, adults I have counseled, have recalled that at the age of five or so they already knew what they wanted to do, yet most of them didn't think it was possible, because they were told 'that's not a decent profession'.

Fred, as noted, personifies a person who from a young age had the permission to follow his heart's desire. Creating worlds and stories by gazing at the clouds was actually a form of expression, and many years later it became his way of life. Fred derived great pleasure from his right to individual expression, and his parents respected this. His first "articles" were in fact written at the age of five. Fred was practicing the skills and techniques of creative expression while lying on the grass and playing with words. Twenty years down the road the tools had changed, but the same creative imagination was still serving him well. It took Fred a while to understand that the stories and his journalism were the same thing. It was only years after working as a journalist that he was retroactively able to "give himself permission" to integrate his hobby with his career and enjoy it.

DEFINING YOUR VOCATIONAL IMPASSE
A. WHY AM I STUCK?
B. WHERE AM I STUCK?
C. HOW CAN I MOVE ON?

A. WHY AM I STUCK?
Ten Categories of Vocational Impasse
The following ten categories of vocational impasse are based on experience drawn from observation of my patients' journeys. It is important to note that further categories do exist, but I have chosen the following categories as the basic examples for a starting point.

1. I am "forbidden" from realizing my true career choice.
Unlike Fred, who knew and chose what he loved to do, Erik knew what he wanted but felt that realizing his wish was somehow forbidden. A successful financier, Erik came to me at age fifty, looking for a career change. Though successful in his work, he felt vocationally stuck. "I just don't know what I'd really like to do," he told me.

"If you had no limitations and could make your career dream come true," queried I, trotting out the magic question. "What would you choose to do?"

"I don't know," said Erik, "but I know what I want to do when I retire."

"What's that?"

""I'd like to study philosophy and work in education," he said decisively. "The truth is, I'd like to be a philosopher."

"What makes you feel you are not a philosopher already?" I pursued.

"Oh, come on, there's no way I could go and study now. I was never a great student. But you know what? Even if I don't study philosophy, deep down, I'll always be a philosopher."

Erik's psychometric assessment showed a very high learning

ability and a pronounced bent for culture, education, and abstract thought. Since Erik was financially independent he could afford to work part time and begin studying right away. We both knew the path was there for him to walk. The choice was in his hands.

"Who's keeping you from choosing freely right here, right now?" I asked him.

"I don't know," he answered. "I just feel stuck; something is prohibiting me from following my true choice. Maybe I'm not allowed to. How can a respectable middle-aged man suddenly go and do whatever he pleases?"

"Why not?"

"You know what? I always thought that when I would retire, I would be able to study philosophy – so why not now?"

It was the start of a long, hard road. His difficulty with permitting himself to reach for fulfillment was embedded in the past. Erik had to struggle, not only with himself, but also with his dead father, who eighty years earlier had lost his own father and been obliged to make an overnight transformation from outstanding student – a real philosopher – to family breadwinner.

"Even after he became wealthy," Erik recalled, "his eyes shone with excitement every time I discussed philosophy with him. Then very quickly the light would be extinguished and he would say, 'Let's cut this nonsense and deal with reality.' We both knew that he dreamed about philosophy, ethics, and the human spirit. But how could someone with a family to support allow himself to spend time on this sort of spiritual luxury? In those days, I guess people didn't think in terms of integrating philosophy with making a living."

Erik adopted his father's prohibition. He came up against the classic conflict of the unfulfilled parent – the parent who wants to see their offspring's dreams come true, but can't let it happen. The inner pain and the unconscious jealousy are connected with the parent's feelings of having missed out themselves. Parents for whom permission was denied to fulfill their true choices are in turn unable to hand it down to their children.

Erik was one of those people whose careers were stuck even though they knew what they really wanted to do. Their inner inability to gain self-actualization generally derives from their identification with a vocationally unfulfilled, frustrated parent with whom the child wouldn't want to compete.

2. I am "forbidden" to know that it is my right to choose.

This category describes people who are not allowed to know what they want to do and how or what to choose. This often happens to children whose parents are divorced, formally or emotionally.

Tammy described her parents' "emotional divorce" very clearly: "I can recall when in the middle of a family conversation they would suddenly ask me: 'Tammy, sweetheart, who do you love more, Mommy or Daddy?' I never answered. I thought that if I said that I loved one of them more, something terrible would happen and one of them would leave home. I felt as if it would be like choosing only one of them, and therefore it was impossible for me to answer."

Tammy learned not to choose. She didn't know how to choose a name for her daughter, she couldn't decide whether to order meat or fish at a restaurant, and she was ambivalent about what to major in at college. Her inability to choose, dating back to her childhood, infringed on every imaginable sphere of her life. Through intensive counseling, comprehension slowly dawned on Tammy that no child can hold together their parents' failing marriage.

The prohibition on knowing and choosing can also come from another source – our own sense of responsibility. Choice and self-knowledge imply action. Many people have trouble implementing the necessary action. From an early age they learn that not knowing is preferable: when you don't know, you don't have to make a choice; and thus there is no need to implement a responsible action.

Change also requires the assimilating of new knowledge, and incorporating it as Tammy did, when she understood that she couldn't save her parents' marriage. Unlike Tammy, Fred's prohibition was manifested in the way he related to his actions. For Fred, the journalist, knowing what he wanted was linked with the permission to choose and the obligation to act; once he knew, he would have to do something about it. When not knowing is a person's primary, existential defense, knowing becomes a threat.

To know what you want means being committed to act upon it. Taking action leads to performance which in turn implies a measurable benchmark of success or failure.

3. I don't know what to choose or what to do.

This category describes people who opt not to know what they want to do, period. The most famous of these is Peter Pan. Being grounded in reality certainly doesn't appeal to Peter Pan; free flight without commitment is his preferred lifestyle. Peter surrounds himself with children, almost as if it's his unpaid calling. Possibly not even one of the millions of children who have come to love Peter Pan over the years has ever asked the question: What does Peter Pan do? What is his job?

The eternal student who can never commit is the modern incarnation of the Peter Pan character. He rambles around from one faculty to another, constantly changing courses, and when asked what he does for a living falls back on the standard reply, "I'm still at university." In other words, "I haven't chosen yet, because I still don't know."

The 'I don't know' category also includes children who are obedient to their parents' vocational wishes and, later on, to social mores. Many of the best of these become dissatisfied teachers, doctors and engineers, choosing vocations that are expected of them, yet often deny their inner needs. This may lead to chronic dissatisfaction and a never-ending search for career fulfillment.

Naomi was a typical "good daughter" who didn't know what to choose. She had been sent to study at a teachers training college, a presupposed track that would enable her to make a respectable living and be a good wife. Lacking maturity, Naomi was unable to oppose the vocational course chosen for her by her parents, who knew very little of her inner world and her deepest needs. Since Naomi had little self-confidence, she accepted the choice her parents made and became an average, ordinary teacher. Only when she recognized that a fulfilled career is all about identifying one's needs, did she understand that she was allowed to take responsibility for the path she would walk and the vocation she would pursue.

My own father, himself a frustrated teacher, told me more than once, "Forget about all this psychology stuff and go be a teacher. Teaching has everything: a reasonable salary, vacations, and women who help each other." When I qualified with a Masters Degree in Clinical Psychology, something to make any parent proud, my father mildly disappointed, and perhaps slightly envious, said to me, "So does that mean you're not going to be a teacher?" And I, to comfort him, smiled graciously, "Don't worry Daddy, I can teach psychology at university," and decided to begin working as a teaching assistant.

A fair share of those who choose a "secure profession" such as engineering, law, or medicine, do so thinking that they will be ensured of a steady income. Affinity for the field is less important in their eyes. Nor is much importance attached to the fact that sometimes their talents turn out to lie in a completely different discipline.

"You're right," a father once told me, acknowledging the contradiction between his son's talents and his son's occupation, "but it's important to me that my son should have a good profession, even if he never practices it…"

The myth of choosing a good profession has changed with the spirit of the times, since choosing a "good profession" should be defined by an individual's best qualities, skills, and their inner desire.

4. I am "forbidden" to recognize that my choices suit me.

The fourth type of impasse involves those who are permitted to choose and to find fulfillment, but are not allowed to acknowledge and enjoy it either internally or externally. Daniel, the multimedia professional whose story was told in chapter one, belongs to this group. He worked in the multimedia world but was convinced he was in the wrong profession. He projected such flagrant dissatisfaction that eventually he was almost fired from his job.

People who experience this kind of prohibition tend to be children of parents who themselves lived with an ongoing experience of non-fulfillment. Despite having chosen a career path they liked, they were never able to recognize having done so. Daniel's father was a graphic artist, but because of the grandfather's verdict that "only a painter is a true artist," both Daniel and his father lived with the feeling that being a graphic artist was never enough, even though this was their true calling.

In such cases, awareness of the vocational multigenerational trap is the first step out of it. The second step is being able to rethink negative family perceptions and being able to reconstruct your own definitions without losing sight of a traditional family calling.

5. I don't know how to realize my choices.

This category includes the people who know what they want to do, but don't know how to go about doing it or what vocational tools should be acquired. These people are high-risk candidates for missing out on fulfillment. Among them are many charismatic people with proven talents, perseverance, and courage who are unable to focus their resources and take the plunge. They see the objective clearly but fail to identify the road or the means to take them there.

Stuart was a talented businessman who had no idea of how to set boundaries in his work environment. He was unable to anchor a contract in reality, or conduct negotiations to achieve his targets. The commercial spark burned relentlessly in his belly, yet Stuart seemed doomed to an ongoing Sisyphus-like struggle of success and failure.

Stuart came from an extremely deprived family. The physical hunger of his childhood was transformed into a desire to gobble everything up as a businessman. He had no clear boundaries whatsoever. For example, as a child his parents had never bought him ice cream, so the adult Stuart strived to own the entire ice cream store. Paying little attention to food costs or inventory, his uneconomical decisions jeopardized his investments. When he learned to analyze his mistakes and gradually build new, reparative experiences, he was able to take a more studied approach to building new business ventures, without rushing into things in the destructively impetuous manner of his earlier years.

Stuart learned that by setting boundaries and creating order – rules, policies, and protocols – he could set up an effective system that would survive in times of both crisis and prosperity.

6. I don't want to know what my real calling is.

This category describes people with overly high expectations of themselves, who find it almost impossible to accept their real calling, because making a commitment demands their total being and may even compromise their inner truth.

Knowing this, and because in their conceptual world there is no room for compromise, they sometimes prefer to remain on the outside until conditions improve.

Perfectionists fall into this category. They set precise tasks for themselves but the path to realization is so tortuous that some prefer to give up before even starting. The need for perfection is cruel. Giving up on realization is such an easy way out, that sometimes the perfectionist prefers to merely examine the pros and cons, and rarely moves into the implementation stage.

The perfectionist typically wonders: Is all of this work worth my while? He or she doesn't take into account two critical things: One, this is my life we're talking about here. Two, can I achieve a less perfect goal but at the same time, paradoxically, find myself in a much happier world, and ease off my expectations?

Leo was such a case. Leo's mother died immediatly after he was born. He was an exceptionally wise and logical child. His tyrant father was an immature control freak who inwardly blamed his son for his wife's death, partly so as to absolve himself of any involvement in his wife's pregnancy and tragic death. Until the age of five, Leo's father educated him in an uncompromising, rigid manner devoid of any kindness or warmth. Only total perfection was permitted, only excellence pleased him. Compromise was not a word Leo learned from his father as part of the vocabulary needed for life.

"I reduced my world to a minimum of needs, and applied myself to each new task so thoroughly that there was nothing left for me in life other than completing each new mission," related Leo.

Although Leo was an extremely gifted child, he was never able to choose one single area of activity for himself, or define his true calling. He was never able to tell himself what he would really have chosen had he dared taken the leap.

When expert after expert repeatedly commented, "If only you would choose, the Nobel Prize would be a piece of cake for you."

"So maybe not choosing is preferable," was Leo's standard reply.

Leo was so wrapped up inside his expectations of absolute

perfectionism that he was never able to free himself of his chains – committing to only one area of his multi-talents would lead him to suffering total commitment, yet with little reward because of his painstaking self-criticism that nothing would ever be good enough in any way.

For many people in this category, accepting their true calling is an almost impossible mission; only long and dedicated self-work can eventually lessen their unrealistic expectations of themselves.

7. I'm indecisive yet deep down I know what I want to do.

A wise man I once knew described the seventh category best: On a flight, once you decide to order chicken, you have simultaneously decided against ordering the beef. Making decisions involves setting limitations, which is problematic for many people who have trouble making up their minds.

Still, there are those who are capable of deciding what they want when they are quite young regarding love or vocational choices. Such people often feel as if a clear inner voice helps them to make the correct choices. For example, a young woman of twenty can choose a spouse with whom a happy marriage will ensue for the next fifty years.

These clear inner voices help people make decisions in their career choices and in all areas of life. There are many people who acquire their chosen profession when they are still quite young and continue with it happily through old age.

8. I'm indecisive and can't commit to any decision.

In contrast, there are many talented people who cannot decide. Some, for example, can't make a decision to study law because this may prevent them from studying something else. I call this kind of person a 'Vocational Don Juan'; a person who wants to keep all their options open. These folks enjoy vocational conquests and change occupations as often as possible. They are constantly seduced by the opportunity of a more romantic prospect. They go on deluding themselves that somewhere out there is a profession they have yet to discover. Even when they recognize that moving from one profession to another means failure, they still have trouble in committing to a specific choice. A person who chronically avoids making critical vocational decisions, tends to avoid the possibility of finding the profession that is already there, deep down inside him.

"Fear of deciding is driving me nuts," I was told one day by a talented, successful man named Richard, who constantly changed jobs. "Now I want to go back to school to study architecture, but what will happen if after four years I suddenly find that this profession bores me yet again?"

"So what would happen?" I asked him.

"I'd change it," replied Richard.

We both knew that with vocational change, the process was liable simply to repeat itself, unless Richard would accept his liabilities and find his calling within his untamed boundaries. Richard's problems centered on his difficulty to committing himself, rather that deciding on a profession. These kinds of people find difficulty in committing to long-term relationships in all aspects of their lives. The more they become involved with something or someone, the more they feel suffocated and quickly seek the nearest escape route; only to repeat the never-ending cycle.

9. My career choices are influenced by a personal trauma.

The ninth category includes people who have suffered some terrible trauma that deflects their original choice away from its natural course. In such cases, the trauma may only find its expression later on in a person's life. For example, a talented artist to be, following the traumatic loss of a parent to a difficult illness, may suddenly register for a different track, completely unrelated to his authentic desires. Such children can invest long, hard years of study in a challenging profession only to reach the age of forty with the notion that only now are they entitled to choose their true calling.

Craig's situation illustrates this conflict well. His mother had been ill with multiple sclerosis for many years and the disease had fascinated the inquisitive child. He was convinced that if he became a specialist in that field, he could personally find a cure for his ailing mother.

"I thought that if I studied intensely," said Craig, "I would discover a new drug that would save her life. I was determined to become a doctor, and that's what I did a few years after her death. Today I'm an excellent doctor, but I always have this feeling that something is missing in my soul."

A short historical review of Craig's family background brought an interesting finding to light. Other than Craig, all the members of his family were successful businesspeople. Through gaining an understanding of what Craig really wanted, I clearly saw that the family talent had not passed him by, and that he had simply been sidetracked by the trauma of his mother's lengthy illness and slow death.

I counseled Craig to avoid making any sudden transitions. He began his new career slowly by importing a drug for skin diseases which turned out to be an outstanding success on the domestic market. "When I'm sure that the business world is really right for me," Craig said at one of our last sessions, "I'll integrate all my medical knowledge with my business skills. Until now I've always felt that as long as I'm saving lives and healing people, I'm saving my mother. Maybe now I'm ready to let go of the illusion that I can cure her and the rest of the world. Lately, though, what really turns me on is the passion of unleashing my entrepreneurial skills."

Craig reached the stage where it was permissible for him to bypass his life trauma and move ahead with his true choices. He was liberated from the burden of his self-imposed duty to save his mother's life, and could redirect his energies fully to the business ventures he really wanted to pursue.

10. My career is influenced by coping with my childhood experiences.

The last type of impasse includes people who underwent early life experiences that continue to block them from making full use of their talents or exploring their core vocational choices. Some of them even feel compelled to turn these experiences into their life's work.

Geraldine came to me in a state of total despair. She was twenty-six and had no profession. "Nothing really interests me," she told me. "I don't feel that there's any one vocational area that I really like."

The key to this puzzle was buried in her childhood. Geraldine was an emotionally abused child. "My father was constantly hounding me," she said. "He was always checking what I hadn't done well, which homework assignments I hadn't completed, what housework I had shirked. I was the daughter who got the short end of the stick. Misery was my permanent state of being."

Geraldine's passport to life finally came from her career in the army. Far from home, she found a niche of her own by specializing in helping soldiers whose commanders abused them. She knew all the relevant laws and military protocols by heart and would unabashedly let those in charge know when they had broken regulations. Many officers on the base didn't like her, but the soldiers adored her.

"And now, several years after your discharge, do you feel you have a profession?"

"No," said Geraldine.

"What if I were to tell you," I said, "that you actually do have a profession and all you have to do is translate it into your life?"

At subsequent sessions we looked at several possibilities for Geraldine where she could counsel people on how to cope with intimidating bureaucrats and government offices of higher authority. Eventually Geraldine went back to school and studied tax consulting. She ended up specializing in helping people who felt threatened and exploited by the income tax authorities.

Geraldine leveraged her childhood experiences and her coping skills by putting all of that to work in her professional life. All she needed from me was a process of recognizing and accepting that her style of coping was actually a respected vocation and her personal calling.

B. WHERE AM I STUCK?
Four Dimensions of Insight

Once you have identified which category/categories you fit into – you may find parts of your impasse overlap with more than one category – or otherwise figured out where you are vocationally stuck, we can add four additional dimensions to help you understand your career impasse. They are listed here in descending order of difficulty in bringing about transformation or career change.

1. Vocational Change

This dimension refers to a person's specific vocation or profession that no longer provides fulfilling vocational self-expression. Impasse of this kind is long and difficult because moving beyond it requires a fundamental change in the nature and content of a person's work; a complete change of profession. This change in turn demands a transformation in the way a significant part of a person's inner self is reflected by their career and work environment. People at this stage of impasse feel that their basic need to express who they are, via what they do for a living, is in need of profound modification.

2. Vocational Growth

This dimension refers to when a person has maximized a certain stage of emotional development and self-development and is unable to move on because of a need to grow and advance within the same career direction. Often this type of person is unequipped to understand or function at a more sophisticated emotional level. Although this may be experienced as a crisis, it can actually become the catalyst that will drive the person to a higher level of emotional maturity. This demands inner emotional development and new perspectives in terms of self-image and relationships with others. The result of this process is sometimes manifested in a change in a person's inner vocational dimensions – for example, moving from a mediocre income to an increased income; moving from being an ordinary manager to a strategic manager; moving from being a supporting actor to a protagonist.

For something like that to happen, a person needs a greater capacity to deal effectively with themselves and their environment. Sometimes what is needed is an improvement in self-image, or the ability to face and be liberated from certain fears that are holding the person back. This can include fear of expressing aggression, fear of failure, fear of success, and so on. Thus, a person's self-development is often expressed when undertaking a new level of responsibility, creativity, management, or other work related element.

3. Context Change within a Profession

A third dimension of impasse involves the context of a person's work. This refers to how a person is stuck in terms of work context, position, and scope and moving forward requires understanding of all these dimensions within the system or organization where a person functions. Often, there is a deep, inner need to grow further within the context of one's chosen profession. This may demand specific understanding of the person's present work context – as well as recognition of intergenerational family patterns and role relationships – for optimizing work performance and satisfaction. Changes may include moving from a big organization to a smaller one, and visa versa; or moving from being an employee to becoming self-employed, and visa versa; or moving from partnership to working alone, and visa versa.

4. Wider Self-Expression

This dimension of impasse relates to a person's need to widen and enhance self-expression through work or non-related work activities. A person's 'Activity Pie' includes the sum total of their scope, variety, and undertakings in terms of work and home. Career burnout can sometimes happens when a person lacks the existential need, in whatever proportion, for self-expression which can sometimes lead to quenching the desire to perform, and draining any hope of satisfaction. Often the simple act of exploring, identifying, and integrating a meaningful pursuit or new hobby – whether work related or not – into a person's life formula can heal a vocational frustration and infuse a sense of satisfaction.

C. HOW CAN I MOVE ON?
Six Stages of the Journey

When you are stuck in one way or another in your vocational life, I have found that a commitment to a journey that will lead you to breakthrough has six stages on the path towards moving beyond impasse.

Stage 1 – Awareness

In the first stage of a career change, you need to recognize and identify the situation in which you find yourself, and be able to declare, "I am stuck in my career; I am at a career impasse," as opposed to being stuck in some other place or in some other part of your life.

You need to be able to recognize that what is happening to you is a situation involving work-related impasse. People in this stage will typically say things like "I'm stuck in my career and can't get moving," "I'm unmotivated at work," "This just isn't it," "I have to change jobs but don't know what new job to choose," "I don't feel like getting up in the morning," "Every day at this job is torture," etc.

People are scared of the idea of facing up to the knowledge that they are experiencing a career crisis and sometimes suppress their awareness of the impasse. But, generally, coping with it becomes inevitable, since stress intensifies with time.

From my perspective, I have seen that getting stuck on a career path is a healthy and dynamic part of life for a developing human being. When people experience their work as something they are in control of, they allow themselves to do a little stock-taking once in a while. Sometimes they are satisfied with what they are doing; sometimes they feel stuck. Some people are frightened of this sense of impasse and rush to circumvent it or dig their heels in and oppose it, yet others see impasse as an opportunity for change and for creating a breakthrough. Either way, awareness of work-related impasse is a precondition for the next stage.

Stage 2 – Diagnosis

The next phase is the diagnostic stage where you need to identify what is causing your career to be stuck. (Please refer to the earlier sections in the Appendix where ten categories and four dimensions of impasse were explained.)

When you are able to examine or diagnose the impasse you are experiencing, you are more than likely to discover more than one category of impasse with more than one way-station along the journey. That is because by nature, human beings are complicated and cannot be categorized into exact boxes. Still, you will find that a clear diagnosis helps clarify the stages of dealing with each category. By focusing on the relevant challenge, you will be able to define action items for implementation – a necessary step towards making progress along your journey.

Stage 3 – Confrontation

The next phase in the journey is confronting the void or the sense of emptiness. This is a complex and difficult stage, if not the most difficult step of the journey. You are by now aware of the problem, have diagnosed it, but you have still not discovered the best way to solve your impasse. This stage demands intuitive listening to one's inner self, which usually demands a quiet time-out from your work or home life in order to cope with the turmoil and confusion. You can help yourself to move forward by finding a sympathetic ear, reading self-help books, or consulting with a professional. In order for new data to be absorbed, there has to be room for it. A quiet period is necessary in order to hear the cry from within and focus on reconnecting to your root sources while rediscovering your personal vision. Paying attention to your inner voice, is a must in order to move on to the next stage. Sometimes, the void can be experienced as a kind of catastrophe, but only from this state of emptiness can one be filled anew. The knowledge that this stage is temporary makes it easier to bear.

Stage 4 – Vision

The fourth stage of the journey lies in identifying your vision and deciding where you want to go and where you are headed. For many people who don't know where they are headed, or haven't yet defined their vision, it is usually because either something unknown or some concrete fear is holding them back. You may very well be undergoing similar feelings.

Over the decades, I have learned to respect this lack of recognition of a person's will or vocational dream. Rushing things is inadvisable. If you feel you are unable to accept certain truths about yourself, or unable to reconcile your life's dream with reality, you may have a good reason, without understanding why. Sometimes the prohibition relates to a lack of permission – from family and society; or obedience to morals and preconceptions – in order for you to fulfill your dream.

Sometimes the tools needed to make your dream come true are missing, and not knowing what they are is a way of fending off frustration. People want to feel they have maximized their options in life. Missing out on one's vocation is a devastating feeling, not only for you, but also for your family.

Deep down, most people intuitively know what road they were meant to take in life. Sometimes, fulfilling the dream demands a confrontation with uncomfortable scenarios that may include envy and rivalry, greed and fear, and so on. Moreover, acknowledgment of a dream begets almost a self-imposed command to accomplish it or be forever banished to face the knowledge that you are living with an unfulfilled dream. An even more painful punishment is handed out to those who prefer to ignore their dream or bury it completely. Living with the feeling that one's life is passing by without fulfilling one's true calling, career or dream, is possibly the closest to a living death.

Stage 5 – Training

This stage of the journey refers to equipping yourself with tools and mentors who will train you and help you pursue the path to fulfillment of your vision quest, or your next step towards change.

Once you have figured out where you want to go vocationally, you have now reached the practical stage where you need to ask constructive questions such as: How do I proceed from here to reaching my goal? What route should I take? What tools do I need? What pace should I set? Who will guide and advise me? Who will share my journey? Who will I separate from along the way?

Obviously, the clearer your direction and goal, the greater potential you will have for success. Wherever you invest optimal effort, you will be granted maximum help and your passion will instill passion in others; in other words, "God helps those who help themselves."

During this phase, you need to gather all your strength and carefully plan your way by paying attention to detail without being tempted by shortcuts or being vulnerable to opportunists. Proceeding attentively shortens the route to fulfilling your dream.

Stage 6 – Fulfillment

The last stage is arriving at a sense of accomplishment. However, this is an ongoing process, and you must always be aware of the fact that one day, you will more than likely face your next impasse… and the next… and so on. People who feel that they're doing the work they were meant to do and achieving their vocational vision describe their fulfillment as "Every day brings me new excitement," "Finally I'm doing what I always wanted to do," "I never felt so whole before," "I'm full of energy."

During this phase, it's important to note that there will always be ups and downs, and one day, when you may hit impasse again, you will be able to decipher it as a breakthrough to your next stage of development.

Conclusion

So, dear reader, the tale is told… but the story's not over yet.

In this appendix, I have described some of the processes and tools that can be of help to you. Each process of figuring out what is happening and what it means requires considerable investment and commitment. I have chosen to view these processes as journeys on the way to further developing your life and career quests. In all of these shared journeys, beyond the pain and the frustration, there is the happiness and satisfaction that come with growth and fulfillment, with finding your path, and walking it.

To all of you who have traveled this literal journey with me, I wish for each of you a personal journey that will be true, enduring, and fulfilling.

Learn from others and teach yourselves.
Seek your path.
Trust its wisdom.
Never give up on your dreams.
Go out there and find your Promised Land.

BIBLIOGRAPHY

Adler, A. (1959). *Understanding Human Nature*, New York: Fawcett

Bank, S.P. & Kahan, M.D. (1982). *The Sibling Bond*, New York: Basic Books.

Barner, R. (1996). The new Career Strategist: career management for the year 2000 and beyond, in E. Cornish (ed.), *Exploring Your Future*. Bethesda Maryland: World Future Society, 12-18.

Barnett, E. & Barnett, S. (1988). *Working Together: Entrepreneurial Couples*. Berkeley: Ten Speed Press.

Beck, E.D. & Cowan, C.C. (1996). *Spiral Dynamics: Exploring the New Science of Memetics* (eds.), Cambridge: Blackwell Publishers Inc.

Becker, E. (1973). *The Denial of Death*, New York: Free Press.

Bowen, M. (1980). *Key to the Genogram*, Washington DC: Georgetown University Hospital.

Bolles, R. N. (1996). *What Color is Your Parachute?* Berkeley, Ten Speed Press.

Bordin, E.S. (1968). *Psychological Counseling* (2nd ed.), New York: Appleton Century, Crof.

Bratcher, W.E. (1982). The influence of the family on career selection: A family systems perspective. *The Personnel & Guidance Journal* 61, 87-91.

Brill, A.A. (1949). *Basic Principles of Psychoanalysis*, New York: Doubleday.

Dagley, G. (1984). A Vocational Genogram (mimeograph), Athens: University of Georgia.

Datan, N. & Ginsberg, L. (1975). *Life-span Developmental Psychology*, New York: Academic Press.

Dawkins, R. (1989). *The Extended Phenotype*, Oxford: Oxford University Press.

Dawkins, R. (1989). *The Selfish Gene*, Oxford: Oxford University Press.

De Vries, M.F.R. Kets & Associates (1991). *Organizations on the Couch*. San Francisco: Jossey-Bass.

Fairbairn, W. R. D. (1952). *An Object Relations Theory of the Personality*. New York: Basic Books.

Fenichel, O. (1954). On the Psychology of Boredom, in *Collected Papers of Otto Fenichel*, I. London: Routledge & Kegan Paul.

Fores, B.R. (1953). Personality Factors in Occupational Choice. *Educational Psychological Measurements* 13, 361-366.

Freud, S. (1959). Instincts and Their Vicissitudes, in *Collected Papers* 4. New York: Basic Books.

Galinsky, M.D. & Fast, I. (1966). Vocational choice as a focus of the identity search. *Journal of Counseling Psychology* 13, 89-92.

Ginsberg, E., Ginsberg, S.W., Axelrad, S. & Herman, J.L. (1951). *Occupational Choice*. New York: Columbia University Press.

Greenvald, H. (1964). Why do so few people find work satisfying? in L. Freeman, M. Theodore (eds.), The Why Reports Purchase, New York: Arthur Bernhard.

Gysbers, N.C, Heppner, M.J. & Johnston, J.A. (1998). *Career Counseling: Process, Issues and Techniques*. Boston: Allyn & Bacon.

Hall, D.T. (1996). Long live the career, in D.T. Hall & Associates (eds.). *The Career is Dead – Long Live the Career*. San Francisco: Jossey-Bass.

Holland, J.L. (1964). *Making Vocational Choices: A Theory of Vocational Personalities and Work Environment*, Englwood Cliffs, New Jersey: Prentice – Hall.

Holland, J.L. (1962). Major Progress of Research on Vocational Behaviors. In Borow, H. (ed.). *Man in a World of Work*. Boston: Houghton Mifflin.

Hoppock, R. (1963). *Occupational Information*, New York: McGraw-Hill.

Ilan, E. (1962). The Problem of Motivation in the Educator's Vocational Choice. *The Psychoanalytical Study of the Child* 18, 266-285.

James, J. (1996). *Thinking in the Future Tense,* New York: Simon & Schuster.

Klein, M. (1959). *The Psychoanalysis of Children*, London: Hogarth.

Krau, E. (1997). *The Realization of Life Aspiration through Vocational Careers,* New York: Draeger.

Lamb, M.E. & Sutton-Smith, B. (eds.) (1982). *Sibling Relationships – Their Nature and Significance across the Life Span*. Hillsdale, New York: Erlbaum.

Leibowitz, Z. & Lea, D. (eds.) (1986). Adult *Career Development: Concepts, Issues and Practices*. Alexandria: National Career Development Association.

Maddox, R.J. (1995). *INC. Your Dream*. Penguin Books USA INC.

Marshack, K. (1994). Love and work: How co-entrepreneurial couples manage the boundaries and transitions in personal relationship and business partnership. Doctoral dissertation, Santa Barbara: The Fielding Institute.

Maslow, A.H. (1954). *Motivation and Personality*. New York: Harper.

McClelland, D. (1962). On the psychodynamics of creative physical scientists, in Gruber H.F., Terrell, G., Wertheimer, M. (eds.) *Contemporary Approaches to Creative Thinking*, New York: Atherton Press.

McGoldrik, M & Gerson, R. (1985). *Genograms in Family Assessment*, New York: W.W. Norton & Co.

McKelvie, W.H., & Friedland, B.U. (1978). *Life Style: Theory, Practice and Research*, Dubuque: Kendall/Hunt.

Nachmann, B. (1960). Childhood experience and vocational choice in law, dentistry and social work, *Journal of Counseling Psychology*, 7, 243-250.

Obholzer, A., & Roberts, V.Z. (1994). *The Unconscious at Work*, London: Routledge.

Okiishi, R.W. (1987). The Genogram as a tool career counseling. *Journal of Counseling and Development*, 66, 255-259.

Osipow, S.H. & Fitzgerald, L.F. (1996). *Theories of Career Development.* (4th Ed.) Boston Allyn & Bacon.

Parsons, F. (1989). *Choosing a Vocation*, Garrett Park: Garrett Park Press.

Pines, A.M. (1993). Burnout: An Existential Perspective, in W. Schaufeli, C. Maslach, & T. Marek (eds.) *Professional Burnout*, Washington DC: Taylor & Francis.

Pines, A.M., & Aronson, E. (1988). *Career Burnout*, New York: Free Press.

Pines, A. M., & Yanai O. (2000). Unconscious Influences on the Choice of a career: Implications for organizational consultation. *Journal of Health and Human Services Administration* 21, 502-511.

Pruyser, P.W. (1980). Work: Curse or Blessing ? *Bulletin of the Menninger Clinic* 44, 59-73.

Roe, A. (1964). Personality structure and occupational behavior, in H. Borrow (ed.). *Man in a World of Work*, Boston: Houghton Mifflin, 196-214.

Roe, A. (1956). *A Psychology of Occupations*, New York: Wiley & Sons.

Rohrlich, J. B. (1980). *Work and Love: The Crucial Balance*, Summit Books.

Savickal, M.L. & Walsh, B.W. (eds.). (1996). *Handbook of Career Counseling: Theory and Practice*, Palo Alto: Davies-Black Publishing.

Segal, S.J. (1961). Psychoanalysis of personality factors in vocational choice. *Journal of Counseling Psychology*, 8, 202-210.

Siegelman, M. & Peck, R.F.Z. (1960). Personality patterns related to occupational roles. *Genetic Psychological Monograph* 61, 291-349.

Stern, G.G. Stein, M.I. & Bloom, B.S. (1956). *Methods in Personality Assessment*, Glencoe: Free Press.

Sulloway, F.J. (1997). *Born to Rebel*, Boston: Vintage Books.

Super, D.E. (1965). *Vocational Development*, New York: Colombia University Bureau of Publications.

Vroom, V.H. (1964). *Work and Motivation*, New York: Wiley & Sons.

Walsh W. B. & Osipow, S.H. (1995). *Handbook of Vocational Psychology*, Hillsdale, New York: Erlbaum.

Watchtell, E. F. (1992). The family psyche over three generations: The Genogram Revisited. *Journal of Marital Therapy* 8, 335-343.

White, M. (1995). *Re-Authoring Lives: Interviews and Essays*, Adelaide, South Australia: Dulwich Centre Publications.

White, R.W. (1954). *Lives in progress*, New York: Drydem.

Winnicott, D.W. (1965). *The Family and Individual Development*, New York: Basic Books.